Calculating the Human

Calculating the Human

Universal Calculability in the Age of Quality Assurance

Luigi Doria

CNRS at Centre Maurice Halbwachs (CNRS – EHESS – ENS), Paris, France

palgrave
macmillan

First published 2013 by
PALGRAVE MACMILLAN

Palgrave Macmillan in the UK is an imprint of Macmillan Publishers Limited, registered in England, company number 785998, of Houndmills, Basingstoke, Hampshire RG21 6XS.

Palgrave Macmillan in the US is a division of St Martin's Press LLC, 175 Fifth Avenue, New York, NY 10010.

Palgrave Macmillan is the global academic imprint of the above companies and has companies and representatives throughout the world.

Palgrave® and Macmillan® are registered trademarks in the United States, the United Kingdom, Europe and other countries.

ISBN 978–0–230–35374–9

This book is printed on paper suitable for recycling and made from fully managed and sustained forest sources. Logging, pulping and manufacturing processes are expected to conform to the environmental regulations of the country of origin.

A catalogue record for this book is available from the British Library.

A catalog record for this book is available from the Library of Congress.

To my parents

Contents

Acknowledgements

I would like to thank Massimo Amato and Luca Fantacci, with whom I have shared a long journey of friendship and collaboration, Michele Bee for discussions, suggestions and support, Bill Maurer for his encouragement and Alexandre Schild, to whom I am very much indebted for discussing with me parts of this work and for his invaluable comments.

The fellowship I took up some years ago at the Nantes Institute for Advanced Studies has been the initial source for some of the ideas developed in this book. I am grateful to all the colleagues that I had the opportunity to meet in Nantes, and particularly to Alain Supiot and Muriel Fabre-Magnan for their support and encouragement.

This work is also the product of the research activities carried out at the Centre Maurice Halbwachs, for the research project 'Mesurer la qualité de la vie. Les enjeux démocratiques d'un processus de rationalisation', funded by the Ville de Paris, within the framework of the programme Emergence(s). Thanks are given to the colleagues working on the research project and particularly to Alexandra Bidet.

I would also like to thank my editors at Palgrave Macmillan for their support and patience.

I am, naturally, solely responsible for the views and opinions expressed in this book and for any errors or omissions.

A note on grammatical style

In the interests of using gender-inclusive language, I switch between male and female pronouns throughout the text.

Introduction

Contemporary debate in the social and human sciences bears witness to an intense and growing focus on the issue of calculation.

Various lines of thought explore – from a variety of points of view – the morphology of calculative practices, their ability to shape organizational and socio-economic realities, the relationships between calculation and power and between calculation and democracy.

However, the multifaceted debate on calculation, which often opens up to philosophical investigation, continues to be riddled by a certain disquiet. The latter surfaces, in a very particular manner, with respect to the way in which calculation touches on man. Calculation tends to encompass 'objects' – such as emotions, affects, psychological well-being, social relations, intellectual labour – which historically have been at its periphery. What appears before us is an unlimited calculative proliferation ever more directly involving human life, down to its most 'incalculable' aspects; and precisely when we are faced with the calculation of the incalculable human, the awkward question on the *unconditional* character of calculation is projected as a disturbing shadow.

In this volume, I intend to renew questioning on the calculation of the human, considering the relationship between calculation and quality.

Indeed, it would seem that, precisely in the age of extreme calculability, calculation proceeds comfortably under the banner of quality, as the calculation of the quality of everything: quality of environment, of work, of social relationships, of political experience, of cultural practices, of death and of life itself.

Why does the age of unlimited calculation coincide with the age of quality, to the extent that the latter comes to be perceived as a disquieting keyword, endowed with enigmatic power?

How should we consider the phenomenon of the calculation of quality? And how, from the perspective of quality, can we renew questioning on the very nature of the calculative?

In considering calculation and quality, how can we reflect on the relationship between calculation and enhancement of *life*?

What does it mean that, precisely under the banner of quality, life appears as a total of dimensions, moments, experiences to be calculated, with a view to the *total quality* of life itself – and that human development comes to be represented as a constant increase of the calculable quality of life? And what can possibly be meant by the fact that quality of life will remain in force, even when that life no longer resonates on the human scale, but on the scale of the post-human?

In order to tackle these questions, this work will carry out, through a constant interchange with the social science debate, a phenomenological investigation based on the interpretation of various moments of Heidegger's thought.

From these initial notes, it can already be seen that this volume adopts a very particular perspective with respect to the debate on calculation which has arisen over the past few years.

This debate, it is worth pointing out, inherently involves the distinctive ambiguity that surrounds the term 'calculation' – a term that is commonly used to refer to measurement; to ordering; to classification; to control; to translation; to manipulation; to arrangement.

As we shall see in the chapters that follow, this debate centres, on the one hand, on the range of operations and practices that should be considered as having a calculative character and 'performativity', and thus on the way in which the borders of the calculative itself should be understood. On the other hand – and these two approaches are obviously often intertwined – the debate investigates the increasing role that calculation plays in the economic, managerial and socio-political sphere.

The theme here is thus the ability of calculative languages, technologies and devices to 'construct' economic phenomena, to shape organizational structures and practices and to define the identity of individual and collective actors. But what is stake – see the rich debate on biopolitical calculation – is also the weight of calculation in the most diverse dimensions of social life. And the ubiquitous proliferation of calculation is often referred to as a vehicle for that managerialization and commodification of the social that is commonly considered as a worrying characteristic of present times.

Reflection on calculation thus often addresses the calculative as the score in which is inscribed the transformation of nature itself and of the forms of power.

From a slightly different perspective, however, attention is also concentrated on the incomplete, provisional and open nature of calculation practices and on the social construction of calculative processes. From this perspective, the focus is not on the risks of a universal calculative rationalization. Instead, the subject is the forms and implications of a 'politicization' of calculation. Calculation emerges increasingly as a political process and, vice versa, the political sphere – the theories on *technical democracy* spring to mind here – appears to be increasingly 'calculative'.

In the midst of this complex debate, a question can be heard in increasingly decisive tones, asking all the various lines of interpretation: what does it mean when humankind itself becomes a matter of calculation, when man and his life become the object and the outcome of calculative operations?

This is a question which arises in the face of calculation's unstoppable advance towards the most intangible and secret dimensions of the human. But this question resounds – in a very peculiar tone – when calculation occurs within the realm of the so-called *post-human*.

In the post-human scenario – which is so important that it reshapes the entire debate on calculation, including sociological reflection – what is presaged is the transition from a calculation of human life that, however detailed and intrusive it may be, nonetheless leaves intact a certain idea of man to a calculation that, due also to the frenetic development of the bio-genetic, cognitive and computer sciences, radically calls into question the nature of man and the relationship between the human and the non-human.

Genetic manipulation; the advances of cyborg sciences; the advent of intelligent, emotional, conscious, *living* machines: these are all phenomena that appear to profoundly reconfigure the calculative treatment of the human, provoking concern or even alarmed reactions. The very 'essence' of man and the sense of life and death as human phenomena seem, indeed, to be profoundly implicated.

Life no longer appears as an object to be perfected, on the basis of a 'traditional' conception of humankind, but as something that obeys an unconditional demand for transformation and expansion, in the direction of post-human life.

The relationship itself between man and things appears ever more decisively as a question that plays out on the level of calculative manipulation and transformation. And, indeed, the issue of the relationship, the interchange and the translation between the human and the non-human stands out as one of the cutting-edge areas in social science and philosophical reflection.

Precisely with the intention of casting a fresh look on the phenomenon of the calculability of the human, this work will undertake a dialogue with Heidegger's thought. This refers to the way in which Heidegger invites us to consider the essence of the calculative, the meaning of the perfecting of calculation and the relationship between humankind and beings in the age of the calculative perfection. But it also refers to the way in which some of Heidegger's works, albeit in a non-explicit and indirect manner, provide hints for understanding the hidden core of the connection between quality and calculation.

According to Heidegger, the age of the extreme deployment of the *calculative thinking* coincides with the age of the *completion* of the history of philosophy – which, for Heidegger, is the history of metaphysical thought. This completion corresponds with the perfecting of modern technology – a perfecting in which man's relationship with things and with himself becomes an increasingly complete techno-scientific manipulability, that has the character of *cybernetic* control, and in which man and things both become standing reserves, available for all forms of mastery and enhancement.

Without doubt, this has to do precisely with the extreme perfecting of man's 'calculative' attitude towards himself and all beings. For Heidegger, indeed, the calculative decisively marks the entire history of the metaphysical West. It takes its place at the heart of the decisive phenomenon of modern metaphysics – the transformation of all beings into representable objects for man who self-assures himself as a subject – and characterizes the whole parabola of modernity right up to the time of its completion.

However, it is a case – and this task is as important as it is arduous – of understanding ever more precisely the true nature of calculation (and its non obvious relationship with numerical measurement) and the relationship between the calculative and the 'technological'. This requires challenging some seemingly solid and convincing interpretations of the dominion of calculation in present times: those referring to a quantitative possession of everything, to a demand for unconditional numerical measurability, to a *reduction* of everything to the rank of the countable. This also means preparing to distance oneself from some conceptions of the calculability of the human that appear obvious: those that allude to the *annexation* of man to a calculative regime in continuous expansion and to the paradoxical submission of humankind to a universe of calculation which man himself has created, up to the extreme outcomes of the *reification* of the human.

The opportunity to renew the question on the calculative arises, in a most striking way, precisely in the face of the enigmatic complicity between quality and calculation. This requires, once again, calling into question (although this in no way implies the slightest condescension or undervaluation) some of the current readings of that complicity.

The debate on the nexus between quality and calculation – and I will return to this point in more detail subsequently – has developed in a particularly intense and lively manner recently, and attention has been focused as much on the ambiguous power of quality discourses and technologies in the management of contemporary organizations and societies as on the growing role of the issue of *quality of life* as a central reference in the socio-political dimension.

A major part of the critical attention is focused on the movement through which each and every quality is reduced to an unconditionally measurable, controllable and auditable object. On the basis of this reduction (which is surrounded by a particular form of managerial rituality), quality is seen as establishing itself as an ideological umbrella under which a controversial universal quantification occurs, which is complicit in the demands of managerialization and marketization that characterize the realm of neo-liberal governmentality. The measurement of quality of life is also often addressed, in a similar interpretive vein, as the framework within which a technocratic demand for biopolitical calculation develops, connecting the increasingly pervasive diagnosis of the life of the individual with the management and maximization of the well-being of the population.

From another perspective, attention is concentrated on the social and political nature of quality measurement. In both the economic-commercial sphere and the socio-political sphere the processes of 'qualification' are seen as an eminent field of the 'politicization' of the calculative. The definition, construction and measurement of quality is thus regarded as a precarious and contestable process, open to constant reflexive questioning within the socio-technological networks that are interwoven throughout the field of *technical democracy*.

However, in my view, the issue of the calculation of quality cannot be adequately considered merely from the perspective of a commodification-oriented quantification of quality itself, or from the perspective of quality measurement as a socio-political battlefield.

What is the very meaning of the fact that under the banner of quality – that word which, in Western history, points towards incalculable individuality and the incalculable individuality of the human – life emerges as being obviously and unconditionally calculable and enhanceable?

On reflection, precisely by examining the nexus between quality and the question of life, the possibility emerges of renewing the investigation of that relationship which Heidegger invites us to consider as very decisive: the relationship that, in the entire history of metaphysics up to its technological completion, links the calculative (and thus the sphere of assurance, control and manipulation) with that which seems to have nothing to do with it, to the extent that it seems to be its complete opposite: *lived-experience*.

The calculation of quality, as I will seek to demonstrate throughout my interpretive trajectory, concerns the movement by which the individuality of life and of things is represented, maintained and *assured* as a matter of *lived-experience* – of that lived-experience that, for Heidegger, banishes in a most decisive way every element of mystery and enchantment in man's relationship with himself and with beings.

By virtue of the calculation of quality as 'lived' quality, man's relationship with the individuality of his own life and of things becomes something that resonates in the register of lived-experience; and something that can be taken into account by measuring how it is experienced, felt, lived. It is on the ground of this basic calculation of quality, I argue, that the systematic measurement of the human – through the measurement of every quality – can proceed in an ever more complete and obvious way.

Precisely when the individuality of life and of things resonates in the obligatory orchestration of lived-experience, life, in its totality and individuality, can easily become available to the unconditional demands of management and enhancement.

It is within this interpretive horizon that, in my view, it is possible to shed new light on that which is so often evoked, in contemporary social science and philosophical debate, as the 'vitalistic' character of calculation and of enhancement; I refer to that proliferating 'power of life' that marks the age of the extreme calculability of the human, up to 'transcending' the human itself, in the post-human scene.

The more one moves, through the lens of the quality-calculation nexus, towards a clarification of the nature of calculation, the more it becomes possible to regard calculation neither merely as a condition to be accepted by living it 'politically', nor as a menace to be countered in the name of an endangered humanity.

Extreme calculability may appear – difficult though it may be to grasp this possibility – as something that has, at one and the same time, characteristics both of danger and of *opportunity*.

I refer here to the very peculiar 'ambivalence' that characterizes, in Heidegger's thought, the age of technological-calculative perfection. When calculation develops in the most complete way, it hides the fact that its dominion is the way in which man is challenged and claimed by that which is not under his control, as it does not belong to the realm of the self-securing of man as a calculating subject. Yet, precisely against calculative perfecting – and the way in which it involves man, things and their relationship, – man has the opportunity of experiencing the openness of human life to that dimension of radical incalculability in which the human being can relate to her own essence. When quality becomes nothing else than a matter of calculability and lived-experience, I argue, it somehow silently points towards the basic relationship of the human with the dimension of the incalculable.

The work is set out as follows.

Chapter 1 gives an account of the density that the relationship between the issue of the calculation of life and the issue of quality has taken on in recent social and human sciences debate. Whether on centre stage or in the background of current reflection on quality and calculation, some important questions emerge that will be my focus in the subsequent chapters.

In the first part of the chapter, which is a prologue with respect to the argument on quality and calculation, I focus on the meta-question concerning the 'transformation' of the human as the object of calculation and manipulation that occurs on the post-human scene. I will give a first glimpse at this transformation by showing how it reshapes one of the most influential theoretical perspectives on calculation (as well as on the quality-calculation nexus): the one based on the interpretation of the Foucauldian thought on government, power and biopolitics.

I then review the emergence of quality as a controversial *mot d'ordre* in contemporary managerial, socio-economic and political spheres. I will focus attention on two levels, which have important links connecting them.

On the one hand, attention will be directed at the sphere of business and public management, in which, starting from the final decades of the last century, the discourses and technologies of quality (among which auditing, ranking and standardization) have played a dominant role. On the other hand, I will focus on the concept of *quality of life* and on the ways through which it has established itself as an increasingly important reference for contemporary political and socio-economic debate.

I will then discuss some interpretations of the issue of the present-day 'complicity' between the calculation of life and quality. Without intending to set out a comprehensive summary, I will touch on the replete and cogent debate in which some of the key topics in the contemporary thought on calculation can be found.

Different lines of interpretation will be addressed: those investigating the link between the rituality and 'self-referentiality' of calculative practices and the ambiguous, elusive or even ideological nature of quality; those interpreting the ubiquitous quality measurement as a configuration of governmental rationalities; those addressing the measurement of quality of life as a manifestation of the increasingly perfected complicity between the calculability of the citizen's soul and the management of the populational well-being; those focusing on the incomplete and contestable character of the processes of 'qualification' and thus on a politicization of calculation, which calls its hegemony into question.

It is also through critical analysis of these debates that my investigation will proceed; my argument, however, as pointed out above, will refuse the possibility of properly investigating the quality-calculation relationship merely on the basis of an interpretation of quality as an element of bio-political rationality or as the linchpin of the processes of politicization of calculation.

Chapter 2 is devoted to a long phenomenological journey into the core of the relationship between calculation and quality. The analysis will be carried out through the reference to several Heidegger's works, including the posthumously published *Contributions to Philosophy* (Heidegger, 1999a).

The *Contributions* provide indeed clues to think the qualitative, the quantitative and the calculative in a certain perspective – in which, as I will try to show in my interpretation, the relationship between quantity and quality is not a matter of a relationship between categories and the calculation of quality is not to be understood primarily as its numerical *quantification*.

The first question addressed in this chapter concerns what Heidegger considers as *calculating*, in the sense of the German verb *Rechnen*.

Although numerical measures have a very important and specific role in calculation, in order to understand the dominance of calculation and of *calculative thinking*, according to Heidegger, we must not bear in mind first and foremost numerical measurement and the reduction of everything to a countable entity.

I will focus on how Heidegger recognizes at the heart of calculation the movement of *taking for*, of *considering as*; and it is precisely that movement that I will keep in view in my entire interpretative path.

In order to prepare the ground for my interpretation of calculation, quality and life, I will then focus on the crucial question concerning the correspondence between what Heidegger designates as *Machenschaft* and *Erlebnis*.

Machenschaft (machination) denotes that decisive determination of the being of beings according to which a being is nothing if not what *makes itself by itself*. This determination completely permeates and decisively marks the entire history of metaphysical thought; it lies at the roots of the modern calculability of beings and ultimately establishes itself at the heart of modern technology and its constant 'calculative' perfecting.

Erlebnis on the contrary, denotes, in the *Contributions*, that demand according to which every being counts as a being only in the dimension of *lived-experience*.

It is then through the reading of the Heidegger's argument on the (long-hidden and, even now, difficult to grasp) co-belongingness between machination and lived-experience that I will seek to raise anew the question of the calculation of quality.

I then develop the above outlined argument on the calculability of quality. By virtue of the movement which assures quality as *lived quality*, life in its individual relationship with itself and with things, can easily appear as a mere matter of 'liveability' and can be measured as a totality of dimensions, occasions and moments of lived-experience.

Chapter 3 further stresses the approach taken in the previous section, and with regard to the issue of quality, questions the intimate relationship between the calculability of the human and the demand for life enhancement – that enhancement which tends to be felt as an 'ethical' demand when it takes the shape of *integral human development* and as something which is instead rather disquieting when it points to the so-called post-human enhancement.

In the face of the contemporary power of quality, the 'relationship' between calculation and enhancement seems to come up against us in a very particular way. This is so, precisely where modern times seem to proceed under the 'incontestable' demands of *making quality*, of unconditionally increasing quality, assumed as unconditionally calculable.

I will revisit two questions which were previously investigated in Chapter 2. The first of these questions concerns the relationship between *life* and *things* in the regime of quality. The second relates to the decisive complicity between the question of the calculability of quality and the question of totality – a complicity which arises on the 'mundane' grounds of management, under the heading of *total quality*.

The centre of attention will be the phenomenon through which all 'things' (assumed as 'components' of human life) are calculated in their quality, in view of the quality of life as a total – where, according to Heidegger, human life can never be a totality of components.

Precisely under the heading of the increasable *total quality of life*, I will argue, an idea of life as a totality of components (of domains, moments and possibilities of life) advances as if it were obvious, in its relationship with an idea of the development of life as a constant *expansion* of this totality.

This conception of human development as a continuous expansion of a totality of 'manifestations' of life is something that has marked Western thought from Marx onwards. It is, in fact, precisely in Marx – the metaphysical thinker in which the demand for *self-making* is conveyed, in a peculiar way, to the heart of human life – that we find the root of a conception of man (and of the constitutive *richness* of the human being) as a totality of manifestations and possibilities of life. It is also in Marx that we find a conception of man as a being that has a constitutive need to develop himself and as a being whose development coincides with the reappropriation of that totality.

I will then consider some theoretical positions – such as those of Sen and Hardt and Negri – which diversely relate to the Marxian conception of man and of his development.

However, it is not by simply focusing on what takes place in Marx, I argue, that we can understand the extreme deployment of calculation and of power that occurs in the age of the 'cybernetic' completion of the history of metaphysics.

It is precisely by questioning the meaning of the dominion of calculation in the age of technological perfection, that I will investigate post-human dimension – that dimension in which the enhancement of life takes places within things: human cells that live outside the human body, human brains uploaded into computers or intelligent, 'living' machines.

The age of the completion of metaphysics is the age in which the correspondence between machination and lived-experience becomes ever more complete and, at same time, it is the age in which calculation reaches perfection; this means also that the 'calculative' relationship between man and things assumes a new meaning. What is at stake is not man who calculate things from the standpoint of man and in view of the enhancement of human life, but instead the phenomenon in which non-human beings are taken and considered as human and vice versa.

In the light of the interpretation of this phenomenon, I will critically discuss some theoretical stances – I refer in particular to the work of Bruno Latour – on the translations between man and beings and on the symmetry between the human and the non-human.

I will show, in the last part of the chapter, how, resulting in the most extreme enigmaticity of quality, the calculable and increasable quality of life continues to be a reference even on the post- or trans-human scene, in which the question on what qualifies life as human life resonates in an unprecedented tone.

Chapter 4 presents some concluding considerations. These dwell on the way in which we should understand the *extreme* to which a significant part of the literature on calculation refers.

How should we interpret the extreme development of calculation and power? We must not interpret it, I will argue, as merely the extreme annexation of man to a realm of manipulation and technological power. Even less should we understand it as merely the extreme outcome of the evolution of the capitalist process or of biopower (which remain, of course, two questions of the utmost importance and worthy of the greatest attention).

If we take heed of Heidegger, the age of the perfection of calculation is the age in which human life closes on itself in the most decisive way, refusing in the most extreme way the relationship with finitude. However, extreme calculability, far from being an inescapable fate, contains a possibility, difficult to grasp as it may be: *precisely* in the era of the extreme denial of finitude, man has an unprecedented chance to relate to his own finitude as an access to a dimension which is radically other to the sphere of the calculative self-securing of man himself.

The more precisely we consider the very nature of calculation and of its perfecting, the more we can prepare ourselves to grasp this opportunity; and the latter, in my view, comes to us in a very distinctive way, when we are confronted with the calculability of quality and with the distinctive *emptiness* in which quality resonates today.

Looking in a new way at quality does not require any denunciatory approach towards neither calculation nor calculable quality. Neither should we turn our eyes away from what happens on the scene of calculation. Precisely on the frontier of the unconditional calculation of every quality, I argue in the last part of the book, we may sense how the question of quality hints towards a dimension of radical incalculability. And this can be seen not only on the frontier of the post-human but also looking at some 'traditional' issues that are at the core of socio-economic science reflection.

Precisely when the issue of quality in the social domain seems to imply nothing else than a demand for assurance, quality alludes to the possibility of a social, economic and managerial life which is other than the unconditional pursuit of security; towards, in other terms, the possibility of experiencing choice, decision-making and measure in their relationship with the incalculability of the human.

1
Calculation, Quality and Life: A First Look at the Debate

1.1 A prologue: Notes on the transformation of the human as an object of calculation

In recent years, the human and social sciences have witnessed, within various disciplinary perspectives, a renewed interest in reflection on calculation. Because of the problematic definition of calculation as the object of analysis, such reflection does not take the form of an organic debate. Instead, it develops as a set of analytical paths, often linked by significant connections, which focus on the various dimensions of contemporary calculative scenarios, from the morphology of calculation processes to the 'performativity' of calculation in organizational and socio-economic life, from the link between calculability and managerial rationality to the ties between calculation, power and institutional structures, and up to and including the relationship between calculation, agency and democracy.

Many of these lines of thought touch on some important issues for my investigation of the calculation of the human and its relationship with quality – they will be the focus of dialogue within this work, starting in the present chapter, in some cases.

It is not my intention, in this prologue, to provide a synthesis of the debate; I will instead make an initial reference to a meta-issue that has recently profoundly marked the entire reflection on calculation, man and life, and that will be the subject of particular attention throughout my analytic trajectory. I refer to the transformation of the human as the 'object' of calculation – and of the nature itself of the calculative intervention on the human – in the scenario defined by the evolution of biogenetic and computer sciences.

Until some time ago, the expression 'calculation of the human' could allude to the calculation (to measurement, normalization, control and administration) of various aspects and ambits of human life.

Certainly the reference to calculation of the human pointed towards different dimensions: from the treatment of the 'quantitative'[1] aspects of life (length of life, natality and mortality) to the calculation of social life in all its determinants, to the increasingly detailed diagnosis of psychological, emotional and affective well-being. In this calculation scene, however, it seemed possible to retain the reference to an image of man (and of man in society). Certainly, this image could be considered as being continually reshaped by the operations of calculation and representation of life, without this then casting doubt on the distinction between the human sphere and that of non-human things.

However, what has come to our attention ever more forcefully in recent decades is a radical transformation of the scenario. This transformation has to do with the advent of forms of manipulation, recomposition and reshaping of man that are so strong that they pose in a new way the question of what man is, and on the way in which the distinction between the human and the non-human should be understood.

I will dwell on how this transformation is borne out by the reshaping of the theoretical perspective that interprets the nature and the proliferation of the processes of calculation in the light of Foucault's reflections on governmentality and biopolitics[2] (see in particular, Foucault, 2007; 2008).

It will be useful to consider, although very briefly, some moments of the Foucauldian studies, not only because they have played a major role in the debate on calculation of social life, but also because the Foucaldian perspective has constituted itself, as we will see later, as a particularly powerful and flexible theoretical framework for the interpretation of the quality–calculation nexus.

The complex branch of research that has developed around Foucault's thought on the transformation of power and government has been one of the richest and most fertile trends in the panorama of human and social sciences in recent decades.

In particular, the school of thought commonly known as the Anglo-Foucauldians has contributed significantly to the investigation on the morphology and performativity of the calculative practices that pervade contemporary organizations and societies (see Hopwood, 1992; Miller, 1992; 2001; Miller and O'Leary, 1994; Miller and Napier, 1993; Miller and Rose, 1990; Rose 1990; 1991; 1992; 1996).

The influence of this branch of analysis – and in particular the studies on accounting practices, understood in the broadest sense[3] – can be recognized not only in the studies on economic calculation[4] (and thus in the analysis of how calculative practices represent and shape economic processes and institutions), but also in the broader reflection on government and power in social life.

One of the ways in which Foucaldian studies have renewed the debate on calculation concerns the analysis of the historically and spatially differentiated ways in which *calculating selves* and *calculable spaces* are produced. What is at issue, therefore, is what Miller refers to as the *individualization, responsibilization, calculation* triptych and thus the close link between calculation practices and the making of subjectivities which are capable of self-regulating and self-governing. The multiplication of calculative regimes is thus seen as strictly related to the production of the possibility for individuals to *act upon themselves* and to be *acted upon* in turn. As Miller (1992, p. 63) wrote:

> Subjectivity or selfhood in this sense is of interest in two respects: it refers to the possibility of being subject to regulation or control by someone else; and yet it also emphasizes how practices of the self operate by mechanisms that tether one's own identity to oneself by self-knowledge and self-regulation.

The subjectivities that appear in the contemporary calculative spaces are therefore the object of control and management operations, and at the same time are free subjects, able to define their own goals, to make choices in view of achieving those goals, and to be responsible for those choices with respect to themselves and to others. This is a result of the multiplication of accounting practices and calculative regimes that bring the actions of 'free' subjects into accord with specific objectives (Miller, 1992).

We are thus faced with an interpretation of the relationship between calculation and government that alludes to the great Foucauldian theme concerning power relations as defined not merely by its effect on others, but by its effect on the actions of others, where the latter are constructed as responsible subjects, endowed with the freedom to act in one way or another.

The relationship between calculation and government is thus considered from a perspective in which government, as an exercise of power, has to do with the definition of the possible field of action of others, and the ability to act upon the actions occurring in that field (Miller, 1992).

The interpretation of calculation from the perspective of governmentality (and its neo-liberal form) endows the Foucauldian perspective with a considerable capacity for interpreting the proliferation of calculative processes and their performativity.[5]

Considering calculative practices as technologies of power has allowed the vast interdisciplinary literature to analyse the differentiated and changing morphology and the multiple rationalities of calculative processes. The reference is, for example, to the Foucauldian studies on human resource management (see for instance Barrat, 200; Townley, 1993) and to technologies of control, auditing, standardization, self-diagnosis and performance measurement that have developed in this field.

The vastly accelerated practices relating to the measurement of emotions, affections and feelings are particularly significant.[6] That field of calculative processes, which aims explicitly at calculating the most incalculable aspects of the self, develops under the heading of the optimization of the performance of the human resource – whose 'exploitational' horizon, by the way, goes far beyond the limits of work to include, ever more completely, the entire life of the worker.

The calculative technologies of the self are then seen as marching, in an increasingly pervasive way, towards the *governing of the soul* (Rose, 1989).

As Rose (1992, p. 142 quoted in Rapley, 2003) pointed out:

> The guidance of selves is no longer dependent upon the authority of religion or traditional morality; it has been allocated to 'experts of subjectivity' who transfigure existential questions about the purpose of life and the meaning of suffering into technical questions about the most effective ways of managing malfunction and improving 'quality of life'.

The pervasiveness of calculation, however, is clearly not merely a question of the unconditional proliferation of disciplinary practices. On the contrary, it is a phenomenon that points towards what Foucault[7] highlighted as the dense intersections between power as discipline and governmental power.

And, as we will see later, the intersection and mutual support between the 'disciplinary' and 'governmental' dimensions of power is a phenomenon that emerges in a distinctive shape precisely in the universe of the calculation and management of quality (of life).

The increasingly extreme calculability of the self – and the related technologies of (self)control, inspection, reporting, auditing and standardization – becomes part of complex and dynamic governmental architectures in which the governing of the individual life and performance, the management of 'targeted' sub-populations and the administration of the population as a whole become ever more closely interrelated.

The link between calculation, production of *responsible subjectivities* and neo-liberal governmentality forms a powerful interpretive key to the phenomenon of the proliferation of calculative practices well beyond the limits of the business and economic spheres.[8]

Public action, in all its dimensions, is seen as being defined by the intertwining of calculative regimes and 'entrepreneurial' actors, who are responsible for their own free choices and measured in terms of efficiency and performance. The multidimensional space of policy and of governance appears as a complex mesh – in continuous and often unforeseeable evolution – of calculative devices, calculable spaces and calculating subjects.

Within this framework has arisen a fertile vein of Foucaldian criticism of managerialist torsion of the public sphere (from health services to education, from scientific research to the field of care and to culture) and of the complicity between 'managerialist' discourse and the trend towards the commodification/marketization of social life. This is a question which, as we shall see, will dominate a significant part of the debate on *quality discourse* in the public sphere.

In general terms, we could say that considering calculation from the perspective of neo-liberal governmentality – and considering government from the perspective of the evolution of calculative processes and rationalities – has become a macro-theoretical framework in Foucauldian studies for interpreting what appear to be two conspicuous manifestations of the phenomenon of human calculability: the proliferation of calculation processes in all social spheres; and the gradual annexation of the most 'incalculable' dimensions of life.

Considering the progress of calculation in its relationship with the set-out of neo-liberal programmes of government (and thus with the morphogenesis of capitalism in the neo-liberal era) also brings with it a tendency to interpret from a certain perspective the crucial question of the 'relationship' between calculation and enhancement (and between calculation and enhancement of the human).

In other words, it becomes possible to consider the relationship between calculation and enhancement of life under the heading of a multitude of relationships between calculability and mobilization of the self: the calculability and resourcification of the self at work; the accountability of the policy actor as a calculating self who is expected to achieve an ever higher degree of performance; the calculability of the citizen as an individual self, whose measurable and always 'optimizable' quality of life is at the service of the well-being of the nation, which in its turn is involved in processes of comparison and competition with other nations. The life of the calculable self thus appears to be enhanced on a growing multiplicity of pathways.

It is precisely the significance of the 'maximization' of life, however, that is called into question in the scenario designed by the new possibilities of techno-scientific manipulation of man and nature. In this scenario, the meaning of enhancement of life seems to evade the possibility of being understood merely in terms of optimization, as we customarily understand it.

The frenetic developments in biogenetic, cognitive and computer sciences define a horizon in which the notion and the limits of life seem to be radically transformed. In that horizon, as Lemke sums up, 'the image of a natural origin of all living organisms is gradually being replaced by the idea of an artificial plurality of life forms, which resemble technical artifacts more than they do natural entities' (Lemke, 2011, p. 93).

Genetic manipulation, the sciences of transplantation and of cyborgs, and also a group of technical and scientific projects that occur at the boundary between biology and computer sciences (such as those concerning the uploading of the human mind to an artificial storage medium) profoundly alter the traditional image of body and mind, and raise the question – voiced by some in tones of considerable concern – about what remains of the human in a life subjected to intense processes of transformation.

The very relationship between life and death is called directly and brutally into question, as is evidenced by the project for the techno-scientific construction of immortal humanity. Death becomes an increasingly manipulable object: an object which one can imagine as being transferable from one body to another. As Lemke (2011, p. 95) summarizes: death can become 'part of a productive circuit and used to improve and extend life'.

Around the issue of the trans- or post-human, a very robust interdisciplinary debate has arisen which extends far beyond Foucauldian studies. However, it is precisely from the perspective of the reflection on biopolitics that the impact of the transformation can be grasped. This impact broadens the scope of the biopolitical issues, modifies the meaning and morphology of the biopolitical processes, reconfigures biopolitical rationalities, and redefines the scenario of the relationships between biopolitics, agency and democracy.

As Lemke (2011) notes, the reworking of the notion of biopolitics has one of its main roots in the overcoming of the Foucault's conception of body as a closed and delimited entity. What various and interlinked techno-scientific developments put in practice is indeed a dismantling, recombination, reprogramming of the body, which goes along with an ever more intense transformation of biogenetic processes and with the production of new forms of life.[9]

In some lines of interpretation, such as that of Rabinow (1992), the focus is on the emergence, amongst the sub-plots of the ongoing techno-scientific revolution, of unheard-of possibilities of self-description and self-conception in biogenetic terms, and therefore on the emergence of a new biogenetic citizenship, new political identities and new *identity politics*.

In Rose's reflection (which I will return to later), the issue of the radical rethinking of biopolitics – and of the forms of biopolitical calculation, broadly speaking – emerges in a particularly decisive and provocative manner.

The developments in the techno-scientific manipulation of life raise question of what qualifies *man as man*, and of the *philosophical status* of man himself (Rose, 2001; 2007).

When the body becomes the subject of new possibilities of manipulation and transformation (and becomes the linchpin of new possibilities of self-perception), what Rose emphasizes is the need to recognize 'a kind of "vitalist" character to the existence of individuals as political subjects' and thus the opportunity to think in terms of *vital politics*.

> If discipline individualizes and normalizes, and biopower collectivizes and socializes, ethopolitics concerns itself with the self-techniques by which human beings should judge themselves and act upon themselves to make themselves better than they are. While ethopolitical concerns range from those of lifestyle to those of community, they coalesce around a kind of vitalism: disputes over the value to be accorded to life itself: 'quality of life', 'the right to life' or 'the right to choose', euthanasia, gene therapy, human cloning and the like.
>
> (Rose, 2001, p. 18)

The novelty that Rose speaks of concerns something such as the entry onto the scene of *life itself*. Life itself would become the object of recursive acts of judgement, evaluation, selection and contestation.

> On the one hand, our very personhood is increasingly being defined by others, and by ourselves, in terms of our contemporary understandings of the possibilities and limits of our corporeality. On the other hand, our somatic individuality has become opened up to choice, prudence and responsibility, to experimentation, to contestation – and so to a 'vital politics'.
>
> (Ibidem, p. 20)

Today's biomedical practices – Rose (Ibidem, p. 22) notes, in particularly evocative terms with respect to the subject of my work – are predicated on the possibility of judging 'about the relative and comparative "quality of life" of differently composed human beings and of different ways of being human'.

It is worthwhile noting that Rose concludes his book on the politics of life itself, keeping his distance from the possibility of reading what is happening to man in terms of the 'traditional' critique of biopower. One of the main criticisms that Rose predicts could be raised of his theses

> is, no doubt, their absence of the familiar tropes of social critique. For all the talk of biopower, who has the power, who wields it to what ends, who gains and who loses? For all this talk of biopolitics, where is the analyses of hidden interests, of the role of class, the new forms of inequality and exploitation that are arising?
>
> (Rose, 2007, p. 258)

For Rose, we should not allow the 'old' forms of political critique to get in the way of grasping the novelty of what is emerging. It is at the same time necessary to let go of any form of melancholic hand-wringing about the intrusion of science into the sphere of what man is *as man*.

> The melancholy refrain of those who condemn the arrogance of biomedicine for meddling in such areas, who convict all references to the biological of reductionism, individualism and determinism, or who predict a new eugenics are of little help to us in understanding the issues at stake here.
>
> (Rose, 2001, p. 22)

If the above-mentioned technological and scientific developments are considered to be a phenomenon that transforms the notion of biopolitics, a parallel transformation is the subject of the debate on the relationship between capitalism and life.

What is at issue in some recent lines of thought is in fact not merely the question of the increasingly intense assumption of the human in all its dimensions in the sphere of capitalist exploitation.

In other words, it is not merely the case of a 'radicalization' of the issue of capitalist calculation, in its relationship with the universal commodification of life. Nor is it merely a case of investigating – as, for example, in Boltanski's and Chiapello's (2005) *new sociology of capitalism* – the link between the new spirit of capitalism and its forms of justification and the ever-closer commodification-oriented encoding of life (which is party to the capitalistic assimilation of every authentic difference).

Instead, it is a case of radical redefinition of the relationship between capitalism and life, which involves both poles of the relationship.

The reference here is, for example, to Sunder Rajan (2006) and his analyses on the emergence, within the new scenario defined by the innovations in the biosciences, of a new phase of capitalism (in which the production of scientific knowledge is intimately related with value production) or to Cooper's (2008) argument on the emergence of *bio-capitalism.*

What is at issue in Cooper's work is an emerging bio-economy in which life is reproduced in an *unlimited* way, within a frame of a morphogenesis of capitalism. Capitalism reinvents itself, assuming a biological nature, or in other words, taking on as the driver of its own development the steady enhancement of life promoted the biological techno-sciences.

When neo-liberal capitalism acquires a biological feature, life is exploited through bioscience in order to continuously generate itself out of itself, beyond any natural limit; this puts the production of a surplus of life at the heart of bio-capitalism.

Thus it is in this scenario that we must be prepared to consider the issue of the quality–calculation link. This is a scenario in which quality is not only the key feature under which a calculation of the human takes place in view of a well-known idea of the perfectibility of life. It is, instead, a scenario in which quality will continue to remain on the scene of calculation even when the question of what *qualifies* man as man plays to an unprecedented tune.

For now, however, it is time to give a brief account of the emergence of the issue of quality and its calculation as one of the key phenomena in the contemporary social scene.

1.2 The rise of the power of quality

Few words have marked the lexicon of science and social practices in recent decades with as much forcefulness and pervasiveness as quality, and perhaps none of these words has manifested, at the same time, such an elusive and indeterminate character and such extraordinary dogmatic power.

Quality has established itself, in fact, as a buzzword – a catchword, a keyword, a *mot d'ordre* – in all the spheres of life: from the environment to health, from family to culture, from research to teaching and from educating children to caring for the dying.

The rhetoric, cultures and technologies of quality – auditing, ranking, standards, indicators, certification schemes – widely and pervasively permeate the domains of business and public management, as well as that of policy making, up to and including those of the national and supranational governance.

While it is certainly not easy to reconstruct the paths that led to quality's 'astonishing' power, it is nonetheless possible to recognize two macro-aspects, which are moreover connected by strong and solid ties.

The first of these concerns the emergence of quality as a keyword in the management discourse (on business management and on public management) starting from the 1980s.

The second regards the establishment of *quality of life* as one of the key concepts in the social, political and economic discourse from the second half of the twentieth century onwards.

The path leading to quality's assumption of power in business management stems from the field of technical control of product quality. Initially, the scene was thus dominated by the concept of *conformity* with respect to predetermined standards. The sphere of quality management was therefore pervaded by increasingly elaborate and complex statistical control techniques, aimed at achieving a reduction in errors and non-conformity.

The 'conformative' dimension of quality was soon joined, however, by a focus on the satisfaction of (present or future, implicit or explicit) customer's requirements and demands.[10] The service economy (with its implications in terms of complexity and differentiation of consumer behaviours) plays a decisive role in reshaping the culture of quality around the client.

Starting from the interpenetration between the domain of control and conformity and the dimension of customer satisfaction, quality has thus progressively become the emblem of an overall tension – with increasingly *cultural* roots – concerning excellence in all areas of enterprise activity.[11]

In this scenario, in which quality sets out to designate a combined mobilization of all the resources (human, organizational, cognitive, experiential and relational) of the company, the *quality discourse* becomes more and more decisively a key element of organizational thinking and procedures.

The mobilization of all the energies towards what appears to be the vaguely esoteric goal of *excellence* requires a rethinking and restructuring of the organizational fabric. It calls for liberating the organization from the rigidity of the Taylorist organization in order to create suitable conditions for individuals and groups within the organization to be able to offer their own contribution to the overall project of self-diagnosis and self-improvement that quality demands.

It is in this context that the famous – or infamous – technological-discursive macro-apparatus known as 'Total Quality Management' emerged in the last decades of the twentieth century. Under the banner of 'Total Quality' – an expression which, as we shall see in the following chapters, deserves careful consideration over and above the meaning that it has taken on in the managerial lexicon – a plethora of rhetorical frameworks, organizational technologies and 'innovative' tools has flourished since the last decades of the 1900s.

The revolution promised by Total Quality (in its various forms and transformations) involved an overall de-bureaucratization of organizational dynamics and a bypassing of rigid subdivision into roles and tasks, with the objective of bestowing responsibility, autonomy and *empowerment* on individuals and groups. The critical debate which emerged on this theme, especially in the 1990s (see, for example, Tuckman, 1994; Wilkinson and Willmott, 1996), cast doubt on the outcome of that ambiguous cultural revolution, drawing attention to, among other things, the paradoxical results of re-bureaucratization produced by this change of tack in quality.

The sphere of influence of *quality discourse*, however, soon extended beyond the limits of the enterprise to assail the field of public management.

The rhetorical and technical arsenal of quality profoundly marks the transformation which, at the turn of the century, affected management and public policies. In particular, the imperative of quality has established itself as a pillar of that controversial phenomenon – the advent of *New Public Management.*

The New Public Management 'revolution' developed around a number of headings: efficiency in the production and provision of public services, accountability of organizational and management processes, performance measurement,[12] transparency and value for money. But quality (as a value, as a 'shared' culture, as a 'philosophy' and, naturally, as a measurable, manageable and upgradeable object) has acted as a sort of unifying heading for that problematic revolution. The reference to quality produces its effects as much in terms of the rethinking of the organizational practices and of management cultures of public administrations, as in terms of focus on the client and the related discourse on excellence.

The English-speaking world has been at the forefront of a process that has since extended, in different ways and at different rates, to all industrialized worlds. While some sectors – such as health, education and research – were the initial guinea pigs of the transformation (and a critical debate has arisen around those very sectors, as I will explain in the following section), the phenomenon has progressively extended to all the spheres of public action.

This has given rise to the ever-growing 'catalogue' of qualities (of the environment, of education, of research, of health services, of cultural activities and so on) that marks the contemporary political–managerial scene.

The scene of *quality-based* public management has thus become characterized by the emergence of new forms of expertise, new bureaucracies[13] and new relationships between the state (in the guise of remote controller) and the organizations providing services (which, precisely under the umbrella of quality, enter ever more convincingly into the role of *calculating subjectivities*).

The extent of the transformation can also be seen from a perspective specifically focused on policy making and governance. On the one hand, the *policy making* universe tends to be structured more and more decisively around the keywords of the production and social construction of quality. On the other hand, the technologies that more or less explicitly refer to quality (auditing, standardization, certification and ranking) take a central position on the stage of the so-called new *policy instrumentation*.[14]

The power and pervasiveness that the logic of quality manifests in the field of policies can be seen particularly clearly in the domain of supranational policy (and particularly European policy). The 'philosophy' of quality pervades the entire field of European administration and policy making. What is at issue is the remarkable development of internal auditing practices in the administrative structures of the European Union (EU), but also the role of quality standards, certification and indicators in EU policy (as well as in other international or supranational policy spheres). Some of the domains involved include industrial products, environment,[15] territorial planning and policy,[16] higher education and research,[17] up to and including that of the quality of regulation[18] (Doria, 2009).

The surprising power of quality settles at the very core of European governance and significantly shapes the scene of the multilevel relationships between EU institutions and local and national actors, with the risk of reinforcing the tendency towards a techno-managerialist turn in both European action and local policy.

On the basis of a surprising 'connective' ability, quality arises as a powerful connecting element between different fields of policy,[19] between different levels of government, and between the actors that interact in the new public–private policy networks (Doria, 2009).

In short, quality shows itself, and evidently not only in the supranational policy sphere, as an ambiguous, if not enigmatic, ethical reference, as an expert system *à la* Giddens, and as an automatic connector between the various fields and dimensions of socio-economic and political life (Ibidem). It stands as a principle which can be 'adapted' to everything, but at the same time it cannot be reduced to any of its determinations – as a reference that stands out as being obvious, even before we consider its significance.

Even when the focus is on the concept of quality of life, the scenario that arises – see, for example, Rapley's (2003) useful work – is one of a discursive apparatus which is simultaneously powerful and controversial, pervasive and ambiguous.[20]

The concept of quality of life (Benzer, 2011; Rapley, 2003) set out on its own glorious path around the 1960s, with the *social indicators movement* that spread throughout the United States and Europe.

The underlying idea of this movement was to propose measurements of social progress that would go beyond the limited horizons of the 'traditional' economic indicators, and in particular the gross domestic product (GDP).[21] The intention was to provide a more organic representation of living conditions, taking into account an ever-increasing range of dimensions of individual and collective existence (which would then become the components of total quality of life).

Thus the methodical pathways concern the construction of a framework for representing living conditions, through the definition of increasingly complex lists of 'objective' items (public order, social mobility, education, weekly working hours etc.; Rapley, 2003).

This fundamental method of calculation of quality of life will continue to be popular to the end of our times – I am thinking, for example, of the lists of components continually proposed by international organizations[22] in their initiatives aimed at measuring and comparing national quality of life or well-being.

These measurements highlight the decisive role of *representation*, displaying or figuring. In this calculative scenario, in other words, the phenomenon of the construction and 'fixation' of an elusive object, by means of representing it within a frame, emerges. This is an issue that alludes to the sociological debate on *qualculation*, which I will return to later.

Unsurprisingly, since the start, the definition of these 'objective' components of quality of life has encountered the problem of *consensus* with respect to those items which actually deserve to be taken into account. This is a question which, as Rapley (2003) pointed out, involves a set of assumptions and positions of an eminently political nature that, even today, form a key element in the methodological debate which is intertwined around the calculation of quality of life.

While the first stage in the history of measurement of quality of life is therefore characterized by the so-called 'objective' measurement, from the mid-1970s onwards (Benzer, 2011) – and with increasing intensity in the succeeding decades (Rapley, 2003) – the 'objective' approach to measurement has been accompanied by a 'subjective' measurement.

The conviction gradually grew that a scientifically rigorous and therefore politically useful measurement of quality of life should take into account the subjective perceptions of individuals regarding the overall quality of their life and the conditions that determine this quality (Benzer, 2011; Rapley, 2003).

The advent of the idea of the feasibility and utility of a subjective measurement of quality of life profoundly marks the scenario of calculation practices; and an extremely wide-ranging methodological debate emerged around the theoretical and ideological assumptions underlying the measurement of subjective perceptions.

While I will come back later to some questions raised by that debate, it is worth mentioning here one of the most significant issues at stake. I refer to the possibility and opportunity of addressing quality of life in terms of an overall judgement about one's life or of measuring feelings (positive or negative) on a moment-by-moment basis.

As outlined in a recent report edited by Stiglitz, Sen and Fitoussi:

> Subjective measures of well-being have been very prominent in recent discussions about measuring QoL [quality of life], but this popularity has also generated some ambiguities and misconceptions.
>
> Most prominent among these is the assumption that all dimensions of subjective well-being can somehow be reduced to the single concept of 'happiness'. In reality, as argued by Diener (1984), subjective well-being (SWB) is best understood as encompassing three separate aspects:
>
> - life satisfaction, that is, a person's overall judgment about their life at a particular point in time;
> - the presence of positive feelings or affect, that is, the flow of positive emotions (such as feeling happiness and joy, or a sense of vitality and energy) from moment to moment;
> - the absence of negative feelings or affect, that is, the flow of negative emotions (such as feeling angry, sad or depressed) from moment to moment.
>
> Life satisfaction, positive affect and negative affect are separate aspects of SWB, and accord with different conceptions of QoL. Satisfaction with life as a whole (and with particular domains, such as work, housing and family life) involves an *evaluative judgment* of how one's life is faring, which requires making an effort and remembering past experiences.
>
> Conversely, positive and negative affect involves measuring the hedonic *experiences* experienced by people in real time, or shortly after these experiences have occurred.
>
> (Stiglitz, Sen and Fitoussi, 2009, p. 145–146)

Above and beyond the methodological debate (whose openness to crucial issues can already be glimpsed in this brief mention), the taking root of the idea itself of subjective measurements not only became the preferred target of many critical stances, but also was singled out, in some parts of the debate, as a connecting element between the sphere of quality of life and the sphere of 'managerial' quality.

When, with increasing intensity throughout the 1990s, the calculation of quality also became a matter of subjects engaged in measuring the quality of their own lives, it emphasized some of the basic elements of the quality discourse in the political and management field: the increasingly marked tendency towards the proliferation of *responsible calculable selves*,[23] the focus on the customer in the management of public services and the associated drift towards marketization (Rapley, 2003).

> The idea of QOL has become much more than a social policy analogue for the GDP – and is now tightly enmeshed with a set of other, and explicitly ideological, knowledges and unashamedly 'American' political and commercial projects. QOL has become not just a concept that ties together a variety of social indicators to offer an index of the success of public policy, but an integral part of the *marketing* of public policy.
>
> (Ibidem, p. 9)

Today, the methodological debate continues, recognizing the opportunity of preserving both the objective and the subjective macro-perspectives of measurement.[24] Precisely by developing around the two major axes of measurement, the debate has gradually become richer, involving some of the most relevant techno-scientific apparatuses, amongst which is that of the *economics of happiness*.

Bearing witness to the richness and density of the debate is the above-mentioned report (Stiglitz, Sen and Fitoussi, 2009) which, due to the reputation of its authors, is expected to play an important part not only in the scientific history of quality of life, but also in the trajectory of its political influence. This report, commissioned by the French government,[25] is devoted to an exploration of the issue of a means of measuring social progress that goes beyond the traditional economic indicators. The subject of quality of life, not surprisingly, plays a very significant segment of that report,[26] and the way in which it treats some of the conceptual and methodological issues will be the focus of attention in the present work.

While the issue of calculation of life at the national level has emerged as the focus of significant media interest and political relevance, it should be pointed out that also at the local level – and in particular at the urban level – initiatives aimed at measuring quality of life, or *liveability*, have proliferated over recent years.

These initiatives are of various types and have wide-ranging instigators: from the rankings promoted by the press bodies[27] (which are the subject of increasing attention from both the public and local governments) to indicator-production in the field of policy processes.[28]

On the one hand, the measurement of quality of life at the urban level presents methodological affinities with the measurement of quality of life at the national level. I refer, in particular, to how the breakdown into components of quality of life is mirrored by the disaggregation of urban quality in areas such as administration, environment, level of public services, provision of infrastructure, cultural attractions and urban security. Much of the methodological debate on quality at the urban level arises precisely around the definition of the list of components and the definition of suitable indicators for each of these.

On the other hand, urban/local quality of life, on a conceptual and methodological level, recalls regional quality-based policies. In these policies, the regional space tends to be subject to a diagnostic-evaluative investigation that breaks down the territorial capital into distinct components. SWOT-type analyses then contribute to defining the current and potential contribution that these components may offer to the total local quality. As a result, a multitude of diagrams, figures, projections and schemes throng the calculative – or qualculative – scene of the measurement of the 'liveability' of local spaces (see Doria, 2009).

More and more often this diagnostic investigation is also directed at more elusive, more difficult-to-calculate components: namely identity, local atmosphere, quality of cultural life and so on. These components are constructed as policy objectives precisely through *qualculative* operations. This is the case of local identity, a notion that is commonly recognized as having an 'existential' nature, and that therefore lends itself to being listed among the most difficult to calculate dimensions of the territorial/regional 'capital'. The construction of this elusive entity as a policy object develops along a twofold path. On the one hand identity is broken down into components; on the other hand, it is put side by side with the other 'hard' determinants of the *total quality* of the territory.[29]

Unsurprisingly, the cultural and artistic dimension also forms one of the most controversial aspects of the measurement of quality of life at the local level. Precisely in the field of the measurement of culture[30] (which develops, for example, through the production of indicators of the intensity and richness of cultural and artistic life or of *cultural vitality*), issues may emerge, with peculiar intensity, concerning the meaning, the feasibility and the potential 'instrumentalist' nature of the measurement.

Even the domain of local quality of life thus appears particularly dense and controversial. Precisely in this domain, moreover, a sort of bifurcation of the political rationalities on the calculation of quality of life emerges in a particular form.

On the one hand, the calculation of regional/urban quality of life is associated in a more or less critical tone with the important phenomenon of competition between urban systems.[31] This has given rise to a perspective of critical thought on urban quality as an element of the trend towards the marketization of the urban space and its complicity with the technocratic twisting of territorial policies.

On the other hand, the local dimension is assumed to be a privileged place for the participatory construction of quality. The local is assumed, in fact, as a privileged space for the emergence of forums for debate (open to a diversity of conceptions and interpretations of quality) in which measurement can be far removed from its 'technocratic' outcomes. The mobilization (on a cognitive and relational level) of local actors is seen as an element capable of improving the quality of life of the local community.

The link between the reference to *localness* and the participatory nature of the process is today at the core of the initiatives for measuring local quality, which are promoted in the context of national and supranational policies; and this link can be seen throughout the trajectory of the history of quality measurement, referring for example, as Rapley (2003) notes, to the history of *community consultation* practices, oriented to meaningful and cooperative governance.

1.3 On some lines of interpretation of the quality–calculation nexus

As previously mentioned, a very extensive debate has grown around the singular power of quality and the universe of arguments, technologies and practices that have developed around it.

At this time, I will merely retrace this debate – by no means exhaustively – bearing in mind the argument that I will develop in subsequent sections.

A substantial line of argument – which has developed with regard to the ambiguous power of quality in business and public management – targets a macro-issue concerning the questions of rituality, self-referentiality and hyper-reality in the management universe.

Consider, for example, Charlton's criticisms of the regime of auditable, controllable and quantifiable quality. In contemporary management scenarios, quality appears to be reduced to nothing more than an unconditionally controllable and measurable object, to the detriment of all *genuine* excellence or of *real-world quality* (Charlton, 2002).

An initial form of this issue can be seen in quality assurance's constitutive tendency to bypass reference to the product, in favour of compliance in terms of control mechanisms.

> Quality Assurance (QA) is a technical managerial term for that type of auditing which is concentrated upon *systems and processes* rather than outcomes. QA is built on the assumption that any properly-constituted organization should be based around a system of auditing systems and processes.
>
> (Charlton, 2002, p. 20)
>
> [...]
>
> When 'quality' has thus been re-defined in terms of auditable systems and processes, rather than excellent outcomes, this has the effect of liberating 'quality enhancement' initiatives from the need to *define* desirable outcomes or best practice. This is of particular relevance to education, since it has proved impossible to agree upon valid and reliable definitions of the real-world 'quality' (i.e. excellence) of teaching.
>
> (Ibidem, p. 21)

The explicit reference here is to Michael Power's vast and fertile reflection on the universe of auditing, on the emergence at of an *audit society* at the end of the twentieth century, and on the ambiguous and epistemologically obscure nature of auditing itself.

The discursive and technological universe of auditing and the sphere of quality are closely related, although audit may be regarded as just one of the technologies of quality assurance. This is not only because the lexicon of auditing can be translated (for the most part, and perhaps in its entirety) in terms of the audit of quality (of managerial quality, organizational quality, environmental quality, quality of administration, quality of public services), but because, as Power himself points out, 'Audits do as much to construct definitions of quality and performance as to monitor them' (Power, 1994, p. 33).

It is precisely from the perspective of its relationship with quality that the ambiguous nature of auditing as a control of control can be grasped. Let us consider the following passages:

> Audits are often not directly concerned with the quality of performance, whether environmental, educational or financial, but rather with the systems in place to govern quality. This 'policing of policing' distinguishes the audit explosion from an older tradition of engineering-based quality control and its statistically grounded methods. (p. 6)
>
> Audit has thereby become the 'control of control', where what is being assured is the quality of control systems rather than the quality of first order operations. In such a context accountability is discharged by demonstrating the existence of such systems of control, not by demonstrating good teaching, caring, manufacturing or banking. (p.15)
>
> Detailed conceptions of quality may be very different if a supermarket is compared to a hospital. But the general principles of quality control systems for both can be made to look very similar, enabling one to compare them at an abstract level. (p.16)

Auditing – that calculative technology that brings to the forefront the self-enhancement control and assurance – proceeds comfortably under the banner of quality; the quality of everything we might add, since in Power's text we see once again quality's surprising ability to develop in all directions, encompassing all things, despite their 'differences'.

Calculation thus seems to advance smoothly, hand in hand with quality, but without ever encountering the *quality of a thing*.

Because of its relationship with quality, it develops as the constant assurance of itself, and as the assurance of its own quality. This also means, however, that in the management regime illustrated by Power, quality appears, in a way, as nothing more than a matter of calculability, or, in other words, as a matter of assurance of its own calculability.

Here, we recognize that aura of ambiguity, almost of inscrutability, that surrounds managerial calculation and that Power (1999, p. 142) alludes to in his famous argument on the unconditional and self-referential nature of audit:

> Audit has put itself beyond empirical knowledge about its own effects in favour of a constant programmatic affirmation of its potential.

What is at stake is the tendency of certain calculative practices to resist any investigation that seeks to justify them in terms of empirically proven benefits.[32] This issue is, in some way, related to the question of the demand for *unconditional measurement of everything* and the way in which this demand pervades contemporary management (Power, 2004). These are important issues that Power interprets in terms of the influence, perhaps destined one day to be overcome,[33] of an almost ideological belief and a fashion for audit and quality (Power, 1994) or as the effect of *cultural* and *psychological* reasons (Power, 2004).[34]

The issue of the distinctive self-referential nature of the quality and audit regime has been the object of great attention in the interdisciplinary literature. See, for example, Vollmer (2003) who, in his reflection on the state and prospects of the sociology of calculation, highlights the possibility of understanding the *auditable quality* regime as a form of the production of those hyper-real spaces that characterize some fields of contemporary economic calculation, and whose most significant manifestation is in the sphere of financial calculative practices.

One line of thought that insists explicitly on the eminently ambiguous nature of the notion of quality in public management was already followed in the 1990s (and thus at the height of the quality boom) by Loughlin (1996; 2002).

Loughlin's critical target is the pervasive spread of the reference to quality in all spheres of public life – and, in particular, in the management of public services, such as those related to health.

The discourse of performance measurement and improvement takes place under the banner of quality as an ethical-cultural reference and of the measurement and maximization of quality as an incontrovertible mission. This is despite the fact that the meaning of the term 'quality' and the reasons for its use remain obscure.

The debate about how to achieve quality is phrased in 'a pseudointellectual "management-speak", whose quasi-economic ugliness fails to disguise a shocking lack of precision' (Loughlin, 2002, p. 67). Why – Loughlin asks – is the tension towards the improvement of performance expressed in terms of improving the quality of everything? And why, although this question cannot be answered in a logically rigorous way, does quality remain in force as an imperative to be willingly obeyed? Why can quality be something to which one can be 'wholeheartedly committed' before it has become clear what this means, and despite the fact that the problem of its indefinability is to some extent recognized by the apologists of quality themselves?

The questions that Loughlin poses point towards important issues for my own analytic path. The phenomenological investigation that I will subsequently carry out will, however, lead me far from Loughlin's answers. For the latter, in fact, while the power of quality has no basis in logical or rational terms, quality's persistence on centre stage is seemingly justified on two grounds:

> The first is that the word 'quality' has emotive properties such that, other things being equal, the very fact that the word has been applied to something inclines us to view it positively, irrespective of any rational considerations.
>
> (Loughlin, 1996, p. 93)

The second concerns the fact that the success of the quality discourse and of quality technologies serves an ideological apparatus based on the free market model, and thus on universal marketization. 'Contained within the hollow jargon of quality is the mentality of the market' (Ibidem, p. 93).

In general, a macro-line of interpretation can be perceived in the debate which combines the reference to the ambiguity of the *quality discourse* (and its connection with other controversial discursive frameworks such as those based on transparency,[35] accountability and efficiency), the focus on the self-referentiality of calculative processes, and the interpretation of the 'power' of quality in terms of disciplinary and governmental rationalities.

The analyses take place (within but also beyond Foucauldian perspectives) on different levels, which are nonetheless interconnected: the level of interpretation of the morphogenesis of contemporary governmental regimes (with particular reference to New Public Management and to its effects on the managerialization and marketization of the public sphere), and the level of the analysis – often carried out using ethnographic methods – of the micro-dynamics of power.

Some sectors, such as education and academic research, are the subject of particular attention.

Shore and Wright (1999; 2000) view auditing as a political technology which, in the frame of neo-liberal governmentality, develops through the internalization by individuals of normative frames and through processes of *self-activation* and *self-policing*. The anthropological analysis of the universe of quality and audit culture in the educational field identifies the presence of forms of *coercive accountability* (Shore and Wright 2000).

The regime of quality is analysed by Morley (2003) with regard to both the macro-systems of accountability, control and regulation and the micro-dynamics through which quality influences the cultural and relational environments in universities. Quality operates as a 'universalizing metanarrative', while the definition of what constitutes quality becomes a fundamental dimension of power. 'The definition of quality in quantitative terms in the public domain is one of the ways in which discursive regulation takes place' (Ibidem, p. vii).[36]

An emphasis on the transformation of the identities of calculating subjectivities can be found in the arguments of Ball (2003) on the culture of competitive performativity which goes hand in hand with the management panopticism of quality and excellence. The policy technologies of education based on performance tend to produce a transformation of the nature of work and interpersonal relations that potentially affects both the identity of the subjects involved and the authenticity of their working life.

A focus on the effects in terms of *institutional self-strangulation*[37] can be found in Lock and Lorenz's (2007) analysis of the quality and audit regime in universities. The attention is concentrated on the proliferation of a hyper-bureaucratic discourse aimed at codifying academic research and teaching and at making academic life accountable in terms of measurable efficiency criteria.

> The important point is that academic quality – of both teaching and research – is coming to be *defined* in terms of such auditable indicators. It is rather as if truth were to be *defined* as equivalent to particular values for blood pressure, heart rate, respiration and skin conductivity, as measured by a lie detector (polygraph). It is a rash justice system that would base its policy on such an equivalence. It is a rash education system that would base its policy on 'audited quality'
>
> (Lock and Lorenz, 2007, p. 416)

Self-referentiality and rituality are also addressed in some studies on the quality-based evaluation of cultural policy. Evaluation, if carried out under the auspices of a technocratic quality discourse, appears as control for the sake of control (Nielsen, 2003), which develops through a complex of managerial rituals.

Some contributions go as far as considering quality as radically compromised with a managerialist ideology with neo-liberal roots and thus as something which should be left aside (see Dahlberg, Moss, and Pence, 1999).

The debate on the technologies of quality (such as standards and indicators) also touches, of course, on the role played by those technologies in the overall transformation of the forms of government and of the relationships between levels of government (international, national and local).[38]

The politics of standards and indicators holds a particular importance on a critical analysis level from the perspective of the theory[39] and anthropology of law. Consider the important thoughts advanced by Supiot (2006, p. 117) on those devices which, by providing a 'caricature of self-oblivious normativity', tend to legitimate a normative Darwinism embedded in the neo-liberal doctrine.

The managerial regime of unconditional and unlimited evaluation proceeds by formatting law (and the normative dimension of law) as something that can be evaluated in term of *efficiency*. In the background of Supiot's argument, there is the very important issue concerning the dogmaticity of management and the way in which management is not aware of its own dogmaticity.[40]

Finally, we should mention a perspective centred on the social construction of quality measurement practices and on the political dimension of the calculation of quality itself.

This is a theme that manifests itself in various forms and on different levels. In works such as that of Nielsen (2003), the focus is on the opposition between an abstract and technocratically disposed discourse on the quality of cultural processes and the possibility of 'contextualizing' the practices of definition and measurement of quality. When the evaluation and definition of quality become the object of context-specific and 'participatory' public debate, the quality imperative is weakened as a problem and instead becomes the potential heart of a 'progressive' discourse. A sort of 're-qualifying' of quality as an antidote to its 'instrumentalist' drift lies at the heart of the debate, above and beyond the sphere of culture, and identifies a kind of resistance strategy in fields such as that of quality of research or education, or quality of life at a local level.

From another perspective (see, for example, Salais' works on indicators), the focus is specifically on the technologies involved in measuring and comparing quality – particularly the quality of crucial political 'objects', such as work and social rights.

For Salais (2006), understanding the intrinsically social nature of the process of producing indicators (which, like all social data, do not reflect any state of nature, but are the result of social dynamics which are inevitably embedded in specific social, institutional and cultural realities) entails moving away from the illusion of being able to use the indicators themselves to carry out a mechanistic comparison of everything with everything else (and of a given country's historical and cultural trajectory with that of any other country).

The use of indicators is, on the contrary, an extremely delicate operation that should be considered in its character as a local and social operation. In other words, it should be acknowledged as an open process that requires the active role of local actors 'under certain conditions of public discussion' and involves the 'development of knowledge and of the capacities of action and initiative of each of the participants (individuals, administrations, organizations)' (Ibidem, p. 243).

The issue of the politicization of quality measurement takes on a distinctive tone and meaning within the perspective of the actor-network oriented studies. In this perspective, the primary object of analysis is the incomplete and provisional character of calculative practices and the implications for the question of agency.

I am thinking here of the recent contributions by Callon and his colleagues, and in particular of the debate on the so-called *economy of qualities* (Callon, Méadel and Rabeharisoa, 2002).

In today's economic scenarios (and, in particular, in the sphere of the service economy), a crucial role is played by processes designed to define and stabilize the distinctive properties of tangible and intangible goods. In the interpretative key proposed by Callon and his colleagues, these processes represent a fundamental point in the operations that make a good calculable and therefore transform it into a marketable good (Callon and Muniesa, 2005).

The analysis of market transactions is not based on the properties of goods as intrinsic characteristics of the goods themselves, but stresses the crucial role of the complex dynamics of co-construction of these properties. Through processes of qualification,[41] producers cooperate with consumers (in a scene involving a multitude of other social actors, including civil society organizations and public institutions) in order to shape and reshape the qualities of the goods and 'adjust' them to the world of the buyer.

The qualification processes[42] are, therefore, practices of treatment and manipulation of technological and socio-cultural phenomena, intended to translate those phenomena into the form of quality of products/services. In this way, the profile of a particular good and the limits of a given market are defined. The protagonists of these qualification operations are complex *calculating agencies*, which, in line with one of the fundamental assumptions of the *actor-network* theory, take the form of socio-material networks – of networks, in other words, which are constituted not only of human agents but also of technical devices. The latter take widely differing forms, including, but not limited to, schemes of classification, of measurement criteria, of certification formats, of *accounting* methods and of quality standards.

The socio-political character of the *economy of qualities* is thus linked to the open nature of qualification and to the constitutively precarious and *contestable* nature of products and markets. Qualification is understood as a movement that leads to the continuous deconstruction and reconstruction of qualified objects. The making of markets is, therefore, exposed to a constant, reflective investigation that recursively reopens and restructures their boundaries[43] (Callon, Méadel and Rabeharisoa, 2002; Callon and Muniesa, 2005).

While from the *economy of qualities* perspective the definition of qualities is addressed with reference to the market (and therefore involves the issue of the relationship between qualification and alienation of goods[44]), the issue of the incompleteness and contestability of calculation practices (and particularly of quality measurement processes), as it is interpreted by Callon and his co-authors, overtakes the whole socio-economic and political scenes. The focus is on the possibility that the socially distributed nature of calculation and its *politicization* bring into question its potential hegemony in socio-economic life (see Callon and Muniesa, 2005). This is an issue that clearly alludes to the subject of *technical democracy* and thus to the emergence of important areas of public debate and of democratic participation on issues of technical-scientific origin (Callon, Lascoumes and Barthe, 2001).[45]

The contribution of actor-network oriented studies is thus, unsurprisingly, addressed in several recent works on the calculative technologies of quality. This is the case of Higgins and Larner (2010), who, in the conclusions of a recent book they edited, interpret the phenomenon of standardizing focusing on the intersection of the actor-network theory with some of the themes dear to Foucauldian studies.

The attention is on the differentiation of *standardizing practices* (which are local by nature, and are shaped by local processes of adaptation, negotiation and implementation), on the hybridization between technical and methodical frameworks and local bodies of expertise, and on the incomplete and *impure* nature of the processes that frame agents and goods through standards. The interpretation of the phenomenon of standardization (although the analysis could be extended to other calculative technologies) thus does not point to a universal rationalization process. Instead, attention is turned to the work of standardizing and to *how* standards are involved in the construction of different forms of rationality and social organization.

It is expedient to emphasize, however, another important issue that is addressed by Higgins and Larner. The latter, referring to Foucault (2008), note that the neo-liberal forms of governing do not primarily develop by standardizing, meaning the use of 'rigid' mechanisms to govern individuals; rather they construct spaces which are open to fluctuating processes and political unknowns. Referring to the Massumi (2009) re-reading of Foucault, Higgins and Larner also emphasize a shift from standardization and normalization to processes that are characterized by instability, spontaneity and self-organization.

The issues that Higgins and Larner raise can be read with regard to the debate on *qualculation*.

On the one hand, what is at issue is the question of the calculative capacity of practices that are not directly involved with the sphere of numerical measurement (and in particular with cardinality[46]). Such practices include figuring, displaying, framing, labelling, ranking, the arrangement of objects in a given space–time framework and the definition of new relations between such objects (see on qualculation, Cochoy, 2002, 2008; Callon and Law, 2005).

This is a range of practices that must be understood as being constitutively open, and which also incorporate practices that are neither rigid nor rigidly predetermined. 'Quantitative methods, qualitative procedures, professional judgments, or the tinkering of daily practice, all of these are qualculative' (Callon and Law, 2005, p. 731).

Qualculative processes develop 'in indefinitely many ways' (Ibidem, 719), which means that the borders of qualculation are fluid: 'the character of comparability, and manipulability, this needs to be left open' (Ibidem, p. 720). On the other hand, however, our thoughts turn in the direction recently taken by the debate on the qualculative sphere, in the article by Callon and Law quoted above.

From Callon and Law's theoretical perspective, the issue is not merely the fact that, in contemporary calculative scenarios, 'spaces' of incalculability are bound to constantly emerge (to become the subject of new calculative operations, which result in the emergence of new areas of incalculability). Instead, what is more specifically at issue is the *co-othering* relationship between the dimension of the calculable and that of the incalculable.

> all calculation builds itself with and against noncalculation – and vice versa [...]
>
> This approach suggests that they are Other to each other – indeed, separate but also mutually implicated [...]

> Incalculabilities, we argue, are enacted just as much as calculabilities.
>
> (Callon and Law, 2005, p. 718)

The calculable and the incalculable are considered to be living in a relationship of co-othering, precisely on the basis of their common nature as enacted entities. *Incalculabilities* are enacted, precisely like calculabilities, through a wide range of material arrangements and practices.[47]

However, it is worth noting already here, as a foretaste of the argument I shall advance later, that from the perspective in which Heidegger invites to think the calculative, the issue of the dominance of calculation (which is a danger, but which is not to be demonized as an inescapable fate) is in no way weakened or removed by the 'recognition' that calculation does not deal exclusively with numerical operations or with any other operations exhibiting the nature of 'rigid' determination.

Nor is the power of calculation called into question by the constant emergence of spaces of incalculability, destined sooner or later to become related to calculation, and even less by the acknowledgment of the congenital co-implication of calculability and incalculability.

What the dominion of calculability denies, according to Heidegger, is rather the relationship with that *incalculable* that denotes a dimension of radical unavailability and of radical otherness with respect to any representation, production or manipulation.

Returning to our recognition of the debate, we must note that many of the issues (and much of the disquiet) that permeate the analyses on 'managerial' quality, can be found also in the reflection that focuses specifically on quality of life.

This is the case, above all, of the question concerning the ambiguity and elusiveness of the notion of quality of life. In the face of the increasingly intense efforts involved in operational definition and measurement, quality of life retains, even in the opinion of those undertaking the work of measurement, its nature as an *inconsistent* concept. As Cummins, Gullone and Lau (2002) write, mentioned by Rapley (2003), quality of life stands as one of the most inconsistently used terms in the human sciences. Rapley himself also mentions Edgerton's definition (1990, p. 149) of quality of life as the 'shibboleth of the 1990s', where the term alludes to the importance as well as to the eminently contentious nature of the field of quality of life.

One of the angles from which the ambiguous power of quality of life can be interpreted is that referring to the spread of governmental rationalities and the way in which these connect the increasingly precise diagnosis of the state of individual well-being and that of the population at large.

Under the umbrella of quality of life (and of its measurement at the individual and population level) the construction of the 'responsible subject' occurs, which means conceptualizing the individual's own responsibility and freedom in terms of capacity and duty to set up a diagnostic and evaluative inspection of his or her own life, in its entirety.

For Rapley, thus, the calculability of life, under the heading of quality, appears to be a very important moment of the 'transfiguration' of existential questions into technical matters which Rose (1992) referred to.

As I have previously mentioned, for Rapley, the quality-based construction of the self as an *enterprising self* – involved in the management and maximization of its own life as a contribution to the 'total quality' of the population – highlights its own complicity with the tendencies towards the neo-liberal marketization of the public sphere. This is typically shown by the way in which the concept of quality of life is used to measure the level of satisfaction of a group of target populations of public policies; these populations are invited to participate actively in measuring their own quality of life as an 'indicator' of the quality of the services which they are 'clients' of (Rapley, 2003).

An interpretation of the issue of quality of life as the frontier of the transformation of biopolitical rationalities (and as a moment in the construction of a new biopolitical humanity) is also proposed by Brusa and Tarizzo (2009). In their line of interpretation, which I shall return to later, the bond between the extreme calculability of the self and the administration of the populational well-being is examined with regard to the *economistic* roots of the emerging technical and evaluative rationality which is revealed under the heading of quality of life.

Thus, attention is focused on the decisive role of the techno-scientific apparatus of economics, as a science that is ever more decisively tending to become a science of the calculation of everything. This super-science, and particularly behavioural economics, is charged with the ever more precise and 'rigorous' calculation of the degree of individual well-being. On the techno-scientific scene of measurement – in particular of measurement of quality of life on a 'subjective' level – a formatting of individual happiness is carried out, that serves as a building block in calculating well-being at the level of the population. Following this path leads to an increasingly marked 'economistic' reduction of the individual lived-experience, which then becomes drained of all historical depth (Ibidem).

From the Wahlberg's (2007) perspective, the population comes to be redefined as an object precisely on the basis of the morphogenesis of biopolitical calculation that takes place under the banner of quality of life. The population is ever more completely manifested not just as the subject of biopolitics that administers mortality rates, life expectancy or morbidity rates, but as the subject of *anthropopolitics* that deals with a collective subjectivity as a psychological, sociological and anthropological problem.

In this calculative scenario, a decisive role is played by the technoscientific complex organized around the psychological and cognitive sciences, biology, genetic engineering and computer science.

This very mobilization of these scientific systems (and particularly psychological and cognitive disciplines) is interpreted by Rapley as being central to the establishment of the 'subjectivist' concept of quality of life that calls for a psychological–biological diagnosis of well-being. Rapley's (2003) critique thus focuses on the tendency to replace 'phenomenological, social or sociological understandings of human experience and the quality of life' (p. 23) with biological or cognitive science calculations. According to him, this trend can be seen in its typical form in a few major fields of scientific research that are intensely focused on trying to explain the overall well-being of the individual in terms of genetically determined brain mechanisms or of homeostatic balances or imbalances.

The biogenetic sciences are considered by Brusa and Tarizzo (2009) as a field in which arises the *epidemiological* dimension that, in its constant morphogenesis and its relationship with the above-mentioned economistic roots, characterizes the scene of the calculation of life.

The epidemiological rationality of contemporary biopolitical calculation must be understood, however, by investigating a decisive transformation of the meaning of the epidemiological project, which also corresponds to a transformation of the concept of risk and its management.[48] At issue here, according to Brusa and Tarizzo, is a futuristic epidemiology that ever more decisively takes as its own biopolitical goal not just to *enable better living* but to *enable the best living possible*, and therefore the unconditional maximization of quality of life, in all directions. In this perspective, in which quality of life does not appear as an object to administer but as a resource to enhance unconditionally, quality as a biopolitical 'discourse' hints at the disquieting issue of post-human enhancement.

Therefore, while quality of life tends to take on the aspect of a highly charged question (which is, at the same time, undoubtedly relevant and decidedly ambiguous and controversial), a fundamental interpretive stance seen in the literature is that aimed, in a typically Foucauldian tone, at highlighting the non-natural, non-obvious character of the power of quality. When Rapley summarizes the Foucauldian view on the matter, he seems to allude to the issue of the *problematization* (and to the Foucauldian tone of this term) and hence to the necessity of examining the historically determined contingent nature of the project of calculability of the human being which is revealed through quality.

In Rapley's perspective, therefore, it is a case of recognizing that the way of thinking about the self which the quality regime demands is a historically and culturally determined possibility, and not something that can be taken for granted in its own character of evident inevitability.

This stance goes hand in hand with the question of how to act with regard to that eminently ambiguous object which is quality of life.

Rapley refuses to recognize quality of life as a formally operationalized and measurable construct, precisely on the basis of an argument – which contains an unsurprising, albeit fleeting, reference to Heidegger – on the impossibility of accounting for all humanity and its 'behaviour', assuming humanity itself as a totality which can be broken down into measurable components: memories, attitudes, beliefs and moods. The relationship with life and its quality is not a matter of measurability of an object which is unconditionally knowable by the living subject. Instead, it is something which involves a radically different dimension – which Rapley qualifies as *aesthetic* – with respect to that of the techno-scientific measurement of components.

Thus, while it is neither possible nor politically useful to consider quality of life itself as an unconditionally measurable object, quality of life itself may continue to play a role as a *sensitizing notion*; or in other words, as a reference capable of stimulating a debate that can only be in the nature of an *ethical public* debate. This debate, unlike the promises of calculative assurance of life, must constantly deal with the weighing of moral questions.

Against the backdrop of Rapley's arguments, some important issues can be glimpsed that will be at the heart of my own interpretive journey. Except that, in my opinion, the question of the attitude to maintain in the face of quality – and its enigmatic power – cannot be adequately posed until the very roots of the calculability of quality have been thoroughly investigated, and thus until the opportunity has been called into question of considering such calculability in terms of the reduction of quality to the level of unconditional measurability that the sciences seem to demand, working eventually as vehicles of governmental rationalities.

What the debate I have briefly described gives us, over and above the different interpretative perspectives mentioned, is the distinctively ambiguous if not enigmatic tone in which quality and calculation resonate, when they go hand in hand.

Precisely in the season of its increasingly extreme calculability, quality asserts itself as something that is simultaneously powerful and vague, ubiquitous and elusive. It is around this very elusiveness, however – even when it takes the shape of an extreme *emptiness* – that the greatest 'calculative' energy is unleashed.

Then again, precisely when calculation takes place under the heading of calculation of quality, it seems to occur in an increasingly unlimited manner (as the calculation of every thing, and as the increasingly complete calculation of all things). Furthermore, this unlimited proliferation manifests itself as something that resists critical investigation in a very specific way, and tends to stand out in a basically undeniable manner.

It is precisely by grasping the perplexing mark left by the quality-calculation issue on the contemporary scene, that I will address the issues that I alluded to in the introduction.

However, doing so will involve distancing ourselves from some conceptions of calculation and quality that I have referred to above. This will entail, for example, not considering the calculation of quality (and of the human through quality) immediately and above all in terms of unconditional quantification, nor in terms of some sort of *reduction* or reductive assimilation of quality itself. But it will also mean not merely looking at quality as an element of biopolitical rationalities, as a mask behind which a process of managerialization/marketization takes place, as the linchpin of a possible policitization/socialization of calculation, or even as an uncertain object that should nonetheless be accepted as a *sensitizing notion*.

This does not in any way mean that my work considers the critical contributions I mentioned to be of little importance, nor that my work will not continue to deal with them. Instead, it means that my intention is to further insist on the question which asks what is truly meant by the fact that, when calculability moves towards perfection, it advances precisely under the heading of quality. This question deserves to be seen in a light in which its enigmatically fathomless dimension can resonate freely with respect to some of the interpretations which seem to lead that enigma to more solid and known levels.

From this perspective, in the next chapter I will undertake a phenomenological investigation, accepting the fact that this may result in no more than a contribution towards preparing for ever better scrutiny.

2
Quality and Calculation: A Phenomenological Journey

2.1 Preface

In a paragraph from the *Contributions to Philosophy*[1] (Heidegger, 1999a, p. 94) to which this work will pay particular attention, Martin Heidegger writes: 'Quality is meant here as the basic character of the *quale*, of the what, of the ownmost, of be-ing itself.' This sentence seems surprising because quality is, at the end of the sentence, associated with the word 'being' and, not least because the word is written in such a strange, obscure form. Quality is 'the basic character of be-ing itself',[2] where we would have felt much more familiar and comfortable with a reference to humankind and that which is human.

Moreover, Heidegger, in the very same paragraph, goes on to address the 'quantitative' as that which 'is *not* ownmost to be-ing', suggesting that the unconditioned *quantification* of all things, being something that we commonly recognize as coinciding with the quantitative and with its dominion in modern times, is only the *appearance* of the quantitative, an appearance that in an absolutely distinctive way, veils the *original essence* of the quantitative itself.

These propositions alone already seem to localize the question of calculation and of its relationship with quantity and quality on a plane that is most unfamiliar to the current interpretation.

We will now turn to a passage which offers us a more reassuring reading of the issues to be addressed when the relationship between quality, quantity and calculation is at stake.

Georg Simmel (2004, p. 278), in a famous passage from *The Philosophy of Money*, writes about:

> The growing preponderance of the category of quantity over that of quality, or more precisely the tendency to dissolve quality into quantity, to remove the elements more and more from quality, to grant them only specific forms of motion and to interpret everything that is specifically, individually and qualitatively determined as the more or less, the bigger or smaller, the wider or narrower, the more or less frequent of those colourless elements and awarenesses that are only accessible to numerical determination – even though this tendency may never absolutely attain its goal by mortal means.

This passage provides a precise summary of the way quantity, quality and calculation have been understood in the modern West, which feels quite familiar.

According to the interpretation that Simmel puts forward, what is the root of the cognitive tendency that dominates the modern world? It is an unstoppable movement that progressively enables quantity to dominate quality. More precisely, it is a perversion of the dialectical play between the *categories* of quantity and quality, between quality and quantity as categories.

This progressive domination of the category of quality by the category of quantity happens by hollowing out and appropriation: the more quantity dominates quality, the more quality is dissolved into it. What precisely is it that is dissolved by this quantitative possession? The individuality, the incomparability, the incomparable individuality of things; thus, what is dissolved is the possibility for humankind to relate to a thing as the individual thing that it is.

Money, which for Simmel is 'the most perfect representative' of the cognitive tendency to reduce qualitative determination to quantitative determination, does precisely this: 'irreparably it hollows out the core of things, their individuality, their specific value and their incomparability' (Simmel, 1950, p. 414).

The dissolution of quality is thus, for Simmel, a question of the preponderance of one way of determining things over another. The dissolution of the incomparable individuality of things is the progressive process by which humankind is denied the possibility of determining them *qualitatively*. The qualitative is 'everything that is specifically, individually and qualitatively determined'.

The quantification of quality is extremely worrying for Simmel, because it indicates the definitive movement by which calculation proceeds. This quantitative reduction of quality is the most precise way of describing calculation, the dominance of modern calculation, the configuration of modernity as the era of calculation. This is worrying because it touches humankind and with this touch comes the deprivation of man's relationship with the core of things; and this is something that we find still today, when in late modern managerial scenarios, quality is seen as being more and more reduced to quantifiable quality, leading to a an ever more complete *annexation* of humankind to the realm of calculation. The obsession with quantification and calculation will culminate in calculating the entire life of man, resulting in a dehumanization of life itself by way of a progressive hollowing out of the qualitative.

What is more, calculation will begin not only to dissolve quality but to proceed in the name of the quality it is dissolving, proceeding as unconditional calculation of everything there is in quality and as calculation of the quality of everything. Quality will end up appearing so compromised that, according to some, as we have seen in the paragraphs above, it can be left aside.

As anticipated, my analytical path will call into question the possibility of interpreting the issue of calculation as a perversion of the relationship between categories to be eventually faced through a 'requalification' of quality; and this precisely on the basis of the interpretation of some passages of the *Contributions* and of Heidegger's other works.

It is now time to catch a glimpse of some of Heidegger's thoughts on the calculative.

2.2 Calculation, representation, objectification and assurance

What Heidegger refers to as the dominion of calculation and *calculative thinking* has much to do with the obstruction of the possibility of relating to the individuality of things and with human life in its individuality. However, in order to understand the meaning of the relationship between calculation, quantification, quality and individuality, we must try to see calculation for what it is, without allowing ourselves to be dazzled by its most ostentatious manifestations.

The modern manipulation and mastery of beings and of man is rooted in the dominion of the *representability* of all beings as objects for a representing subject.

In the representability of beings is the very root of the condition of the beings under the power of modern technology, that is, the conditions of beings as *standing reserves*, unconditionally available for manipulation, organization, management and planning.

But what does representing mean? And what does this representation have to do with the objectification of beings? Heidegger (2002, p. 69) writes in *The Age of the World Picture*:

> Representation *[Vor-stellen]* here means: to bring the present-at-hand before one as something standing over-and-against, to relate it to oneself, the representer, and, in this relation, to force it back to oneself as the norm-giving domain.

This *Vorstellung*, the movement to bring and hold before oneself, is a movement in which the *being of beings* and their truth is decisively fixed.

Beings become beings by way of representation. This means that beings are only beings as the objects of a representation that fixes them as that which pertains to their beingness.

This happens together with the establishment of the essence of man. Man, as the *representer*, becomes the referential centre of all beings.

> When, however, man becomes the primary and genuine *subiectum*, this means that he becomes that being upon which every being, in its way of being and its truth, is founded. Man becomes the referential center of beings as such. But this is only possible when there is a transformation in the understanding of beings as a whole.
>
> (Ibidem, p. 66–67)

In fixing the being and the truth of beings, the relationship between man and beings is in play and, in the same movement, what man is in truth is fixed: the representing subject.

> This is the fundamental equation of all calculating belonging to self-securing representing. In this fundamental certainty, man becomes certain that, as the representer of all representation, the setter-before of all setting-before, and therewith the realm of all representedness and hence of all certainty and truth, he is securely established – which means, now, that he *is*.
>
> (Ibidem, p. 82–83)

Through representation and through the dominance of the 'representability' of beings, man confirms and assures himself as the subject that represents beings as something of which he can be *certain*.

The beginning of modern philosophy[3] (of modernity as an era in the history of metaphysics), is marked by precisely this determination of beings as objects of the representation and of truth as the *certainty of the representation*. This determination first appears in Cartesian metaphysics and its 'power' is maintained throughout modern metaphysics, Nietzsche included.

What happens with Descartes? It is opportune to read two passages that shed light on the relationship between the modern interpretation of freedom and man's self-assurance of his certainty as subject.

> What is decisive is not that humanity frees itself from previous bonds but, rather, that the essence of humanity altogether transforms itself in that man becomes the subject.
>
> (Ibidem, p. 66)
>
> [...]
>
> That was only possible in that self-liberating man himself guaranteed the certainty of the knowable. This, however, could only happen through man's deciding, from and for himself, what was knowable for him, and what the knowing and securing of the known, i.e., certainty, should mean.
>
> (Ibidem, p. 81)

> Descartes' metaphysical task became the following: to create the metaphysical ground for the freeing of man to freedom considered as self-determination that is certain of itself. This ground, however, not only had to be one that was certain. Since every measure taken from other domains was forbidden, it had, at the same time, also to be of such a nature that, through it, the essence of the freedom demanded was posited as a self-certainty. Everything that is certain from itself must, at the same time, however, certify as certain that being from which such knowledge is certain and through which everything knowable is made secure.
>
> (Ibidem, p. 81)

It is man as a subject engaged in his own self-confirmation that can be installed at the centre of the totality of the beings; he can put himself forward as the setting in which the beings must be maintained as objects.

> The *subiectum,* the fundamental certainty, is that always secured entity which representing man always co-represents along with human or non-human beings, along, that is, with the objectified. The fundamental certainty is the me-cogitare = me esse which is, at all times, indubitably representable and represented.
>
> (Ibidem, p. 82)

The modern interpretation of man as that being who positions himself in the midst of the totality of the beings makes it possible for things in their totality to become something that man can grasp the idea of and something upon which to orient himself. The world therefore is only what man, the *subjectum* who installs himself in the midst of beings, can grasp the idea of, in the sense of 'being in the picture' about it.[4]

This means that within the modern philosophical interpretation of man, inaugurated by Descartes, man is that subject which explains and evaluates everything from the standpoint of himself and in relation to himself. When, for the first time, something is referred to as man's position, this position must be assured by man, starting from himself, meaning to say, starting from man's self-confirmation as subject.

The appropriation of this position is what makes it possible for the world to become, for man, a picture – *Bild*. Beings are that which man produces, representing them as that of which he has a complete picture.

What then is the attitude, the fundamental disposition of man in the face of a world that has become a picture? This attitude is *Weltanschauung*. *Weltanschauung*, Heidegger suggests, should be understood as meaning vision and conception of life. The disposition that man has in relation to beings is a disposition in which beings are for man's *life*. The measure that beings receive from the standpoint of the subject is a measure defined in terms of man's life.

When, in the last part of the essay, Heidegger poses the question about the correspondence between *Weltbild* and *Weltanschauung*, he points to the essential co-belonging between the movement that brings and fixes the beings before the subject and that which defines the beings as something that is within the measure of and which is related to the life of man.

This is the tone that the *abandonment of beings by being* assumes in the modern era: in modern times, being 'abandons' beings letting beings count as far as they are available for objectifying representation, as far as they can be assured for the human subject and her life, that in turn has to be assured. This means also that the predominance of representability is the way in which, in modernity, being abandons *man*, leaving him under the injunction to assure his own self-installation as the representing subject.

Man is left under the injunction to calculate, to deal with beings (and with his own life) as something calculable to calculate. The only possibility of thinking that is left to man is *das rechnende Denken* or calculative thinking: thinking that proceeds by calculating, by constantly assuring beings, man and the relationship between man and beings.

It is opportune now to linger on the way in which Heidegger invites us to understand the relationship between the calculative – *das rechnende* – representation and assurance. Reading another passage of *The Age of the World Picture* (Heidegger, 2002, p. 82):

> To represent means here: of oneself, to set something before one and to make what has been set in place *[das Gestellte]* secure as thus set in place. This placing-in-securedness must be a calculating,

> since only calculation guarantees being certain, in advance and always, of that which is to be presented.

The assurance that pertains to representation is 'calculative'. The only guarantee of being certain is the possibility to calculate, in advance and constantly, that which is to be represented.

To understand this intimate relationship between representation and calculation, it is useful to refer to another of Heidegger's works and a passage dedicated to clarifying the meaning of the relationship between the German verb *rechnen* and the Latin verb *reor*, which is also the root of the word *ratio*.

> *Ratio* belongs to the verb *reor*, whose guiding sense is 'to take something for something'; that for which something is taken is placed under, sup-posed. In such a placing-under, that under which something is placed is readied for what will be placed under it. 'Putting something in order for something,' 'to take one's bearings from something' is the sense of our verb rechnen [reckon].
>
> To reckon with something, to take something into account means to keep one's eye on it and to act accordingly. To reckon or count on something means to expect it and thereby to figure it as something upon which to build. The genuine sense of 'reckon' is not necessarily connected to numbering. This also holds for what one calls calculus.
>
> (Heidegger, 1996, p. 100)

Rechnen, (of which 'numerical calculation', is just a very particular kind) means this: to take something for something, to take something for a particular thing and to consider this thing *as* that which has been taken for it. It also means to adopt that which has been taken for that thing as the basis for proceeding.

> 'Reckoning' means 'to orient something in terms of something', 'to represent something as something.' That *as which* some particular thing is represented [*vorgestellt*] as being, is what it is imputed [das *Unterstellte*] as being.
>
> (Ibidem, p. 102)

It is only by this movement of 'taking for' that it is possible to represent something, place it there and keep it there, in a manner that is certain, before the representing subject.[5]

> When we reckon, we represent what must be held in view, namely, that with which and in terms of which we reckon with some matter.
>
> (Ibidem, p. 100)

That which is assured in the representation is something assured in advance and at the same time yet and ever to be assured. The assurance of this anticipated and constant certainty of the *repraesentandum* is a reckoning, or calculation. Only 'calculatively' can this anticipated certainty be guaranteed: the certainty of being able to count in advance on the totality of beings *as, and only as,* the object of a representation for a subject.

Modern sciences, in the sense of all branches of knowledge that follow the path of scientific research, take upon themselves the duty of giving an account of beings in terms of calculation and they do this by means of that which Heidegger calls the prioritization of *proceeding* upon the subject matter of calculation. This proceeding is performed under the injunction to produce results that, in turn, must be assured by other results; *science as research* therefore relates to beings and their truth according to the sole availability of the results of research and the ability of these results to drive science itself toward new results.

> The decisive question for science as such is *not* which essential character a being itself has that lies at the basis of the field of the subject matter, but rather whether with this or that procedure a 'knowledge', i.e., a *result* of the research, may be expected. What is key is the view of the arrangement and readiness of 'results'. Results and, in the end, their immediate appropriateness for use guarantee the accuracy of the research – a scientific accuracy that counts as the truth of a knowing.
>
> (Heidegger, 1999a, p. 103)

In proceeding by way of calculation, science fixes that which, for science, counts as the truth.

If, with Descartes, truth becomes the *certainty of the representation,* the way in which modern sciences undertake to maintain assured that truth is assuring the results through new results. The more truth resonates in this register, that of *performative truth,* the more modern scientific research demonstrates its own alienation from *knowing,* recasting itself as 'a mechanism of accuracies of a region of explanation' (Ibidem, p. 103).

Techno-scientific modernity therefore proceeds by calculation, under the injunction of calculation and by means of calculations. It is precisely by proceeding in this way, that modern technology does not let itself be recognized as something that belongs to the sway of being; as the way in which being, by withdrawing, holds sway in modern times.

The dominion of calculability proceeds *from out of itself,* as something that 'simply' goes on its own, in that dimension of *emptiness* which is the ever more complete absence of any referent. It is in this light that we have to understand the perfection that the demand for calculation pursues in the era dominated by modern science and technology.

This refers to that perfection which we will return to in the next chapter when we question the meaning of the perfected calculability of the human.[6] It is that perfection that Heidegger, in *The Principle of Reason,* alludes to in terms of its essential nature: the ability of calculation to go by itself, to go in its own direction, to secure the possibility itself of calculating.

> This perfection consists in the completeness of the calculably secure establishing of objects, in the completeness of reckoning with them and with the securing of the calculability of possibilities for reckoning.
>
> (Heidegger, 1996, p. 121)

Now we should ask: what is the relationship of that which we have seen, albeit in a provisional manner, with the risk of losing the *individuality* of things? The answer is that the relationship is very close, so close indeed that what we will be trying to do will be nothing other than an attempt to understand it and appreciate it better.

What risk does modern man run when he is left under the injunction to assure, by way of calculation, the world and his own life as objects to be represented for a subject who assures himself in that very representation? What risk does he run when things only count according to the degree to which their explanation can be assured by calculation?

It is the risk, as Ricci (2008) reminds us, of losing the sense and meaning of things, the risk of not being able to encounter a thing as *that very thing*; the risk that no one thing has anything left to say to man about the thing that it is. And this risk involves the possibility of losing the relationship with that which immediately and without interruption concerns each one of us individually in our own being.

Before proceeding along this path, we must once again start speaking a language that we seem to have forgotten: the language of the quantitative.

2.3 The 'quantitative' is calculated quantitatively

How is it that, speaking about representation and calculation, as something we are assuming has much to do with the 'dissolution' of individuality, we distance ourselves so much from the question of quantification, and the quantitative reduction of things, the question that for the modern West has something directly to do with that dissolution?

Yet, says Heidegger, in the *Contributions*, the dominion of calculation coincides with the dominion of the 'quantitative', the point being, however, that this 'quantitative' is not to be understood in the usual way.

We should not grasp the essence of the 'quantitative' by concentrating on the numerical quantification of everything, on the reduction of the totality of beings to a numerically quantifiable object. Nor should we concentrate our vision on that which appears as a progressive annexation of all things to the domain of numerical measurement – that annexation that proceeds by measuring what is ever greater and ever smaller, by measuring phenomena that are ever more difficult to measure (including all the 'components' of human life), and therefore by the accelerated production of numbers and numerical measurements.

The essence of the quantitative is precisely in the *representing as such* and in the *objectification of beings*. That which belongs to the quantitative and to the dominion of the quantitative is the representability of beings as objects for a representing subject.

The unlimited and unconditioned quantification of the world gives only the *appearance* of the quantitative.

'Possession' of the world by numerical quantification is the way in which the quantitative represents itself. 'The "quantitative" is dealt with, i.e. calculated, quantitatively' (Ibidem, p. 95).

The dominion of the 'quantitative', that being the dominion of calculative representation of beings, allows itself to be grasped as a progressive process of quantification. The quantitative appears as an unbounded process, which has to do with large numbers and measures.

This means that the 'quantitative' holds itself to *beings*; it allows itself to be grasped starting from beings, and more precisely, starting from beings as *quantified* unconditionally and without limits; starting from beings that are always larger or smaller (let us think of modern physics and how it deals with that which is infinitely large or small).

By proceeding in this way, the quantitative does not allow itself to be grasped in its essence, that is, the representability and calculability of beings; and the 'quantitative', as representability, does not allows itself to be grasped as that which it is, a matter of *being*, the way in which being holds sway by withdrawing and the way in which being abandons man and all things in modernity.

It is precisely when the essential root of the quantitative becomes ever more difficult to recognize,[7] that the quantitative dominates in a particularly decisive form, that being the *gigantic*.

> That which claims large numbers and measures for its representability is only the *appearance* of the gigantic, which, of course, belongs to the gigantic, since it legitimizes that kind of magnitude that relies essentially in setting down and representing.
>
> (Heidegger, 1999a, p. 311)

The quantitative becomes *gigantic* when it becomes a *quality* of its own. It was in writing about this that Heidegger wrote the sentence on quality that I quoted at the beginning of this chapter.

The quantitative transforms into a *quality*, thus becoming something *singular*; something that *goes by itself* and whose own-ness is within itself and cannot be obtained through its relationship with something else. As a quality of its own, the quantitative becomes the form of magnitude that belongs to the era of the perfection of modern technology.

Let us ask now why numerical measurement can play that legitimizing role which Heidegger refers to in the above quote? Why does this capacity for legitimization belong specifically to the numerical?

One of the routes Heidegger takes to deal with this important question is when he investigates the meaning of the *mathematical*.

What is mathematics for modern man? What relationship does it have with what mathematics was for the Greeks, he asks in 'The Age of the World Picture' (Heidegger 2002, p. 59)?

> Τά μαθήματα means, in Greek, that which, in his observation of beings and interaction with things, man knows in advance: the corporeality of bodies, the vegetable character of plants, the animality of animals, the humanness of human beings. Along with these, belonging to the already known, i.e., 'mathematical,' are the numbers. When we discover three apples on the table we recognize that there are three of them. But the number three, threeness, we know already. That is to say: the number is something 'mathematical'. Only because numbers represent, so to speak, the most striking of the always-already-known, and therefore the best-known instances of the mathematical, is 'the mathematical' directly reserved as a name for the numerical. The essence of the mathematical, however, is in no way defined in terms of the numerical.

For the Greeks, the mathematical names that which is *already known* and which is known in advance, in the relationship between man and beings. The mathematical therefore lies at the core of the metaphysical interpretation of beings; and it will become the decisive feature of that pre-determination which lies at the core of the representation and objectification of beings.

Number does not in any way define the mathematical. However, it does belong to the mathematical in a very particular way. The fact that three is three is something we already know in a very particular way, and that four is more than three is the way in which it is utterly irrefutable and thus particularly familiar.

It is no accident that the quantitative (being that which is in essence representation) appears in the forms of numerical quantification. This special relationship that numbers have with the *already known* is the basis of the particular role that numerical measurement plays in modern scientific procedures and, in particular, the oldest of these, *mathematical physics*.

The fact that physics is mathematical means that, in advance something, that is nature, is convened before the representing subject as that which is already known.

> When, therefore, physics assumes an explicitly 'mathematical' form, what this means is the following: that through and for it, in an emphatic way, something is specified in advance as that which is already known.
>
> (Ibidem, p. 59)

For physics, all phenomena must be determined in advance as the spatio-temporal quanta in order to be able to achieve their representation as natural phenomena.

In what Heidegger refers to as the *mathematical design of nature*, the natural world is projected in advance as spatio-temporal quanta. This predetermination is confirmed and constantly assured by the production of numerical results or, more precisely, by the incessant proceeding from one numerical result to another.

Physics is rigorous because it is *exact* and therefore it predetermines phenomena through numbers. It must calculate *numerically* because the relationship it has with the realm of the objectification of beings which pertains to it is of the order of exactness. The 'quantitative' representation of natural phenomena that physics employs can only happen by means of their fixation in space and time as numerically measurable objects.

All the sciences are 'calculative' (and thus 'quantitative') and the more rigorous they are, the more they are so. However, not all sciences are rigorous by being exact. Human sciences (the sciences of the spirit) need not be exact in order to be rigorous.

While it is true that the human sciences are sensitive – and ever more so – to the power of numerical measurement, the route taken by the human sciences towards scientific rigour should not be understood in terms of their becoming increasingly similar to the natural sciences, possibly subsequent to the former's colonization by the latter. In order to rigorously deal with their object, they follow their own particular path, that is, as Heidegger suggests, more arduous in comparison to the path taken by the exact sciences (see Heidegger, 1999a, section 76). It is indeed by addressing the issue of quality that it will be possible, as I will attempt to do further on, to shed light on the way in which the scientific-calculative treatment of the human becomes ever more stringent and rigorous.

2.4 The 'quantitative' shows itself as the quantification of qualities

On the basis of what we have seen about the quantitative, about its essence and its appearance, we will now try to return to the words of Simmel, who we have taken as the representative of a way of thinking about quality and quantity.

As we have seen, the dominance of the 'quantitative' appears as the quantification of everything; but this, so to speak, takes in the whole history of the metaphysical West, a very peculiar form: that of the quantification of every quality.

This quantification of qualities appears as all the more dangerous when human things are at issue: deeds, facts, happenings, all the phenomena that concern human beings and therefore quality as a human 'attribute'.

Let us focus again our attention on the fact that, for Simmel, the problem revolves around the relationship between *categories*. But why should this surprise us? In what other way, other than as categories, are we accustomed to dealing with quantity and quality?

Yet Heidegger provides us with the possibility of seeing the relationship between the 'qualitative' and the 'quantitative' in another way.

Referring to paragraph 70 (Heidegger, 1999a, p. 94):

> We know quantity-quality and ποσόν-ποιόν as 'categories', i.e., in relation to 'judgment'.
>
> But here it is not a matter of reversing one category for another or of a 'dialectical' representational mediation of the forms of representation; rather it is a matter of the history of being.

Metaphysics treats quality and quantity as *categories*. In modern metaphysics, the qualitative and the quantitative will be seen as ways in which man relates to beings. Moreover, the metaphysical representation of the relationship between quality and quantity as a dialectic between the forms of representation, runs through the whole history of modern metaphysics, characterizing the modern conception of the calculation of all things human. To modern eyes, the unlimited and unconditional dominion of calculation is something that derives from the 'perverted' relationship between the forms of representation and, therefore, between the ways in which man deals with beings.

If we follow Heidegger, this means that, when the quantitative and the qualitative are conceived as categories in modern metaphysics, they are considered as starting from beings, from man (as the subject of the quantitative and qualitative determination of things) and the beings–man relationship. The qualitative, in the end, designates a human way of dealing with things and a way that is particularly 'suitable' for dealing with the things that belong to the sphere of the human.

In this guise, quality is constituted as a human attribute, as something that, by its very nature, is close to the human and defines it: what is human is a question of quality. By taking this route, quality can be perceived as a sort of guarantee of the humanity of man and therefore as a defence against the predominance of quantitative measurement.

Now, that which the Heidegger's notes in the *Contributions* invite us to sense is, at the same time, the 'quantitative' – as something that does not coincide with quantification – and the qualitative – as something that is not of the order of the human rational subject and of his relationship with things.

Quality: the basic character of be-ing.

Quantity: basically what is ownmost (as what is *not* ownmost) to be-ing.[8]

Let us take these two propositions thus. Let them accompany us, in their unfathomable nature, towards a path that we have only just started out on.

2.5 A first glimpse at the 'surprising' co-belongingness: Machination, calculation and lived-experience

Representability denotes the way in which being lets beings count in the modern age. But the dominion of representability is nothing other than the modern form of the essential sway of being that is at work from the beginning of the history of metaphysics. The name of this essential sway of being is *Machenschaft*.

Machenschaft, that the translators of the *Contributions* render as *machination*, does not designate a determination of the being of beings that characterizes a certain era of Western philosophy (see Schild, 2013). Rather, it refers to that basic determination that is destined to claim sovereignty over the metaphysical interpretations of the being of beings, from Plato to Nietzsche.

How do we understand the idea of *making* that *Machenschaft* entails? This idea of *making* must not be thought of as starting from human behaviour, of humankind's inclination to make beings, to make something of them, to consider them something that may be made out of. What must be considered, in contrast, is *Machenschaft* as the interpretation of beings according to which beings are nothing if not what *makes* themselves *by* themselves.

This interpretation has its origins in the interpretation of *physis* accomplished by *techne*.

> That *something makes itself by itself* and is thus also makeable for a corresponding procedure says that the self making by itself is the interpretation of Φύσις accomplished by τέχνη and its horizon of orientation, so that what counts now is the preponderance of the makeable and the self-making (cf. the relation of ιδέα to τέχνη), in a word: machination.
>
> (Heidegger, 1999a, p. 88)

Beings seem not to be able to hold their being in any other way than by *making themselves by themselves*; they cannot recognize anything else except what arises out of themselves.[9]

This happens through interpretations of *physis* that move even further away from the Greek experience of *physis* itself. The Greek experience[10] of *physis* – and of the basic movement of the *self-opening* which physis is – comes to be more and more disempowered. This happens in particular by way of the interpretation of physis in terms of *aletheia*, then in terms of *techne* and of *poiesis* (Schild, 2013).[11]

It is in the interpretation of beings in the perspective of the *ens creatum* that a decisive step is taken, enabling *Machenschaft* – which

Schild translates as *empire du se-faire,* the empire of self-making – to put itself forward more clearly; thus making it possible for *Machenschaft* to prepare itself for its prime position in the modern interpretation of beings (Ibidem).

When the modern 'season' of the dominion of machination begins with Descartes, the 'machinational' truth of beings resonates in the register of truth as the certainty of the representation.

> The step taken by Descartes is already a first and decisive consequence, a 'compliance' by which machination assumes power as transformed truth (correctness), namely as certainty.
>
> (Heidegger, 1999a, p. 92)

Heidegger, in Section 61 of the *Contributions,* goes on to say that machination withdraws, concealing itself. Indeed, the more decisively it dominates, the more decisively it conceals itself.

> Machination itself withdraws; and since it is the essential swaying of be-ing, be-ing itself withdraws.
>
> (Ibidem, p. 89)

We have previously focused on how representation does not let itself be grasped in its own essential essence. Now, because calculative representability is the form taken by machination in the modern era, we have to consider that concealment of representability is the way in which, in modern times, machination conceals itself.

Now, in the *Contributions* Heidegger addresses the following phenomenon: the more decisively machination withdraws, the more (and this happens in a peculiar form in the modern era) it conceals itself behind that which appears to be its *opposite,* but which totally *belongs* to it.[12]

What is that which in the modern era appears as the opposite of machination, so that it is called upon to oppose the power of calculation? It is called *Erlebnis,* lived-experience. *Erlebnis* is that behind which *Machenschaft* hides and that seems the opposite of machination itself, 'even as it remains totally and solely its own making' (p. 89).

> If machination and lived-experience are named together, then this points to an essential belongingness of both to each other – a

> belongingness that is concealed but is also essentially *non simultaneous* within the 'time' of the history of be-ing.
>
> (Ibidem, p. 89)[13]

In modernity, a being counts as a being only as a calculable/representable object but, at the same time, it counts as a being only as far as it is a *liveable* being, a being lived through lived-experience.

> Only what is lived through live-experience and is *so* liveable, only what presses forth into the sphere of live-experience, only what man is able to bring to and before himself, [only that] can count as 'a being'.
>
> (Ibidem, p. 90)

This correspondence between machination and the sphere of lived-experience seems surprising. What seems surprising is the fact that, according to Heidegger, beings obey the dominion of representability (and therefore of calculable explainability and manipulability) only in so far as they are 'experientially lived'.

Considering the correspondence between the *machinational* (which will be the root of all we know as objectivation, 'calculative' manipulation, and technological arrangement of things) and the dominion of lived-experience, places the interpretation of calculation, and the calculation of the human, on a plane that is quite unfamiliar to the current interpretation. Heidegger's thought on that basic correspondence, as Livingston (2003) remarks, indicates a yawning gap between Heidegger's ideas and those of Husserl on *Lebenswelt* and thus on the possibility of returning to a foundation in lived-experience against the dominance of scientific abstractions. As well as the argument on *Machenschaft* and *Erlebnis* clearly distances Heidegger from 'a range of projects in the nineteenth-century philosophy of subjectivity, project that identified subjectivity with "life" and saw "lived-experience" as the vital foundation for all aesthetic and cultural productions' (Ibidem, p. 330).[14]

What is this *Erlebnis* behind which *Machenschaft* conceals itself and which essentially belongs to *Machenschaft* itself? And how can we *begin* to approach the correspondence between machination and lived-experience?

> 'Lived-experience' means making what is mysterious, i.e., what is stimulating, provocative, stunning, and enchanting – which makes the machinational necessary – public and accessible to everyone.
>
> (Heidegger, 1999a, p. 77)

How is it possible to understand the reference to stimulus, provocation and enchantment in a non-psycho-anthropological sense, whereas the trivialization of the 'mysterious' is exactly that which is at the root of the anthropological interpretation of man?

How can we understand that dissolving this 'provocative' ability of beings makes it possible to maintain a *superficial* relationship with things, a relationship characterized by *insipid sentimentality* (Ibidem)?

Lived-experience: this expression immediately puts us up against the question of life. And we have already considered the importance of the issue of life, when we saw that in the era of *Weltanschauung*, beings are represented for human life and from the standpoint of human life.

An initial approach to *Erlebnis* and to understanding the way in which, in modern metaphysics, it relates to *Machenschaft*, is to see how the dominion of lived-experience confirms an anthropological conception of man. As Livingston (2003, p. 331) notes:

> Lived-experience, then, inaugurates and confirms the prevailing anthropologistic conception of humankind as *animal rationale*. It does so by restricting 'beings' to a certain limited range, the range of beings that are representable as 'lived through live-experience'. It makes the livability of any being as an experienced representation the criterion of its being altogether, and thereby restricts being to objectivity, understood as set over against subjectivity. The movement of this restriction is that of a pre-delineation, a pre-structuring of the totality of beings to guarantee their representability as objects, their livability in experience, and their comprehensibility to rational man. In the pre-delineation of beings as a whole, lived-experience and experienceability become the univocal standard of their beingness.

What is 'stimulating, provocative, stunning, and enchanting' in life is taken up in the sphere of lived-experience, and becomes 'trivialized' in the dimension of mere *feeling*.

This formatting of the 'provocative ability' of every thing and happening becomes (and this is a truly modern phenomenon) that which confirms the anthropological relationship between man and beings, that is, that interpretation of beings in which beings are understood from the standpoint of man's life and in view of life as the feeling of being alive.

This enables the occurrence of the domination of machination as representability; and this domination occurs precisely by concealing the fact that the determination of beings as lived-experiences is what permits the relationship with beings as representable objects for man.

This concealment occurs where the power of machination as representability and calculability appears as the dominion of pure objectivity – as pure objectivity which counters experienced life.

By showing itself as 'quantitative' objectivity, machination hides itself, by appearing as the *opposite* of lived-experience.

Let us now look at another *Erlebnis* characteristic. It is in the nature of *Erlebnis* that it can only be a transition from one lived-experience to another lived-experience, that it can be nothing other than a straining towards another lived-experience in anticipation of a surplus of lived-experience. This is what Vernon (2008, p. 115), for example, focuses on when he refers to a passage from Section 77 (Heidegger, 1999a, p. 109).[15]

> The very nature of *erleben*, in other words, demands that the world progressively turn 'into a larger, more unprecedented, more screaming "Erlebnis"'.

The 'superficially sentimental' relationship with things is superficial because it can only take place by passing from one lived-experience to another, in view of life as a mere flux of feelings.

Insofar as it is an 'experientially lived' being, no being is capable of halting the characteristic which is inherent to lived-experience: that of being an unstoppable advance towards the search for that stimulus which is the expectation of even greater stimulus.

One of the most direct ways in which this decisive nature of *Erlebnis* can be grasped is that of the production and consumption of 'feelings' in capitalism. In capitalism, which becomes increasingly affective, emotional and experiential (see, on this point, Magatti,

2009), an insatiable desire sets the pace in the run-up to the 'provision' of lived-experiences.

Beings, as lived-experiences are thus all diverse, but are nothing other than 'components' of an incessant flux which makes life 'lived'. As a 'particular', specific provider of lived-experience, no being can interrupt the vortex in which life and beings are enclosed.

Things are therefore there, one next to the other, all of them different, yet all equally liveable, all equally not in relation to themselves, to other things and to man.

What we must bear in mind, also in view of the discussion to come, is that precisely when beings are experienced as lived-experiences, those beings are deprived of their individuality, of the possibility of being as they are. This means that beings are stripped of their capacity to stimulate and to provoke man – the very capacity that a being possesses *as the being it is*. Beings must say nothing more to man that is not of the order of their availability to be lived for man's life, where the latter becomes nothing other than a 'lived' totality of lived-experiences. This phenomenon, as we shall see, is brought before us when life is represented as a total of qualities and these qualities are, in turn, totals of 'lived' qualities.

In this light, we have therefore to consider the superficial relationship with things which characterizes *Erlebnis*, a relationship that essentially has nothing to do with a form of human behaviour that can be overcome, in view of a deeper relationship with things, thanks to a better anthropological interpretation of life.

2.6 What is this: Calculation of quality?

2.6.1 How quality enters the calculation scene

We will now attempt to answer the question: what does calculating quality mean?

What then, does it mean to say that the age of the ever more complete dominion of calculation becomes the age of the calculation *of* quality? What is the meaning of that which appears to us as the entry of quality onto the stage of calculation, becoming an *object, objective* and *value* for calculation itself? What does it mean to say that, under the heading of quality, calculation comfortably proceeds towards perfection?

Does it mean that now *the basic character of the ownmost* will come to be held, with ever greater decisiveness, within the register of representability *and* of lived-experience? And that, precisely by this, calculation will proceed in an ever more complete manner, towards calculating the whole human existence in its 'individuality'?

The above phrases may lead us in the right direction. But, to avoid that them merely sounding evocative, we should try to carry out careful investigation.

Let us proceed by trying, above all, to focus on *how* quality enters the scene and let us start to consider that no mere genealogical analysis can give us a full explanation for the resolute character of that movement.

Modern man is concerned with the certain representation of all entities; he is concerned with calculating and representing all beings for his life, as a multiplicity of lived-experiences.

At a certain point, quality enters the scene directly and decisively. Directly, in the sense that here the qualitative does not appear in one of those guises that it assumes, once it has become the dialectical pole of quantity and therefore in the guise of a category, of a way of determining beings. This is not a question of claiming that a quantitative approach to determining things has been overturned in favour of a qualitative approach, neither is it to defend a qualitative style of scientific research.

Here, quality intervenes precisely as quality and in a resolute and decisive manner. Quality as an object of calculation, as value, as the objective of any calculation. The more we manage to consider the resoluteness of this self-summoning, the more we will manage to understand the dogmatic nature that quality tends to assume in the sphere of management and the difficulty of finding reasons for its surprising power.

Before attempting to examine the phenomenon of the calculability of quality in detail, we will try to grasp, in one go, so to speak, the impact of this entry of quality and thus the effects that it produces in terms of the advance of calculation.

Addressing the issue of the quality of a being (for example, addressing the issue of the *quality of life*) does not take in such questions as: What is quality if the quality in question is of a life? What is life if that life can be described in terms of quality?

On the contrary, it raises the questions: what, for a certain subject, makes quality of life? How is it possible to determine what an individual or collective subjectivity perceives and experiences as quality in our lives? How can the various and diverse experiences of quality of each subject be considered? And the diverse conceptions of quality that one has as a result of her own lived-experience of quality? How is it possible to determine the mix of components that someone perceives as capable of making up the quality of their life? How can these components be measured? And how can we measure the validity of the subjective perceptions of what makes up the quality of life?

All this is simply what calculating quality *does*. The calculation proceeds by posing questions of a methodological nature (which are absolutely 'calculative' issues) and identifying a series of methodological disputes surrounding these questions. It proceeds by producing a collection of calculation operations and results, in the expectation, as in all scientific operations and results worthy of the name, of their confirmation by calculation.

However, there is also what calculation actually is. This is the way in which the calculation of quality confirms itself and assures itself, at the same time keeping its own direction. When we cast our gaze over the nature and the implications of the phenomenon of calculating quality – and we seem to glimpse questions of a certain weight which definitively do belong to the trajectory of metaphysical thought and its fulfilment – we must not forget that the apparent simplicity of the calculative movement belongs entirely to the movement itself, to its power.

Although – as I will attempt to show – the quality's entry on the scene has much to do with the completion of the history of metaphysics, we should not search for a specific philosophical 'theory' that is able to properly explain the contemporary power of quality and its complicity with the calculative.

When considering quality and calculation, we should probably have in view the awkward question that Heidegger refers to in the *Der Spiegel* interview.[16]

> The sciences have today taken over the role that philosophy played up until now. To adequately clarify the 'effect' of thinking, we would have to discuss in more detail what 'effect' and 'effecting' can mean.
>
> (Heidegger, 2009b, p. 327)

The task of 'giving direction' does not belong anymore to philosophy (as what provides the philosophical unity of the sciences);

the development of techno-scientific calculation receives direction in a new way. It proceeds by giving direction to itself by itself; and the more calculation advances towards perfection (and this, I suppose, has something to do with the question of quality), the more calculative thinking goes by itself, proceeding by way of effects.

It is worthwhile noting here that to the range of 'effects' belong also the reactions that the quality's coming on stage may produce. When quality is no longer something at risk of progressive dissolution by quantity but rather appears to be a fellow traveller and accomplice of calculation, it might seem that the task is no longer to merely defend quality from a colonization. Quality may appear to have become something radically different, something radically compromised; and this means that something like a requalification of quality might be needed.[17] Another attitude could appear to strike the tone of a rejection. If quality has become what it has, then it is better to let it go and have nothing more to do with it.

2.6.2 Calculating quality as 'lived' quality

Let us try to further investigate calculation of quality, by focusing on the relationship between *life* and *things*.

Let us think once more of the modern subject who represents – and thus calculates and measures – every being as having value for her life.

She therefore finds herself *measuring a landscape*. This expression is meaningful because it has somehow an automatic completion. Measuring a landscape means measuring it according to values, thus considering the productive, cultural, social, political, aesthetic, emotional, historical (and so on) values of that landscape. The more she manages to take account of all these values, the more she is taking systematic measurements of that landscape. The more she collects and measures information for those values, the better she is able to calculate that landscape for her *life*.

Now let us think about someone faced with the task of *measuring life*, her very own life. What does this expression mean? Why does it sound strange, so much so that it does not seem to be enough on its own, it does not seem to be saying anything?

What does it mean to measure life as an object, if this object is life itself, life *as* life, life as that which is individual for each of us, the whole of life, life as a whole? What does it mean to calculate that 'thing' which is given to each of us individually, that which each of us lives in our own individual way?

We have already glimpsed this: when something happens, something like the entry on the scene of quality, the unease that accompanies similar questions comes to be ever more completely left alone. This *peu de chose* that is the relationship between *human life, individuality* and *wholeness* must resonate in a certain tone and ever more in that tone.

Life as life. Life as it is individually for each of us. As each of us *lives* our own life. As each one of us lives the individuality of our own life. As each of us experiences, by living, the individuality of our own life. As each one of us experiences by living, that which for each of us, makes up life.

The transformation that I was trying to emphasize in the passage above is important and we must not lose sight of it. It is something that we can consider precisely by considering that it is quality that enables it to comfortably proceed.

Life as quality. The quality of life as it is *lived*. How the quality of life is *lived*. The *lived quality of life*. This is what counts, this is what must be counted.

Here we begin to understand how calculation of quality (and calculation of everything under the heading of quality) is basically a matter of *liveability*, in the sense of lived-experience. We begin turn our eyes towards that basic calculation, by which quality is calculated (represented, projected, fixed and assured) *as* experientially lived quality.

By virtue of this calculation, the individuality of things and of life is represented as something that counts *as far as it is lived;* that which is individual in human life and in the human relationship with things is calculated as that which is experienced by each one of us, individually, in the register of lived-experience. The whole movement has, therefore, to do with the projection and constant assurance of individuality as a matter of liveability and, *as such*, as something that man can take into account.

But the more we regard, in a certain way, the calculability of quality, the more it seems that quality turns back on itself. It seems that quality has done an about-face and that, by showing that face, it continues to deny us access to that 'other face' that we may have never seen.

Now, where is quality? What is that thing that now stands before us? What is that thing that is so flat, without depth and without breadth, so flat that it seems to be almost an object? What is that thing that rumbles about everywhere and sounds so empty? What end has quality met? Who has let it slip through our hands?

> So, now I shall say, at the risk of shocking you, that 'quality of life' is a *monstrous* thing.

So said Fédier[18] (2003, p. 66), and also: 'the expression "quality of life" is not sufficiently *qualitative*', and even: 'Speaking of the "quality of life" means precluding ourselves from the possibility of *living*' (Ibidem, p. 66).

We must take these words very seriously, meaning that we must think about them with the maximum rigour we are capable of, that is with the maximum sobriety. I will not comment on these words right now; perhaps I have already done so and I certainly will do again.

Now let us look at the catalogue of qualities we have before us.

The lived quality of a landscape, of an amorous experience, of a relationship with a friend, of a day spent in the woods, of death itself, and so on – all these qualities, one beside another, and besides the quality of life. It seems that, at a certain point, in the quality regime, life and things are suddenly on the same plane, one beside the other.

Let us ask then: is the *quality of a landscape* also a monstrous expression – where the adjective should be intended, looking at the Latin *mostrum*, meaning also something that comes out of the ordinary and catches our attention? What is monstrous about that expression? We are one step away from asking: *when* does it become a monstrous expression? It does so when quality does a sort of about-face and suddenly seems transformed into something else.

Quality seems to resonate as empty in the expression 'quality of the landscape'. And, in turn, it seems that a certain thing transforms itself into something else, calling it in the name of quality.

This happens precisely when quality lets itself be calculated as *lived quality,* and when the systematic measuring of quality confirms and assures quality as lived quality. In the quality regime, the individuality of things – of everything – counts to the extent that it is perceived, felt, *lived* by man individually for the life of man as a 'lived life'.

Under the imperative of quality assurance, human life and things are exposed together, in a seemingly unprecedented way, to the risk hanging over them when the only possible line of thought left to man is calculative thinking. I am actually referring to the risk run by things for man: the risk that things are no longer present for him, no longer say anything to him, no longer speak to him, until they are totally indifferent to him and therefore no longer exist for him and then no longer exist (Ricci, 2008).

Man: that being whose individual singular task is the individual possibility of encountering a thing *as it is*. Man: that being who has a special relationship with quality and who has the opportunity of having a relationship with things through quality. Man: that being of which quality has need.

Suddenly: man, that being who measures ever more precisely the specific quality of everything and of each thing; that being who assures every quality, for the quality of his own life.

Let us return to the words of Fédier (2003, p. 66): 'Speaking of the "quality of life" means precluding ourselves from the possibility of *living*'.

The fact that under the banner of quality (and by virtue of its 'calculative' about-face) the dominion of lived-experience comfortably proceeds, is somehow evocated, in a very emblematical way, by a phrase which Emad (2007) writes, commenting on *Erlebnis* and on the very proximity, in Heidegger, between *Erlebnis* and *Ent-leben*, de-living; this proximity should be understood considering *Ent-leben* meaning not 'killing (*vita privare*) but impoverishment of the living quality of the experience, its de-living' (Emad, 2007, p. 26).

When the measurement of quality is at stake it would seem that everything has been done. There is nothing other than to secure (to confirm, to legitimate), by measurement, the calculation and representation of quality as 'lived' quality; and this, at the same time, means to secure the calculation of life as a matter of lived quality of life and to establish this life as that which life truly is.

The systematic measurement of quality is a job that appears important, noble and urgent because it makes it possible to take account of everything that counts for a human life that is really thus. Yet, as he does this job, modern man somehow denies the possibility of doing another job, that of taking care of quality.

Looking closely, the disquiet we begin to feel is that very disquiet felt when getting ready to go to work, with an incalculable mixture of both anguish and joy. It is the disquiet of someone ready to go to work and who is suddenly informed that her work, that very job, is no longer needed. Everything has already been done; worse still, everything has been done because it was realized that everything was already ready to do. There is still much to do, undoubtedly; we are still needed at work, but *in another sense*.

It seems that the quality of everything, of *all* things and of one certain thing, no longer needs us *in a certain sense*: it has already been done, it is already ready, it is already assured, it is up to us merely to assure it. Only thus can quality count, and count an awful lot.

I have allowed myself to use this somewhat exaggerated and vaguely 'sentimental' tone because, in my view, it is fundamentally this feeling of what is *already done* (and this related feeling of deprivation) that underlies the disquiet that surfaces against today's catalogue of qualities. I am referring to the disquiet that we have seen pervade part of the debate on the social sciences faced with the surprisingly unabashed, 'gratuitous' way in which quality encompasses all things, without a care for the differences between those things.

If quality is the quality that can be calculated for all things, what becomes of the quality of a thing? What becomes of the quality of a thing if things can stand one beside the other and can do so *precisely* as the quality of things?

Let us read for the first time the following words of the *Contributions*.

> What does *machination* mean? That which is let loose into its own shackles. Which shackles? The pattern of generally calculable explainability, by which everything draws nearer to everything else equally and becomes completely alien to itself – yes totally other than just alien. The relation of non-relationality.
>
> (Heidegger, 1999a, p. 92)

If quality is the representable quality of everything, the most general of representation, what has quality become? Let us read on.

> [representation], lets be-ing 'count' as mainly what is the most general (of representation) and as what is the emptiest.
>
> (Ibidem, p. 95)

It is a pity that this phrase actually refers to *being* because it could be extremely useful for the route we are attempting follow in addressing the question of quality.

2.6.3 Quality and totality: Total quality

Total quality. If all managerial formulas deserve attention, few are as important as the above. Total quality is not only a buzzword that has infested our management lexicon in the last ten years, gathering around itself a plethora of management techniques and practices; this expression actually says that when quality enters the calculation scene, it does it in the form of a total, a total sum of components. We have seen in the previous chapter that calculating the quality of a particular thing typically involves a process that identifies the components of that quality. Calculating urban quality, for example, means arriving at an ever more precise definition of the components of quality: the environment, social relations, culture, administration, etc. This means that each one of these components may in turn be deconstructed into components (and, as we shall see, this deconstruction process can, in general, be prolonged indefinitely) that are themselves qualities. For example, we can pose the problem of the 'socio-relational' quality of the cultural life of a city, of the 'political' quality of that cultural life, or of its quality in terms of urban identity, etc.

The phenomenon we now have before us is this: when it is a question of measuring quality, the deconstruction of a thing into its components becomes a particularly obvious operation but, on the other hand, it seems that a particular thing can be comfortably assumed to be a component of a total precisely when we are representing that total as *total quality*.

Only where the components in question are components of total quality (and the latter can, in turn, be thought of as components of different qualities) does it seem that the representation of a thing broken down into components makes it possible to take account of that thing as the thing that it is.

This is valid for those *things* which human beings have something to do with and for that 'special' thing that is human life itself.

It is precisely when human life becomes measurable in terms of its total quality, that things become unprecedentedly 'explainable' as a total of particular aspects, or particular qualities. Nothing seems more obvious, in our relationship with things, than to draw up the catalogue of its qualities, that will be constantly added to and updated: technical, productive, cultural, relational, political, social, emotional quality and so on.

However, when considering life and its quality, the way in which it is represented by calculation as a total, merits some special attention. How can life be a total? What are the components that make up the total quality of life?

Let us reconsider some methodological pathways of quality measurement. In the different ways of measuring ('objective' or 'subjective') we find indeed the question concerning totality.

The first issue that comes to mind is that concerning quality of life as consisting of a set of components, or 'objective' determinants (environmental conditions, political participation, income, etc.) of human life.

But, as we have seen, even when 'subjective' evaluation is at stake, it is still a matter of totality. Let us think of the moment-by-moment measurement of individual well-being; but let us also consider the issue of the, so to speak, inter-individual validation of subjective perceptions.

Let us read the following passage from the Stiglitz Report (Stiglitz, Sen and Fitoussi, 2009, p. 43).

> The specific feature of the subjective measures of quality of life discussed here is that what people report about their own conditions has no obvious objective counterpart: we can compare 'perceived' and 'actual' inflation, for example, but only respondents can provide information on their own subjective states and values. Despite this feature, a rich literature on these subjective measures concludes that they help to predict people's behaviour (e.g. workers who report more dissatisfaction in their work are more likely to quit their job), and that they are valid with respect to a range of other information (e.g. people who report themselves as 'happy' tend to smile more and to be rated as happy by people around them; these self-reports are also correlated with electrical readings of the brain).

The response given by a particular individual to the question about her quality of life can be 'validated' also by comparing it with the perception others have of the quality of life of the individual in question. An individual's quality of life, we might say, can be regarded as the sum total of the evaluations that others make about that quality.[19]

It is as if, once it has become a question of quality, human life can be represented as a total of components, in a previously unprecedented way.

Modern man represents all things starting from his own life and for his own life, but it is only thanks to quality that life seems to be able to be represented as a total of relationships with entities. Once calculated in terms of quality, life seems to be able to be represented as a total, in all directions: a total of 'domains' of life (environment, culture, social relations), a total of temporal states (life's past, present and future), a sum total of representations that others have of us. It is only in the register of quality that these sums can *make up* life, can make up the whole of life, life as life, *in its individuality*.

Previously, I tried to show how calculating the specific quality of each thing means having a relationship with each thing as a specific 'component' of the quality of life. And we began to consider how it has to do with precluding the possibility of having a relationship with the individuality of things. Here we are attempting to see that dealing with things and with life in terms of their *total* quality precludes another possibility (which is the same as the previous one, it is just that we are able to recognize it as such): the possibility of having a relationship with things in their wholeness.

Following Fédier's (2003) advice, we consider a passage from *Being and Time* (Heidegger, 1962, p. 74):

> When, however, we come to the question of man's Being, this is not something we can simply compute by adding together those kinds of Being which body, soul, and spirit respectively possess – kinds of Being whose nature has not as yet been determined.

The sum to which Heidegger refers has a very particular weight, in that it refers to the determining of the human being starting from a certain 'deconstruction' of the human, which has an eminent role in the Western tradition. However, according to Heidegger, every way of determining man as a total of his components is not appropriate to the being of man.

The human being cannot be the sum of its parts; man, as that being that has a relationship of favour and of necessity with being, is individual *in its wholeness*.

What does it mean to say that *totality* and *wholeness* are two different notions? This is a question that is as crucial as it is as difficult to grasp.

The fact that modern man has a relationship with the wholeness in terms of totality is something that derives from the fact that the whole history of metaphysics is the history of the difficulty of having a relationship with the 'all' as a whole.

It is starting from the way in which the metaphysical tradition translates what Aristotle names τό ὅλον. How does Heidegger translate the Aristotelian phrase: τί τό όν ή όν καθόλου? Thus, as Fédier (2003, p. 70) reminds us: '*das Seiende als solche im Ganzen*'.

One possible translation of Aristotle's phrase is 'beings as such in totality'. According to Fédier, what we should be trying to do, so as not to lose right at the outset the possibility of seeing the crucial difference between totality and wholeness, is to translate it as 'beings as such in their wholeness'. We should, in other terms, keep our distance from *summative reasoning,* according to which that taking account of things and of human life itself as a *total* appears to be the most quintessentially human task.

What is more human than considering something in terms of all of its determining features, its aspects, its valences and values? What is more appropriate for considering man in his wholeness, than to take account of all the determining features of his life, in an ever more precise and complete way, in all its dimensions – material, artistic, cultural, relational, psychological, emotional?

Is not perhaps one of the main threads in the debate on *integral human development* the need to take account of the totality of the various dimensions that make up human development, according each one equal dignity?

Has not Marx already, with extraordinary precision (we will tackle this question later on) talked of the truly human development of man, as a development by means of which man appropriates himself as a *total man,* appropriating the totality of his possibilities in life?

Yet the difference between thinking of the 'all' as the total of its components and the other way of thinking of the 'all' is still something that modern man is capable of considering. That difference seems to well up, although in a way that prevents us from properly grasping it, precisely when the calculation of total quality begins to dominate the scene.

This happens in a number of different ways, perhaps in one form more directly that the others. One of the ways of thinking of human life 'summatively', as we have just seen, is to represent it as a sequence of moments for which is possible to measure the degree of well-being and thus their contribution to the total quality of life. Now, such measurements also extend to the very last moments of life. This measurement goes by the name of measuring the *quality of death*.

The wide-ranging scientific debate on the problem of defining the indicators for the quality of death[20] is hardly surprising; nor is it necessary, against similar calculations, to maintain a superior attitude or even less, one of distance, scepticism or irritation. If anything, what must strike us the most is how these forms of calculation, while they may be developing rapidly, are still lagging behind in relation to the possibilities that taking account of death in terms of the quality of life has to offer. Indeed, today, death enters the calculation mainly in terms of measuring increases in well-being generated by the various forms of palliative care and by the social, relational, emotional and communicative contexts in which end-of-life care takes place, on the boundary between bio-medical techniques and socio-psychological treatment.

Should we find it surprising if taking account of death impels us much further than the mere quality of the end of life and attempts to measure the relationship between life and death in the totality of its relations and the ways in which these influence the quality of life at any time and in any dimension? Do we not all know that we have to die? Is not perhaps the degree of happiness (fear or anxiety) that characterizes every moment of our life linked to some 'perception' of death? Would it not be a good idea to take account of all this, in the ways in which calculation will have no difficulty devising, when calculating that peculiar object that is human life?

Faced with this kind of drift in calculation, we are aware of the risk of losing something decisively human; something that concerns the wholeness of human life in its relationship with finitude.

Nothing today is more obvious than calculating things in terms of their quality. But calculable quality is either total or it is not. This means that not only does quality speak the language of totality, but also that totality speaks the language of quality. Only by taking account of everything, in the form of the total of its components, can we calculate the quality of a thing. However, in contrast, only by calculating a thing in terms of its quality can we truly take account of that thing in its totality. Life *as a total* can only really be spoken of when the total is a quality. Only where the total is a quality, will the total be a truly *human* total.

We should try to understand how quality regime prevents us, in a very peculiar way, from being able to relate to the question of the wholeness of human life in its relationship with life's 'individuality'.

A landscape, an event, an encounter are all projected in advance in such a way that man is denied the possibility of recognizing them as those specific things in which, however, the wholeness of human life may spring.

Human life: a sum total of particular relationships with entities that unfolds in a succession of particular moments of lived-experience, up to the point of death, up to the point at which the perception and the lived-experience of mortality are assumed in the summation. This is what the entry of quality on the scene allows us to easily represent as life.

Let us recall what we have seen concerning *Erlebnis*. What must every thing be in order for it to count in the modern era according to the rule of lived-experience? It must be a *particular* lived-experience, a particular provider of lived-experience; a particular component of a totality (in the form of a never-ending flux) of lived-experiences.

What are things particular components of? Of life as a total of lived-experiences; of life as 'lived life', of life as a feeling from beginning to end.

In the succession of feelings that things provide man with, it is only feeling that counts, but feeling only counts on the basis of things as providers of feeling. In the relationship between feeling and the providers of feeling, what is excluded in advance is the possibility of interrupting the movement of assurance that is the movement that assures life as 'liveable', from beginning to end and at 360 degrees.

When beings are components of a total of lived-experiences, we face with the *effacement* of the possibility for a being of being in its individuality, of being in relationship with man as that being which it is and therefore of being able to say something to man.

In the dimension of the particular with regard to the total, the particular and the total are one for the other, but they are not in a relationship. This is precisely because a certain thing (event, happening) is denied the possibility of being in its ownness and therefore of being in a true relationship with the other things.

Precisely by looking at quality, we can try to grasp the phenomenon that I mentioned above: something cannot be that thing that it really is when it is merely a particular source of feeling; a life cannot really be a life when it is a calculable total of particular feelings.

When, under the imperative of quality, we are engaged in the *obvious* representation of life as a total of things and events, it seems that this life is lacking something; more precisely, it is lacking humanity. That living life as a total of lived-experiences is not a human way of living. That thinking in terms of the total quality of life would mean precluding the *possibility of living*, and precluding the possibility of dying in a human way.

Let us return to the previously quoted passage from *Being and Time*. What is the derivation of the impossibility of thinking of the being of man as a summation, as a summation of any kind whatsoever? From the relationship that human life has with death. The feature of wholeness, when human life is in question, is its relationship with death. It is by virtue of the relationship with death that in each individual thing there is always the possibility of relating to the wholeness of life in its individuality; it is by virtue of that relationship that no one thing is for man only a particular component of a sum.

This is the sense of disquiet we experience when quality turns back on itself. As long as we are mortal, our relationship with life and our relationship with quality can never be resolved as a total that can be calculated. Yet, the higher the calculable quality of the life we are living, the more worthy it is; the total quality of life is the highest *value*.

Now I would like to attempt to tackle the question of *total* quality precisely from the point of view of value. The question of value is of crucial importance in Heidegger's meditation on metaphysical thought as calculative thought. As Heidegger (2002, p. 77) wrote in *The Age of the World Picture*:

> No less essential to the modern interpretation of beings is the representation of value. Where beings have become objects of

> representation, there, for the first time, in a certain sense, a loss of being occurs. This loss – vaguely and uncertainly enough perceived – is correspondingly quickly made up for through the fact that we attribute to the object and the thus-interpreted being a value. In general, we assess beings according to values and make them the goal of all action and activity.
>
> Since this latter conceives itself as culture, values become 'cultural values' and these become the general expression of the highest goals of creation devoted to the self-establishment of man as *subiectum,* From here it is only a short step to making values into objects in themselves. Values become the objectification of needs as goals brought about by representing self-establishment within the world as picture. Values appear to be the expression of the fact that, in relation to them, man strives to promote precisely what is most valuable. In fact, however, it is precisely 'values' that are the powerless and threadbare mask of the objectification of beings, an objectification that has become flat and devoid of background.

Values are that which modern man administers to the objectified being and that which makes it possible to proceed with the systematic measuring of beings, silencing that 'loss of being' that, for Heidegger, befalls things once they become calculable objects. Values render a supreme service to calculation, in the guise of the supreme purposes of human activity.[21]

Here I would like to draw attention to the phenomenon because of which, according to Heidegger, the service that value must render to the representation of beings can only be resolved through the objectification of those values themselves. It is only a step, says Heidegger to making values into objects in themselves. The supreme purposes of every human action become themselves objects and, as such, they are subject to systematic measurement.

Now let us think of how quality of life is a calculable object and the value against which we calculate everything. What I suggest we consider is that, when it becomes a question of quality, the fact that the value and the object become indistinguishable takes on a very particular tone.

Contemporary man measures the quality of everything in view of the total quality of his own life.

In what guise does quality permit this step? One could say: in the guise of the unifying value, the supreme value, the most valid of all values, the most 'human' of all values, of the *total* value. Once total value has made an appearance, it seems that a 'particular' value can only unfold as a particular component of quality as the total value.

Quality makes values stand, in an unprecedented way, one beside the other in the form of quality, a phenomenon that recalls the quality catalogue that we commented on in the previous section.

Can we consider this somehow extreme configuration of the question of values from the perspective of finitude? Possibly, yes.

> No one dies for mere values.
>
> (Heidegger, 2002, p. 77)

This phrase means that where values, having themselves become objects, have become the cover for the loss being suffered by beings as objects of the representation, it is no longer possible to go and die in a human way for those values. It means that if death is, for man, that which makes it possible for him to relate to what is not of the order of the calculable, then going to die for a value is a 'contradiction in terms'.

No one dies for mere values, and even less so can we now say, for the simplest and most valid value of all, for the total quality of her own life. At least, not before calculating if such a decision either augments or diminishes that quality.

2.6.4 Quality as an 'immeasurable' total: The incalculable as indefinitely liveable

In the previous section we attempted to interpret the entry on the scene of quality as a movement that belongs to the perfecting of the objectification of beings through calculation. However, we have to attempt to understand even better the sense in which this calculative movement has to do with numerical measurement.

Numerical measurement assures and legitimates – while the very phenomenon of the calculability of quality cannot be in any way grasped starting from its numerical measurement. There is nothing like numbers for assuring us that one life, in its quality, can be *more* than another or that tomorrow it can be more than today.

The production of numerical results allows the science of quality measurement to advance along that which is, for Heidegger, the route of every modern scientific procedure: the production of results and the legitimating of these results by other results. The ability to produce numerical results, and therefore to draw comparisons about quality on an international, inter-subjective and inter-temporal level, is the presupposition for the 'usability' of scientific procedures in a social, economic and political context.

However, at this point we should ask: what is the nature of the numerical measurement of all qualities? What kind of results does it obtain?

Let us look once again at what happens in measurement practices. Numerical measuring can produce a result of this kind: the total quality of life in France (or for a particular French citizen) is 10.5.

But what is the 'foundation' of this number? What is the status of the number associated with the qualities being measured? Can the correctness of these numbers be related to an ultimate theory of quality of life measurement?

Let us focus on 'objective' and 'subjective' measurement.

As measuring experts recognize, it is quite possible to start from the assumption that the total of life is made up of a certain number of components: social relations, culture, political participation, material well-being, etc.

This total has to be understood, in my view, as constitutively *indefinite,* not only in the sense that it is always possible to add some other determinant (affective, psycho-relational, emotional, artistic), but also in the sense that each of these components is in turn made up of a total of sub-components. The component 'culture', for example, can, in principle, be represented by the sum of the social, political, relational, economic, affective and emotional aspects of the cultural experience.

As we have seen, measuring subjective perceptions (that which an individual perceives, indeed lives, as the quality of her own life) also proceeds by the calculation of a total, for example, in the form of an ever more precise calculation of *momentary experiences* of well-being, distress, happiness or sadness,[22] experienced over a certain time period.

A component is itself made up of components; a period is made up of moments. In what way could it be possible to place a limit on this indefinite regression, if the aim is to calculate real life rigorously?

Here, a clue emerges about the fact that determining the components of the total can and must, in general terms, be done in a somehow indefinite manner and that the science of measuring must accept this lack of determination as something that belongs to the specific nature of the measurement exercise.

A clue to what we are trying to grasp can, in my opinion, be found in the Stiglitz Report[23] (Stiglitz, Sen and Fitoussi, 2009, p.16).

> Quantitative measures of these subjective aspects hold the promise of delivering not just a good measure of quality of life per se, but also a better understanding of its determinants, reaching beyond people's income and material conditions.

Let us consider the structure of this sentence and what is surprising about it: according to the normal way of proceeding in the social sciences, the ever better comprehension of the determinants of quality of life must be at the service of good, and ever better measuring of the quality of life itself.

Here the ever better determination of what makes quality of life as a total is as important as the 'correctness' of the measures produced by the measurement process.

In my view, what we should consider is that, when life in its quality is at stake, the scientific rigour of the procedure has to do with the attempt to take into account life itself in the most open, wide-ranging and in-depth manner possible.

Every hypothesis on the nature of the 'determinants' (leading to a certain selection of the determinants themselves) must confront itself with the very peculiar nature of the 'object' of the scientific procedure. This object is *lived* life. The entire issue must be thus understood by considering the issue of liveability in the register of lived-experience and by understanding the latter as *indefinite liveability*.

I have remarked previously that calculating life in terms of quality means calculating the *lived quality of life*. It means representing true quality of life as lived quality of life; this means representing what is individual in life and for life as a matter of liveability and as something that can be measured by measuring how it is lived. Here, I would like to emphasize that calculating quality of life makes possible the representation of the individuality of human life (and of the things that make up life) in its indefinite liveability.

That which makes up life in its individuality (that which makes up life as that individual life that it is) becomes something that is *indefinitely* pursued, calculating the way in which each person lives and *feels* that individuality.

Calculating life as a total means calculating it as an indefinite total, an indefinite total of 'domains' of lived-experience, moments of lived-experience, occasions of lived-experience. We must think of the whole of life as an indefinite total because it is *indefinitely lived*.

When liveability gives tone to life, true life is life in its liveability. And when liveability gives tone to quality, true quality is lived quality. This means that liveability determines the way in which the quality of life is a total: an indefinite total in the way that lived-experience is an indefinite process.

This proceeding down to the bottomless pit of lived-experience can be provisionally interrupted, in order to provide partial results; yet that pit itself remains the proper playing field for the calculative exercise, in order for it to be rigorous.

Let us view this from the point of view of *indicators*.

Calculating the quality of a certain something, and human life itself, proceeds first and foremost by producing and measuring the indicators of that something.[24]

An indicator *indicates* a phenomenon, placing it there before us. We must try to think of the phenomenon of 'indicating', considering the motility and indefinite nature that the process of indicating assumes when the quality of things and of life are in question.

Calculating by indicators means indefinitely projecting (quality of) life as a matter of 'experience', by producing an indefinite number of indicators of its experienced liveability.

The lists of indicators are, by nature, open and every indicator, in principle, can be decomposed into an indefinite number of indicators.

Yet at a certain moment the list may be 'closed' and every indicator can become a number. For example, the number of friends you have relationships with over a certain period of time, the number of artistic events or cultural initiatives in a certain town, the number of periods of time in which positive feelings outweigh negative ones, and so on. It is therefore possible to aggregate all these numbers to be able to assign a number to the total quality of life for an individual or a nation.

However, this operation of reducing to a number is, in a very specific sense, arbitrary. That is not to say, of course, that the 'provisional' definition of the list of indicators and their transformation into numbers is not accompanied by a serious methodological debate employed to determine some form of acceptability for these provisional lists.

That means, instead, that, in my view, no theory of quality of life can definitively solve the problem concerning 'indefinite liveability'. Hence, in my view, the question of the peculiar 'indeterminateness' of numerical measures.

It is in the same vein that we should consider the question that some social science contributions deal with, such as the question of the lack of any 'foundation' for the numbers which continue to intervene in the measuring processes pervading the scene of management.

Measuring the performance of a worker (something that, in my view, could not be more precisely defined as measuring the total quality of her life as a human resource) means also taking into account the most 'incalculable' dimensions: creativity, feelings, emotions, affects, etc.

> Today, personnel departments and management are desperately looking for strategies to attach *true* and measurable values to the immaterial resources that are at the core of immaterial labour and capitalism.
>
> (Vormbusch, 2008, p. 8)

However, this desperate search could end by having to recognize the impossibility of returning to something like the 'truth' and the 'objectivity' of numbers. Measurement efforts result in the continuous production of numbers that appear groundless, in that their truth seems not to be grounded anywhere.

This tends to be interpreted in terms of the relationship between calculation and human resource's mobilization. The incessant assignment of numbers to all dimensions of human resources (social, affective, emotional, relational, etc.) does not seem to justify itself in any way other than as the *communicative mobilization* of human resources toward an ever better level of performance.

> Here, calculative devices are not so much utilized to pin somebody down to a specific and immutable value, but to induce discussion

> about how to continuously work on the perfection of the self and how to adapt one's aspirations to an ever changing space of vocational possibilities.
>
> (Ibidem, p. 10)

The more calculation receives its shape from mobilization, the more the question of the correctness of number resonates in a new tone.

Approaching the question in this way, we could end up saying that the numerical measuring of quality of life bypasses the lack of 'objective' truth because it is driven by nothing other than mobilization toward ever greater quality. And we may even end up thinking of all this starting from a biopolitical or bio-capitalist logic that forces individuals and nations to compete by pursuing ever-higher performance in terms of quality of life.

The co-belonging relationship between calculation and empowerment is undoubtedly a crucial question that I will address later, when I will analyse the nexus between indefinite 'liveability' and indefinite human empowerment.

However, the issue of the 'indeterminate' character that calculation assumes when *calculating the incalculable* cannot be interpreted, in my view, by merely conceptualizing a new nature and role of calculation and a new relationship with mobilization. The nexus between calculation and mobilization should be understood, instead, by keeping in view the above argument on the issue of indefinite liveability.

We should consider more precisely the nature of the incalculable that management seeks to calculate and which constitutes its most precious prey. The incalculability of life is rooted in a representation of life as made of an indefinite multiplicity of dimensions and moments of lived-experience – hence the ambiguous status of numerical measurement, which is not at all an obstacle for the development of measurement itself.

And it is worthwhile noting that, precisely through the representation of the incalculable as a matter of lived-experience – as something that is difficult, but never impossible, to calculate because it has to do with the bottomless pit of lived-experience – the incalculable is ever more securely established as merely *the not yet calculated*. Though this movement, knowledge is refused of that dimension of incalculability which, for Heidegger, escapes every representation.[25]

2.6.5 Qualities as parts of the same type: Life as indefinitely divisible

In other to further consider the issue addressed in the previous paragraph, we must return to the question concerning representation and the 'quantitative'.

The essence of the 'quantitative' is representation, Heidegger says.

But how, reading the metaphysical history of the quantitative (which is the history of the quantitative *as category*), can we sense the 'representational essence' of the *quantum*?

Heidegger traces, in an extremely succinct way, the lines on which this question can be addressed in section 71 of the *Contributions* (Heidegger, 1999a, p. 96). Let us read the first part of the paragraph:

> According to the tradition (cf. Aristotle on ποσόν) the essence of the quantum lies in divisibility into parts of the same kind.
>
> What then is *quantitas*? And the quantitative? And to what extent is the gigantic quantitative as qualitative? Can that be made comprehensible in view of that determination of the *quantum*?
>
> *'Parts of the same kind'* and *'dividing'* and 'dividing and *distributing into parts'* (calculating-λογός, differentiating-gathering)
>
> Distributing into parts and arranging?
>
> Arranging and re-presenting?

Obviously, I do not presume here to comment on the possibilities of thinking the relationship between the quantitative and representation which these few lines point to. I would just like to advance a brief note concerning the 'quantitative' arrangement and representation of human life as a total of parts.

Let us concentrate on what Heidegger says about Aristotle: 'the essence of the quantum lies into divisibility in parts of the same kind'.[26]

What Heidegger invites us to consider, in one fell swoop, is the relationship between the divisibility into parts of the same type and its representation. In order to do this, the philosopher writes a sequential series of propositions. Divide into parts of the same type. Divide into and distribute as parts of the same type. Divide and arrange. Arrange and represent.

What is, for Aristotle a *plethos*, that quantity that is plurality and that can be numbered, thinking, for example, of a flock of sheep? The parts of the same type are the sheep. A flock, divided into sheep, is divided into parts of the same type.

How can we intend the meaning of the expression *parts of the same type*? Being of the same type means, for the parts, each one *not being in relation* to the flock; being parts that are *equally* extraneous to the flock as *a whole*. The sheep are all equally extraneous to the flock in its wholeness.

The divisibility of the flock into sheep is the 'arrangement' of the flock and it is what makes its representation possible. This representation is assured by number. Number tells us the quantity of units of which something is made up. Once divided into sheep we say that a flock of nine sheep is bigger than a flock of eight sheep. Two flocks are thus comparable and this comparability is made possible by number.

Now we make a leap and ask: what does the *quantum* imply when it concerns human life? What does dealing quantitatively with human life mean?

What we can see today is that, when human life comes to be calculated quantitatively, it is represented as a *total*, a total of parts, and this total will be able to be referred to by a number.

But what does dividing into parts of the same type mean when we are dealing with human life? This brings to mind the catalogue, about which we had some misgivings when we considered this previously. Now we might say: those parts are qualities. As we have already seen, only by virtue of the entry of quality on the scene can life be comfortably represented as a total, a total of qualities.

At this point someone may remark: if the parts into which life is divided are qualities, then these parts are indefinitely divisible. Every quality can be always a total of qualities; every quality is a total of qualities *insofar as* it is a 'lived' quality. As I have previously remarked, the quality of environmental conditions, for example, can always, in principle, be decomposed in sub-qualities (the aesthetic, cultural, affective, social qualities of our relationship with the environment which we live in). This is because each 'component' is not 'extraneous' to life as the total to be represented. Each component, so to speak, 'contains' life in itself. In other terms, it is indefinite liveability that gives tone to divisibility of life, in terms of indefinite divisibility.

The arrangement and the representation of life as a total must face this peculiar 'problem'; and this problem is at the root of the particular indeterminateness of number in the calculation of quality, that being the fact that number does not *make up* the total.

2.7 A bridge towards the following argument

Let us therefore attempt, in the wake of what we have seen, a second reading of some moments of the debate on calculation, life and quality.

Let us consider how, according to Brusa and Tarizzo (2009), the emerging biopolitical rationality which develops under the banner of quality of life manifests an economicist and epidemiological character.

On the one hand, behavioural economics plays a specific role in constructing a *behavioural human being*, who is stripped of her historical dimension and deconstructed into economic behaviours, through a segmentation of collective lived-experiences that depersonalizes them, obliterating their psycho-historical depth.

On the other hand, evaluation in epidemiological terms of the determinants of every aspect of human behaviour develops, projecting at the same time, the image of the biopolitical society as a society *at risk*.

For Brusa and Tarizzo, therefore, what is at stake is an ever more intense co-penetration between the techno-scientific approach to human life of the social sciences and the manipulation of the human being that the biophysical sciences exert with growing power and precision. The behavioural man, deconstructed into behavioural segments according to the rules governing economics, is also a man whose behavioural segments can be classified and related to biological markers.

Let us focus our attention on the fact that, with a similar interpretative approach, the techno-scientific calculation of the human is conceived as linked to a set of *reduction* operations: reduction of human experience to behaviour, reduction of human behaviour to classifiable behavioural segments that can be evaluated, reduction of these slices of human experience to the level of population management, where only this level counts. This job of manipulation paves the way for the encounter with the fast-growing biological manipulation of the human.

Quality of life, when it becomes a techno-calculative issue, seems to emerge, in this theoretical perspective, precisely from the warp and weft of these reductionist processes.

Now, in my opinion, the issue of the scientific treatment of the human and its relationship with quality must not be conceived in terms of reduction.

We should not think in terms of a 'quantitative reduction of quality'. Nor should we think in terms of an ever more precise reduction of life to something that can be numerically measured and manipulated. If we take heed of Heidegger,[27] the ever more scientifically rigorous treatment of humankind does not proceed by way of importing the methods of the exact sciences.

We should not then interpret the extreme manipulability of the human merely starting from the convergence between human/social and bio/physical/computer sciences and on the coupling between 'reductionist' techno-scientific rationalities – for example, on the coupling of the reductive rationality of psycho-behavioural economics with the rationality of the biogenetic and computer sciences which tend to format human beings as a set of bits or molecules.

The convergence between human and 'non-human' sciences (and between the way in which they deal with the human[28]) is indeed an extremely important issue. However, we should not consider the path towards ever more complete scientific manipulation of the human, by merely concentrating on the forms taken by the specific developments of sciences.

Although these developments manifest themselves more ostentatiously, and while they are important, our attention needs to be focused on that basic movement by which the scientific treatment of man[29] follows its own rigour – a rigour that originates from the kind of object being investigated.

This means, in my view, that we should concentrate on the phenomenon (and on how it is related to the issue of quality) according to which life come to be, in an ever more complete way, under the 'double jurisdiction' of techno-scientific explainability and liveability in the register of lived-experience.[30]

Let us look again at how calculation proceeds under the heading of quality, by paying attention to an aspect that we have not concentrated on so far.

What is at stake is *calculating* the 'lived' quality of life, meaning representing quality of life (and thus life in its 'totality' and 'individuality') as a matter of liveability and measuring quality as it is perceived and experienced.

But what is at stake is also, *living* the calculated quality of life, meaning living life as *that life* that techno-scientific calculation determines – and continuously redetermines – *as* life.

In order to consider this point, let us come back to the Rose's argument on the *politics of life itself*. The following passage provides a further illustration of the meaning of that 'something new' that Rose identifies in contemporary techno-scientific scenarios.

> 'The philosophical status' – indeed the very ontology – of human beings is being reshaped through the decisions of entrepreneurs as to where to invest their capital and which lines of bio-medical research and development to pursue. It is being shaped by geneticists taking all those small decisions about which family lineages to investigate, which markers to choose, which genes to hunt by which methods. It is being redefined by clinicians working in alliance with their own patients to test out and explore the new potentials of gene therapy or reproductive technology. And it is being developed and contested by all those individuals and groups who are themselves active participants in the new ethics of normalcy – whether as subjects at risk of illness or early death, consumers governing ourselves though diets, selves reshaping ourselves by sculpting our bodies, potential parents deliberating over screening and genetic counselling, gay couples using artificial reproduction to have children.
>
> (Rose, 2001, p. 20)

Living means deciding about what life is – that which makes life as life – and about the different ways of being human. Living means evaluating while living; not merely contesting the 'impact' of scientific manipulations on life, but evaluating in everyday life what sciences continuously projects *as* human life.

Living means evaluating that which life becomes, through its constant reshaping; it means evaluating the *quality* of the new ways of being human.

What we are faced with is, in my view, an ever more complete interlinking of calculation and life. That 'subjectivity' that constantly evaluates life is itself constantly reshaped by techno-scientific developments.

> The new genomic and molecular vocabularies of ourselves [...] are being incorporated within these relations of the somatic self to itself. They render novel aspects of human vitality visible, reshaping 'experience', not only making sense of it in new ways, but actually reorganizing it in a new way and according to new values about who we are, what we must do and what we can hope for.
>
> (Ibidem, p. 18)

It is worthwhile emphasizing that, within this horizon, it is a matter of overcoming certain traditional concepts on the subject of the relationship between calculation and life. It is therefore necessary, above all, to recognize that the distinction between the *natural* and the *artificial* is increasingly losing its meaning in the new ethics of vital calculation.

> Within this new ethics, the human vital order has become so thoroughly imbued with artifice that even the natural has to be produced by a labour of the self – natural food, natural childbirth and the like. Even choosing not to intervene in living processes becomes a kind of intervention.
>
> (Ibidem, p. 19)

This possibility of living 'ethopolitically' coincides with the possibility of a vital *democratic* politics. At the heart of the latter we get an idea of a radical democratization of science; a democratization that calls into question the separation between the places and protagonists of scientific calculation, the scientists and technicians, and the users of the results produced by science.

In the vein of the reflection on *technical democracy*, Rose identifies the scientific mobilization of social subjectivities as the engine of vital politics, with citizens, consumers, patients, social groups and associations becoming the protagonists of the scientific process, interacting ever more decisively with the scientists and discussing, making proposals for and contesting scientific procedures and results.

What calculation does with life must be lived democratically and democracy, as a process, becomes both a vital process and a matter of calculation. At the heart of the democratic process is the possibility of living democratically what calculation makes of us, of what we are and of our human quality.

Against this background, it seems that calculability and lived-experience seem to chime together clearly in a hitherto unparalleled way. However, that cannot in any way lead us to believe that we are in a condition to grasp something *decisive* about that relationship. Even less should we believe we are capable of doing so until we have attempted to further investigate the relationship between quality and calculation, and thus the relationship between calculability, machination and lived-experience.

This is what I will do in the next chapter, precisely addressing the issue towards which the argument developed in this paragraph somehow pointed: the nexus between calculation and the enhancement, both human and post-human, of humankind.

3
Calculation, Quality and Enhancement

3.1 Introduction

In this chapter, I continue along the path which was covered earlier, investigating the relationship between calculation and human development. On the basis of what we had begun to perceive concerning the relationship between calculability and life, I will seek to investigate the phenomenon through which development appears as a *continuous expansion* of vital processes; and once again, I will carry out this investigation from the perspective of quality.

The issue of quality seems indeed to have to do with the question concerning the *enhancement* of life: in an age when quality (of life) becomes a matter of calculation, quality itself seems necessarily to be played to the tune of the 'greater' or the 'lesser'. Nowadays, when someone is asked '*how is* your quality of life?', the most likely answer is 'high' or 'low'.

What does it mean, therefore, when quality of life becomes both the framework within which humankind becomes ever more completely calculated and is, at the same time, the *mot d'ordre* of man's development?

What does it mean when, under the banner of quality, calculation and enhancement seem so closely linked as to give us a glimpse of their co-belonging?[1] And how can we interpret, from the perspective of quality, the question of the 'vital' and 'vitalistic' nature of such empowerment?

I will focus initially on human development as a constant *expansion* of a totality of manifestations and possibilities of living. This is a conception of human development that is at the basis of the contemporary idea of *integral human development* and whose root is to be found in Marx's thought; and this conception proceeds today hand in hand with a certain conception of the calculation and enhancement of the *total* quality of life.

I will then address the above-mentioned issue concerning post-human enhancement: the enhancement in which man and things seem to be called into question in a completely new way. I will ask whether the ever increasable quality of life is still on the scene, when the distinctive quality of the human, in respect to the non-human is called into question.

3.2 Calculation, quality and total human development

3.2.1 Brief notes on Marx and the development of the total man

It is worth stating here that, in this section, I will confront Marx's thought from a very specific viewpoint. To be precise, I will focus – albeit briefly – on only a few aspects of Marx's thought, based on Heidegger's interpretation.[2] While Heidegger's interpretative contribution on Marx is, of course, not comparable to the monumental work on Nietzsche, the notes that Heidegger devoted to Marx are not only extraordinarily important in a general sense, but are also a fertile source as far as the theme of this work is concerned.

According to Heidegger, Marx was the thinker who brought metaphysics to its most extreme possibility; that of its entry into its conclusive phase.[3]

In Marx's thought, we find a determination of the being of beings which holds a very specific place in the history of metaphysics: through this determination, *Machenschaft* comes to the fore in an entirely singular manner. This entry of machination into the foreground should be considered in the light of the original correspondence between machination and lived-experience. As Schild (2011) points out, with Marx the being in the world of the human being consists of obeying *Machenschaft*'s demand *right to the very heart of his experience.*

Marx is, at the same time, the thinker in whom an interpretation is given, in an extremely precise and powerful way, of man's humanity as the totality of manifestations of life. He is also the thinker who advances a decisively important concept of man's development – a concept, we might say, that sets development in the heart of man and of his life. It is through his development that man becomes a truly human being. He is a being who is constitutively in need of developing himself (and the more he develops as a human being, the more he takes on that totality of possibilities of life which constitute the *richness* of man himself); and he is a being who develops as a *social being*.

> Marx demands that 'man's humanity' be recognized and acknowledged. He finds it in 'society'. 'Social' man is for him 'natural' man. In 'society' the 'nature' of man, that, is, the totality of 'natural needs' (food, clothing, reproduction, economic sufficiency) is equably secured.
>
> (Heidegger, 2011a, p. 152)

Marx's theoretical representation of man should be understood in the light of the fundamental ontological thesis which Heidegger invites us to recognize in Marx's philosophy: Marx conceives *the being of beings* as the vital productive activity of the human being in the form of the process of forming all things into objects created by and for himself.

As Heidegger says, for Marx, being is the production process.

> For Marx, being is the production process. This is the representation that he receives from metaphysics, on the basis of Hegel's interpretation of life as process. The practical concept of production can only exist on the basis of a conception of being stemming from metaphysics.
>
> (Heidegger, 2003, p. 52)

Marx's determination of being as a process was prefigured by Hegel, but contains a decisive difference compared to Hegelian metaphysics: for Marx, the process becomes the productive process of life, life as the process of the joint production of the world and of humankind.

This means that, in Marx, *Machenschaft* – that basic determination of being of beings which runs through all metaphysics – takes on a tone of its own, whose influence extends right up to our own times. The *empire of self making* here plays to the tune of the vital process of production of man and of nature; of that process in which man creates himself, establishing the world as an object created by and for himself.

Here we are confronted by the manner in which the relationship between machination, power and life begins to resonate with Marx. The *power* that accompanies the metaphysical trajectory of machination leads back to the heart of man himself. But man's being is vital productive activity; power therefore leads back to the heart of that life, through which man, in the process of living it, becomes man. Power becomes a vital process and the vital process becomes a process of constant enhancement of itself.

Beings do not recognize anything beyond that which arises out of themselves; in Marx, we could say, this becomes the fact that the vital productive activity of the human being does not recognize anything other than itself in its development.

Through the task of elaborating non-organic nature, man produces the objective world; he takes upon himself the historical process of creation of the world through the reproduction of the totality of nature *on behalf of* and *for* humankind. It is precisely through this work that man asserts himself, and develops as a human being. Nature itself, for a man engaged in this work of production, is no more than the inorganic body of man; something which man is a part of, and which is also part of man.[4]

By considering this, we can understand what Heidegger 2011a, referring to Marx, says about materialism. The essence of materialism, Heidegger writes, does not lie in the assertion that everything is only matter, but rather in a metaphysical determination according to which beings appear as a *working material*.[5]

But the vital productive activity – and it is worth emphasizing this – is the process in which man, in becoming total man, becomes truly man. This is the process by which man becomes humanized through that humanization of nature which leads man himself to his human essence.[6] This enhancement of life is no other than the ever more complete *humanization* of man, the ever more complete realization of man's humanity.

For Marx, thus, man's development is the development of the humanization of man himself. Development is the process through which, by living ever more humanly, man regains possession of the richness of the human being. For Marx, man is a being who is constitutively *in the process of developing*, a being who lives in need of developing his own humanity and finds himself under the necessity of such development. Let us consider the famous passage of the Manuscripts (Marx, 1978, p. 91):

> It will be seen how in place of the *wealth* and *poverty* of political economy come the *rich human being* and rich *human* need. The *rich* human being is simultaneously the human being *in need of* a totality of human life-activities – the man in whom his own realization exists as an inner necessity, as *need*.

The humanization of man coincides with the complete emancipation of *all* human senses, and of *all* human qualities: man becomes humanized by retreating ever more completely from the one-sidedness typical of the animal, and attaining the state of 'total man'. This humanization is man's process of becoming total man, a man in need of a totality of manifestations of human life. We can begin to consider this development of man – his humanization – as the constant expansion of the totality of manifestations of life.

Today, nothing seems more natural than to consider human development as the constant expansion of the totality of vital processes. Yet we should always remember the Marxian origin of this conception of man as a *totality in expansion*.

For Marx, however, as I have already underlined, man self-develops as a social man.[7] It is as a *total social man* that humankind reaches the peak of the possibility of enhancing its own human faculties.

Human development is a process which occurs as a process of the ever more complete socialization of man himself. Only as a social man, that is, as a social product, can man achieve his own full humanization: '*just as* society itself produces *man as man*, so is society *produced* by him' (Ibidem, p. 85). It is only as a social human being that man can regain the richness of man himself; and it is only as a social being that man can make himself together with nature and become ever more man. In sociality – and hence in the development of production as social production – Marx sees the key to the overcoming of man's animality.

The communist revolution is, for Marx, the historical process of the appropriation of the human being to his social being, to his true common existence. This process is man's re-appropriation of all the *richness* which constitutes the human being and, at the same time, of the richness of the natural world which is created by man himself.

This is what the overthrowing of private ownership (and therefore the establishment of a truly social society) can achieve: a new manner of relationship between man and things which is also a new opportunity for man to enter into a relationship with himself as a human being.

Overcoming private property allows the overthrowing of that unilateral form of appropriation which is implicit in private ownership itself: that form of appropriation based on possession, on *having*. It is through such overthrowing that man will be able to advance towards his ever more complete humanization, developing the totality of his own abilities as active manifestations of his humanity and thereby developing himself as a total man.

Man is thus truly man inasmuch as he is the totality of human manifestations of life and, at the same time, inasmuch as he is the intuition and real spirit of social existence. Each man, as a distinct individual, is the process of re-appropriation of the totality of the manifestations of life and this is possible as a result of the science of society accumulated in the individual, as a social individual. The means of production are no longer something external, something different with respect to social man, but are 'organs' of the will of man created by human hands, organs of the human brain, which is manifested in the form of *general intellect* (see Bee, 2010).

General social knowledge becomes an immediate productive force. The conditions of the vital process itself of society are monitored by the general intellect, and are reshaped in conformity with it; the social productive forces are produced, not only in the form of knowledge, but as immediate organs of social practice, of the process of real life.

In the third stage of man's evolution,[8] the individual becomes a completely social individual, in the sense that the knowledge of society is accumulated within him. When man fully becomes a social individual, in his most personal existence, he is at the same time also the community (see Bee, 2010).

Here, we are faced with the crucial issue which concerns man as a *particular individual* and as a *social individual*. As Marx writes in the *Manuscripts*:

> Man, much as he may therefore be a *particular* individual (and it is precisely his particularity which makes him an individual, and

> a real *individual* social being), is just as much the totality – the ideal totality – the subjective existence of thought and experienced society present for itself; just as he exists also in the real world as the awareness and the real enjoyment of social existence, and as a totality of human life-activity.
>
> (Marx, 1978, p. 86)

Vital productive activity is a social productive activity which man – as a total and social man – re-appropriates: conscience and language are social products.

> [...] when I am active *scientifically*, etc., – when I am engaged in activity which I can seldom perform in direct community with others – then I am *social*, because I am active as a *man*. Not only is the material of my activity given to me as a social product (as is even the language in which the thinker is active): my *own* existence *is* social activity, and therefore that which I make of myself, I make of myself for society and with the consciousness of myself as a social being.
>
> (Ibidem, p. 86)

As Bee (2010) stressed, for Marx every single individual in its individual existence brings into play the entire species to which it belongs, as much in its existence – which is composed of all existing individuals – as in its essence, above all.

Thus man makes himself through the vital social process by means of which he takes possession of the totality of the possibilities of living. In this way, he is produced as a man, as a truly human being; but in this way he is also created as the human being which *each particular individual* is.

This means that man's relationship with singularity – with the singularity of every man, with the singularity of everything and of all things – plays its part in life as a process. Singularity, precisely because it is truly human singularity, becomes a vital productive process – in this sense, we might say, it resonates to the tune of a 'lived' singularity, to the tune of lived-experience.

The more we appreciate the nature and the power of Marxian thought on man, the more we seem to recognize Marx in that concept of human development that proceeds under the banner of the ever-increasing total quality of life.

3.2.2 Diversely following in Marx's footsteps

Let us now consider some contemporary stances on the development of man which evolve, albeit in different ways, within the dialogue with Marx's thinking.

We begin with the work of Amartya Sen – a scholar who worked thematically on the issue of quality of life – and with his conception of *human development* and the calculation that a truly human development requires.

What does conceptualizing and measuring an authentically human development mean for Sen?

An essay written some decades ago – entitled *Development as capability expansion* (Sen, 1989) – contains some of the basic elements of the Indian scholar's theoretical approach.

The starting point, which Sen links to philosophical tradition, is the necessity of seeing human beings as ends in themselves, rather than as means to other ends.

Assuming human beings as the aim of all economic and social development – and thus refusing any development in which human resources are merely the levers of economic growth – implies putting human life at the heart of the concept of progress. So doing would, in fact, involve countering the temptation of

> treating people as the means through which that productive progress is brought about (rather than seeing the lives of people as the ultimate concern and treating production and prosperity merely as means to those lives).
>
> (Sen, 1989, p. 41)

But this life – a benchmark against which any concept of progress should be measured – deserves to be considered with regard to what makes it truly human life. The criterion against which progress should be evaluated, gauging its degree of 'humanity', is precisely its richness.

> The particular line of reasoning that will be pursued here is based on evaluating social change in terms of the richness of human life resulting from it.
>
> (Ibidem, p. 43)

This idea of human richness is very clearly derived from Marx, whom Sen refers to, mentioning the passage of the *Manuscripts* in which Marx speaks of a man who is in need of a totality of human life-activities.

In other texts, further emphasizing the ascendancy of his thinking on Marx, Sen (1987) quotes a famous passage of *German Ideology* in which the question of totality, considered in the light of total man and of total man as he who is generated through the life of society, is directly at issue. This is the passage in which Marx and Engels speak of what might happen in a society in which everyone can freely develop their own individuality. In a society which regulates general production, it becomes possible for everyone to humanize themselves by cultivating all or any possibilities of life. This society:

> makes it possible for me to do one thing today and another tomorrow, to hunt in the morning, fish in the afternoon, rear cattle in the evening, criticize after dinner, just as I have in mind, without ever becoming hunter, fisherman, shepherd or critic.
>
> (Marx and Engels, 1947, p. 22)

The theoretical perspective which would allow us to move towards a radical transformation of the representation and measurement of development,[9] in order to take the richness of human life into account, is centred on the concept of *capability*. The latter is, in turn, derived from an interpretation of human life as consisting of a set of functionings.

> The primitive notion in the approach is that of functionings – seen as constitutive elements of living. A functioning is an achievement of a person: what he or she manages to do or to be, and any such functioning reflects, as it were, a part of the state of that person. The capability of a person is a derived notion. It reflects the various combinations of functionings (doings and beings) he or she can achieve. It takes a certain view of living as a combination of various 'doings and beings'.
>
> (Sen, 1989, p. 44)[10]

What I would like to further underline here is Sen's acknowledgment of the Marxian interpretation of truly human life – and therefore of a truly human development – as a totality of 'manifestations' of life, meaning such manifestations in the broadest sense possible.

This totality is a totality *in continuous expansion*. We might say that it is a totality of doings and beings, constitutively *in the process of enrichment*.

It is worthwhile noting that Sen transposes this conception of human development to the level of *freedom*, or more precisely, to the freedom of the human being as the freedom to choose the manner of making oneself, in the potential totality of one's own functionings. The free man, according to Sen, is the man who takes possession of this freedom of choice – and does so, we might say, by evaluating his own development such that it measures up to this conception of freedom.

Quoting a passage of the *German ideology*, Sen writes:

> Capability reflects a person's freedom to choose between different ways of living. The underlying motivation – the focusing on freedom – is well captured by Marx's claim that what we need is 'replacing the domination of circumstances and chance over individuals by the domination of individuals over chance and circumstances'.
>
> (Ibidem, p. 44)[11]

Now, what I wish to emphasize is that a certain conception of human life and human development allows itself to be translated, almost automatically, in terms of the conception and measurement of quality of life. Sen himself has a great attention to the notion of quality of life,[12] and the capability theory represents one of the major methodological frameworks for its measurement, as acknowledged in the Stiglitz Report (Stiglitz, Sen and Fitoussi, 2009).

The representation of the human as a set of ways of being and of doing thus coincides with a determination of the quality of life: the quality of human life – that which makes human life a human life, and each person's life the life of each person, as we might say without greatly straining our interpretation of Sen's thought – is the totality of doings and beings, of ways of being and of doing. The more it succeeds in taking account of this totality, the more the evaluation of development will measure up to the richness of the human being.[13]

> If life is seen as a set of 'doings and beings' that are valuable, the exercise of assessing the quality of life takes the form of evaluating these functionings and the capability to function.
>
> (Sen, 1989, p. 43–44)

When the interpretation of human life and its development evolves on the grounds of totality (of total richness and of appropriation of the totality of manifestations of life), quality of life somehow incorporates the reference to totality, making it appear to be something obvious. As I have previously noted, quality is either total, or it is not quality at all. Furthermore, the fact that a *true* quality measurement is a measurement of quality according to how it is *lived* incorporates the fact that this totality in expansion (which makes the human being) is a 'lived totality'.

It is precisely considering the link between a certain conception of human development and a certain conception of total quality that we can return to the question of 'indeterminateness' in the measurement of life.

Sen acknowledges in the above-quoted work the issue, in terms of an ambiguity[14] that surrounds the calculation of human life as a complex of functionings.

What is at stake is the problem of selecting of the functionings to be taken into account, against the possibility of identifying ever newer 'achievements' in the description of functionings.[15]

In the vein of the considerations developed above, I believe that this possibility should be understood as a possibility which must necessarily be kept open whenever human life is represented as a totality of doings and beings.

Furthermore, in my view, the issue manifests itself not only in this dimension – which we might describe as a horizontal dimension – but also can be seen in the fact that every being and every doing can always be represented as being decomposable into an indefinite list of other beings and other doings.

Each doing and each being may appear to be indefinitely decomposable, precisely because – if we acknowledge the Marxian ascendancy in Sen's approach – they are components of man as a vital process.

Might not being an artist be represented as being composed of feeling joy, feeling fatigue, being 'creative'? Might we not consider the appropriation of the totality of the manifestations of life which Marx refers to as the appropriation of the totality of doings and beings that form a given doing or being? As an appropriation, that is, of the totality of possibilities of life which make up a given manifestation of life?

Certainly it is true – and this is a methodological pillar which allows evaluation to proceed – that at a certain point a selection and definition of the functionings can be made on the basis of given criteria of relevance. In other words, it is possible to produce lists of functionings that are worth taking into account in a given evaluation exercise, on the basis of the determination of the relative importance of these functionings themselves. Such a selection can be made in accordance with the specific objectives of the evaluation or with the availability of data relating to one or another category of functionings.

The fact remains, however, that every definition of the determinants of the human has, in actual fact, an 'arbitrary' nature, meaning that the path towards the representation of man's humanity is, in a very distinctive sense, indefinite.

In short, the question I addressed earlier on how to take the human into account (by taking into account quality of life as a 'lived' total quality), now appears as the question of how to take into account human development as a totality of possibilities of life in continuous expansion; in other words, it appears as the question of calculating the human *in its development*. But, let me emphasize once again, as Sen acknowledges in quoting Marx, man *is* his development; he is a being who is constitutively in the process of developing. The totality is a more *truly human* totality, the more it is taken into account as an expanding totality. The measurement of human development might thus find itself confronted with what I referred to earlier as the bottomless well of lived-experience.

Let us now look at a theoretical position that is surely far from that of Sen, but also moves from the interpretation and revising of Marx's thought.

We refer to Negri and Hardt's interpretation of the development of man as biopolitical development.

Negri and Hardt, by emphasizing the difference between biopower and biopolitics, view the latter as an ambivalent process. On the one hand, the latter dictates the framework in which the reproduction of capital as a social relation appears and in which thus arises a morphogenesis of the exploitation and capitalist control of life. On the other hand – and according to Negri and Hardt the recognition, albeit ambiguous, of this ambivalence can be found in Foucault[16] – biopolitics, when viewed as an event, is the construction of a possible liberation, of a vital proliferation capable of producing 'alternative subjectivities'.

> Biopolitics, in contrast to biopower, has the character of an *event* first of all in the sense that the 'intransigence of freedom' disrupts the normative system. The biopolitical event comes from the outside insofar as it ruptures the continuity of history and the existing order, but it should be understood not only negatively, as rupture, but also as innovation, which emerges, so to speak, from the inside.
>
> (Hardt and Negri, 2009, p. 59)

Biopower constantly seeks to react with respect to this vital proliferation, trying to assimilate the potential for liberation that is contained within biopolitical production. The new and numerous forms of biopolitical exploitation are, in fact, articulated within this reaction.

But the biopolitical process – which should be understood as constitutively producing an *excess* – is able to override capitalist relationships, to escape all attempt at recovery and to cultivate within itself the power of innovation and of liberation. The biopolitical process emerges as the production of an excess of life in the dimension of the *common* and, at the same time, as the creation of new resistant subjectivities.

> Our reading not only identifies biopolitics with the localized productive powers of life – that is, the production of affects and languages through social cooperation and the interaction of bodies and desires, the invention of new forms of the relation to the self and others, and so forth – but also affirms biopolitics as the creation of new subjectivities that are presented at once as resistance and de-subjectification.
>
> (Ibidem, p. 58–59)

But where does this productive capacity of biopolitical humanity lie? And in what sense is this capacity linked to a proliferation of vital processes? To find an answer, we can start by examining the characteristics of the protagonist of this mobilization of life: the *multitude*.

The nature of the multitude as a social actor – and its difference with respect to *people* – arises precisely from the fact that it is life *that makes itself by itself*,[17] and that, in so doing, it does not recognize anything other than itself.

> The people constituted a social body; the multitude does not, because the multitude is the flesh of life.
>
> (Negri, 2008a, p. 117)

In the conception of the multitude as the flesh of life – and in particular in the passage which follows – we glimpse the heart of Negri and Hardt's attempt to construct their own ontological thesis which follows in Marx's footsteps.

> Thus the raw material of the multitude is *flesh*, or that *common* living substance in which the body and the intellect coincide and are indistinguishable. [...] Like flesh, the multitude is thus pure potentiality, the non-formed force of life, an element of being. Like flesh, the multitude also is oriented towards fullness of life. The revolutionary monster which is called multitude and which appears at the end of modernity seeks continually to transform our flesh into new forms of life.
>
> (Ibidem, p. 118)[18]

If the multitude is flesh of life, Negri and Hardt could hardly have found a more precise expression than the one which describes flesh itself as a *raw material*.

One cannot help but recall the above-mentioned Heidegger's invitation to find the essence of materialism in the interpretation of beings – and of man – as a working material. The multitude as flesh is working material: it is the existence of man and things as being vital working material; it is vital productive activity constantly extended beyond itself, in the direction, that is, of none other than life itself.[19]

This *being towards life* takes on a particular determination – as a being towards life without end and without limits – when the attempt to come to terms with the very issue of death becomes explicit.

Let us consider a passage from one of Negri's recent works:

> The multitude is the only subject susceptible of launching this creative challenge to death. [...] The multitude's way of being is nothing other than this continuous proliferation of vital experiences which have in common the negation of death, the radical and definitive refusal of that which arrests the process of life.
>
> (Negri, 2008b, p. 70–71)[20]

In the light of the – as yet – briefly described constitutively 'vital' nature of the biopolitical process, we should understand that the surplus that this process produces is no more than the surplus of life, in the shape of ever newer forms of life.

The interpretation and revising of the Marxian theory of man's production by man – which Negri and Hardt refer to in detail – follows a trajectory of reasoning in which such production passes through the living and through the living body and its activity; and it is worthwhile to note that such a theoretical perspective will lead Hardt and Negri to profoundly rethink the biopolitical body and to see biopolitical subjectivities as cyborg-like entities, produced by the ever more intense hybridization between man and machine.[21]

The production of new biopolitical subjectivities advances in step with the immaterial relationships that spread throughout the *common*. The perspective of liberation proper to biopolitical humanity thus occurs in the common, through the interaction and interpenetration of singularities; it arises, therefore, in the proliferation of exchanges, intersections, affective relationships, networks, communications, and immaterial and 'linguistic' productions. Such productions – as Hardt and Negri point out, however, almost as if to emphasize that the process takes place in the heart of man himself – is nonetheless, at the same time and above all, a constant increase of the *capabilities* of feeling, loving, communicating and producing languages.

This production of a surplus of man – as a surplus of vital activity of the multitude – has a constitutively political aspect and, at the same time, defines a new possibility of economic accumulation.

> Accumulation of the common means not so much that we have more ideas, more images, more affects, and so forth but, more important, that our powers and senses increase: our powers to think, to feel, to see, to relate to one another, to love. In terms closer to those of economics, then, this growth involves both an increasing stock of the common accessible in society and also an increased productive capacity based on the common.
>
> (Hardt and Negri, 2009, p. 283)

Such economic accumulation must be interpreted in light of the new aspect that labour takes on in the biopolitical era, in which 'living and producing have become one single whole, and the time of life and the time of production have become increasingly hybridized' (Negri, 2008a, p. 189). This calls, therefore, for an updating of the Marxian argument and an understanding of production through the general intellect in the light of a less 'reductionist' conception of work. In other words, biopolitical production should be seen as a process that is defined on the level of *linguistic* production and of the forms of cooperation that permeate the multitude.

The multitude seeks to take ever more complete possession of this linguistic/relational productivity, developing its own capacity – which is not innate but requires an adequate input of education – to work with language, codes, ideas, and affects.

Here, it is of interest to focus on the fact that a decisive point in Hardt and Negri's theoretical work is their interpretation of the meaning of singularity.

What is the role of singularity – and of concrete singularities, and particularly of single individuals – with regard to the multitude?

For the two authors, the route to finding answers to these questions passes through a radical re-examination of what they call 'the metaphysics of individuality'. In other words, this route passes through the rejection – traumatic as it may be[22] – of the way in which metaphysical tradition has elaborated the relationship between the self, the other and the we. Any metaphysical determination of the notion of identity – and therefore 'all the dialectical illusions that too often plague discourses on identity' (Hardt and Negri, 2009, p. 339) – should be disregarded. Such determinations appear to be constitutively bound to the logic of property and sovereignty, and this arises from the fact that transcendence 'is the key to every metaphysics of individuality, as it is to every metaphysics of sovereignty' (Negri, 2008a, p. 120).

It is particularly significant that the attempt to move away from metaphysical interpretations of the singular takes the form, in one of Negri's other works, of an overtaking of what we might recognize as all the 'qualitative' determinations of beings:

> Materialism introduces into ontology the concept of determination as excedence of being. Not simply as quidditas ['whatness'], as exceptionality or singularity, nor even simply as exemplary (the universal made individual). This excedence is a creative fact which surges forth from labour. It is the ensemble of accumulated human labour, which determines values – excedences.
>
> (Negri, 2011, p. 47)

Let us turn once again to the passage of the *Contributions* I have quoted at the beginning of Chapter 2 – the one in which Heidegger focuses on quality as 'the basic character of the quale, of the what, of the ownmost, of be-ing itself'. Man's relationship with *this* quality – that relationship which metaphysics has gradually made more and more empty, taking it up in the context of a dialectical relationship between categories – seems to be summarily presented here as *nothing more* than a cumbersome legacy of metaphysics itself; and thus as something that biopolitical materialism might enable to be exceeded, in the light of a conception of *determination* as excedence of being (and of being itself as the process of 'exceeding'). This results in disregarding those dimensions of whatness, of singularity, of exceptionality which quality says to the Western man.

How is the metaphysical concept of singularity overcome? The answer lies, first of all, in a redetermination of the relationship between singularity and multiplicity (Hardt and Negri, 2009, p. 338–339):

> the concept of singularity is defined by three primary characteristics, all of which link it intrinsically with multiplicity. First of all, every singularity points toward and is defined by, a multiplicity outside of itself. No singularity can exist or be conceived on its own, but instead both its existence and definition necessarily derive from its relations with the other singularities that

> constitute society. Second, every singularity points toward a multiplicity within itself. The innumerable divisions that cut throughout each singularity do not undermine but actually constitute its definition. Third, singularity is always engaged in a process of becoming different – a temporal multiplicity. This characteristic really follows from the first two insofar as the relations with other singularities that constitute the social multiplicity and the internal composition of the multiplicity within each singularity are constantly in flux.

Singularity, as a flow, is composed of a multiplicity of determinants. It is formed, we might say, as multiplicity *in every direction and in every sense*: as multiplicity of relationships with the other; as multiplicity of relationships with itself; as multiplicity of moments of lived-experience. We are surprised – but not greatly – to find ourselves faced here with a representation, which is precise in its own way, of the question I previously broached as a crucial issue in understanding the calculation and the 'enhancement' of man. I refer to the representation of the singularity of life (of life as life and of each life like as the life that it is) as a 'lived' totality in constant expansion.

For man, singularity as a vital productive flow plays to the tune of totality; and totality resonates in the tune of the 'lived' totality in continuous transformation.[23]

The role of the issue of singularity in Hardt and Negri's reasoning must thus be considered in light of the basic thesis of life as a vital productive activity and of *flesh of life* as the constitutive element of the being itself.

The interpretation of life as a productive activity capable of producing new life is put forward by Hardt and Negri with regard to a conceptualization of the productive and innovative power of *love*. This *love* – considered in the light of Spinozian metaphysics – is defined, precisely, as the capability of creating the new, in the form of the creation of an excess of life, of reinvention of forms of life. At the same time, it is also defined as that which constitutes being. 'Being', Hardt and Negri write, 'is constituted by love' (Ibidem, p. 181). It is precisely this capability of producing life which love holds as a biopolitical event – and as an ontological machine – that sets the tone for the reproduction of singularities in the common.

> Here then is another meaning of love as a biopolitical event: not only does it mark rupture with the existent and creation of the new, but also it is the production of singularities and the composition of singularities in a common relationship.
>
> (Ibidem, p. 183)

And it is precisely the productive power of this love that enables the singular, freeing itself of its metaphysical legacy, to emerge in the multiplicity and as multiplicity.[24]

> Love should be defined, instead, by the encounters and experimentation of singularities in the common, which in turn produce a new common and new singularities. Whereas in the ontological context we characterized the process of love as *constitution*, here in a political context we should emphasize its power of *composition*. Love composes singularities, like themes in a musical score, not in unity but as a network of social relations. Bringing together these two faces of love – the constitution of the common and the composition of singularities – is a central challenge for understanding love as a material, political act.
>
> (Ibidem, p. 184)
>
> [....] As a motor of association, love is the power of the common in a double sense: both the power that the common exerts and the power to constitute the common. It is thus also the movement toward freedom in which the composition of singularities leads toward not unity or identity but the increasing autonomy of each participating equally in the web of communication and cooperation.
>
> (Ibidem, p. 189)

Let us now focus on the problem of measurement and the measurability of the 'products' of the vital productive activity of the multitude. The underlying thesis which Hardt and Negri have expounded at length in a series of more or less recent works is that of a constitutive 'immeasurability' of the value of biopolitical production. In a world where all life is a process of production, labour, in its indistinguishability in relation to life, is defined as a productive activity *outside measure* (Hardt and Negri, 2000). The consequence of establishing biopolitical labour as a vital process – and therefore as something that is no longer distinguishable from life – is the fact that production occurs as the generation of an immeasurable excess of value (Hardt and Negri, 2000). This thesis can already be seen in, for example, Negri (1999, p. 79), where the fact that labour 'finds its value in affect' (defined as the Spinozian *power to act*) is adopted precisely as the precondition for relinquishing any hypothesis of value measurement and thus for a retraction from the value-labour theory.

Postmodern political economy will clearly seek to reactivate forms of biopolitical control over the excess vital proliferation. But these desperate attempts at recovery would appear to be in vain because the biopolitical production of life becomes that which is constitutively beyond and outside *any measure, any control, and any calculation.*

After all, it is worthwhile to recall that the singularities that make up the common (and therefore, we might add, the common itself as composed of singularities) are produced, according to Hardt and Negri, in such a way as to be constitutively intersected by *innumerable* divisions. And this 'innumerability' of the divisions – as I emphasize, drawing on the reasoning set out in the preceding chapter – derives in my view, precisely from the fact that those singularities are 'lived' singularities; in other words from the fact that those singularities are, in the two authors' lexicon, *flesh of life*, which constantly proliferates beyond itself.

The fact that labour and life are biopolitically generated is thus clearly the reason that value is not 'in any sense analysable and measurable in simple quantities of time, and not even in complex sequences' (Negri, 2008a, p. 189). In this sentence, and in the sentence which follows, the issue of the immeasurability of biopolitical value is viewed on the level of 'quantitative' immeasurability.

> The quantitative indicators of professional economists offer little insight on this biopolitical terrain, in particular since production of the common constantly exceeds not only relationships of control but also frameworks of measure.
>
> (Hardt and Negri, 2009, p. 285)

Immeasurability *tout court*, and the impossibility of producing 'quantitative' measurements seem to overlap, since the emergence of the thesis of immeasurability, as a rejection of the possibility of replicating in any form whatsoever the measurement of value.

In *Commonwealth*, however, we find an indication suggesting a 'new' measurement of value; a measurement whose foundation and tone are rooted in the constitutive excedence of life as a productive force. What is at stake is the invention of a new *value theory*.

> We still, however, need a new theory of value that is grounded in exceeding, crossing the threshold. We should note, first of all, that we are not expecting such a theory to reveal value as something other than the perception of a historical event. In the most powerful theoretical experience that runs from Marx to Nietzsche value is already regarded as a historically determined innovation, that is, constituent activity.
>
> (Ibidem, p. 318–319)

Considering value as excedence thus implies imagining a measurement that radically rejects all determinism.

> To exceed is a creative activity. A new theory of value has to be based on the powers of economic, political, and social innovation that today are expressions of the multitude's desire.
>
> (Ibidem, p. 319)

If all this might define a 'new' economy – an economy that would be truly biopolitical – then we might also pose the question of economic value in new terms.

> Whereas capitalists have destroyed economics by turning it into mathematics, it is up to us to bring it back to the terrain of life and the ancient meaning of *oikonomia*. Economic value is defined by the overflowing, exceeding process accomplished by cooperative activity (intellectual, manual, affective, or communicative) against and beyond the capitalist regulation of society exercised through the financial conventions of the market.
>
> (Ibidem, p. 320)

The representation of man's existence as a biopolitical production cannot resist the temptation of measuring that production; whereas, if we follow Hardt and Negri's basic line of reasoning, this measuring should itself be considered a vital process. Here, in the willing surrender to this temptation, the two authors present us with the word we hold so dear: quality. The measurement of the *exceeding* production of life – which is what human development consists of, it should be recalled – should be a measurement *in quality* – through the use of indicators, of course.

> Useful economic indicators instead would have to be qualitative. What are the qualities of the common that constitute society? How accessible is the common to productive social forces? How autonomous are productive networks from forms of control? To what extent do social institutions promote or obstruct access to and productivity of beneficial forms of the common? If such indicators existed, they would trace a biopolitical cycle that is fundamentally arrhythmic, defined by thresholds of social composition and decomposition. But an adequate economic science of biopolitical production has yet to be invented.
>
> (Ibidem, p. 285)

If this measurement took the form of the measurement implemented by a new economic science, then that science could produce a new *Tableau Economique*. In order to do so, however, it will have to tackle the following question: 'How can one create an economic table filled with qualities?' (Ibidem, p. 287).

We are thus faced once again with the 'power' of quality in the calculation of the human. In Hardt and Negri, this 'new' measurement of value which passes for quality is not directly experienced or tackled from the point of view of the 'methodological' problems it might pose. Nonetheless, it should be emphasized, once radically new indicators have been defined, the problem might arise of how these can be translated into numbers along with other related methodological issues.

The fact that the two authors do not dwell on the 'methodological' consequences of this transformation of measurement also stems, clearly, from the fact that the 'new' measurement occupies a perspectival horizon. This new measurement awaits a science of biopolitical humanity – which could also become a new economic science – which has not yet materialized.

But what we are most concerned to ask ourselves is this: why did Hardt and Negri, in conceiving this new science of value measurement, capable of being constitutively beyond all reductionism, proceed under the banner of quality?

They could simply have said that creation of the common can be taken into account only in such a way that, while eschewing the illusion that labour/life can be reduced to controllable sequences, would measure up to the vital nature of the production of value, of its being *flesh of life*.

And yet, in describing the underlying characteristic of this new measurement, they cannot find a more precise expression than saying that the common should be taken into account *in its qualities*. And therefore, we are to understand, if the common is constitutively production of oneself beyond the self, then the calculation of truly human 'development' is a calculation of the quality of the common in its constant increase.

Quality thus enters the scene of the new measurement of biopolitical value. In my interpretation, that entrance on the scene – I repeat once again – occurs precisely when quality becomes available as 'experientially lived' quality. But, in my view, this is, for Hardt and Negri, something which absolutely *goes without saying*.

What is all quality if not something which makes itself as a vital productive process, as flesh of life? What is it, in the light of the above-quoted passages, if not something that speaks the language of the vital process of the common and that therefore makes itself, and goes beyond itself, as flesh of life?

Why then, if quality speaks no other language than that of the 'exceeding' vital productive process, is there any need to bring it into the equation?

I do not believe in the least that the two authors succumb to a lexical fad, replicating a 'discourse' on quality through mere laziness. I believe, rather, that we are once again confronted with the fact that the calculation can easily be carried out without requiring anything more than constantly securing itself, precisely in the name of quality, which means under the banner of the 'calculative withdrawal' of quality itself.

3.3 Calculation, quality and post-human enhancement

3.3.1 Post-human development, lived-experience and machination

Post-human alludes to a set of interventions on man's physical and psychical capacities (through the so-called NBIC[25] sciences) which promises to radically transform the idea of man we have had until now.[26]

On the one hand, this involves transformations of the body and the psyche as a result of the advances in physical and biochemical techno-sciences. On the other hand it involves a *reconstruction* of the human through redefinition of the man–machine relationship: computer sciences and robotics are working with increasing determination on the frontiers of neural interfaces, advanced information management tools, wearable or implanted computers.

The intersection of all these paths promises man's enhancement in all directions: from the extension of human life (to the extent of pursuing the dream of immortality); to the ever more precise control of *genetic* diseases and *congenital birth* defects (moving towards the frontier of biogenetic engineering of increasingly defect-free individuals); to insertion within the body of devices that promise expanded memory capacity or that allow direct access to telecommunication networks; to the 'transfer' of intelligence from the limited storage capacity of the brain to computer-telematic networks in which the ability to calculate and even experience emotions and feelings would take on new life (see Knorr Cetina, 2005).

The prospect of technical reproducibility of the brain – through its ability to be 'copied' and stored on technological storage media – is particularly emblematic.

Nick Bostrom, one of the most important representatives of post-human studies, describes the uploading of the human mind as follows:

> Uploading refers to the use of technology to transfer a human mind to a computer. This would involve the following steps: First, create a sufficiently detailed scan of a particular human brain, perhaps by feeding vitrified brain tissue into an array of powerful microscopes for automatic slicing and scanning. Second, from this scanning data, use automatic image processing to reconstruct the 3-dimensional neuronal network that implemented cognition in the original brain, and combine this map with neurocomputational models of the different types of neurons contained in the network. Third, emulate the whole computational structure on a powerful supercomputer (or cluster). If successful, the procedure would [sic] a qualitative reproduction of the original mind, with

> memory and personality intact, onto a computer where it would now exist as software. This mind could either inhabit a robotic body or live in virtual reality. In determining the prerequisites for uploading, a tradeoff exists between the power of the scanning and simulation technology on the one hand, and the degree of neuroscience insight on the other.
>
> (Bostrom, 2007, p. 22, quoted in O' Brien 2011)

What appears to be prefigurative is an expansion of life beyond the limits of man: a life which lives through the machines and networks, overcoming the finiteness of the body and allowing us to conceive that every human relationship with finitude might be bypassed. Post-/trans-human development resonates in the tone of a constant expansion of man – of what makes up man – within things (machines, networks, cells grown in vitro).

This human 'expansion' is acknowledged in the interdisciplinary debate as something that calls into question the nature itself of man.

As Hellsten (2012, p. 4) points out, according to the predictions of the studies of artificial intelligence and advanced computer science:

> our 'human form of existence' would radically change from a physical, biological being to a nonphysical being living in a virtual reality setup by a digital information system of a super intelligent computer.

Or as Knorr Cetina (2005, p. 78) notes, the developments of science:

> pose a challenge by questioning the sharp distinctions between humans and machines, by appealing to the plasticity of the organic and the technical.
>
> NBIC research creates interfaces between these categories that blur the human/non-human distinction.

For those currents of thought that celebrate the transition to post-human or trans-human, this transition is recognized as offering the possibility of shaping the human and the non-human in a radically new way, to the extreme point of imagining *spiritual*, conscious machines that claim to be human (Kurzweil, 2000).

> Machines, derived from human thinking and surpassing humans in their capacity for experience, will claim to be conscious, and thus to be spiritual. They will believe that they are conscious. They will believe that they have spiritual experiences. They will be convinced that these experiences are meaningful. And given the historical inclination of the human race to anthropomorphize the phenomena we encounter, and the persuasiveness of the machines, we're likely to believe them when they tell us this.
>
> (Ibidem, p. 153)

The numerous critical voices[27] which have been raised against the issue in recent years, however, concentrate on the risk of no longer recognizing man in the being he is turning into. As Fukuyama points out:

> Denial of the concept of human dignity – that is, of the idea that there is something unique about the human race that entitles every member of the species to a higher moral status than the rest of the natural world – leads us down a very perilous path.
>
> (Fukuyama, 2002, p. 160, quoted in Bostrom, 2005)

How, then, can post-human enhancement can be understood within the interpretative perspective of this work? Let us start from a formula employed by an eminent figure in contemporary sociology: the transition *from human to life* (Knorr Cetina, 2005).

In a recent paper, Karin Knorr Cetina explores the distinctive character of the post-human and of the concept of post-human development. In her view, such development should no longer be understood in the context of the concept of *perfectibility* that modern man inherited from the Enlightenment; it no longer maintains its continuity with 'the perfectibility of human society by societal means or the cognitive and ethical perfectibility of the human' (Ibidem, p. 78).

The enhancement that occurs under the post-human banner does not, in other words, adhere more to a certain idea of human progress and to a certain conception of the relationship between human progress and social progress; what we are dealing with is no longer like a 'further expansion of Enlightenment ideals of human reason and social salvation' (Ibidem, p. 76). The root of this decisive discontinuity resides, according to Knorr Cetina, in a cultural transition, of considerable significance and scope, from *human* to *life*.

> I argue that we are experiencing a turn to a 'culture of life' in a broad and encompassing sense that is comparable to the way in which human-centred ideas once dominated our thinking.
>
> (Ibidem, p. 76)

In other words, post-human development arises within a cultural framework centred on the pre-eminence of life, where the characteristics of this life and the nature of its enhancement can no longer be grasped on the basis of the bi-univocal relationship between the perfecting of human nature and the development of human sociality.

> Whereas the concepts of humanity and humanism have inspired intellectual elites and scientific disciplines for centuries, today the notion of life replaces the notion of the human as a concept that bridges developments in several sciences and in practical discourses.
>
> (Ibidem, p. 76)

According to my understanding of Knorr Cetina's argument, the influence of this culture of life must be considered on the basis of the fact that life creates itself as an open process in which new possibilities of living constantly emerge; without any given conception of the human – particularly, as noted above, that conception which we inherited from the Enlightenment – still being able to act as a point of reference for this *open-ended* progression of life.

> 'Life' stands for an open-ended series of biological, psychological, economic and even phenomenological significations and processes.
>
> (Ibidem, p. 76)

This scenario is defined not only by developments in the NBIC sciences – that promise a constant process of *life-enhancement* – but by a set of cultural transformations occurring, broadly speaking, within the field of human sciences. These transformations, in turn, create the conditions for a new encounter between human sciences and natural sciences.

These transformations have to do with complex processes that share the common denominator of the progressive loss of social imagination. This refers to the big question concerning the progressive weakening of both the idea of impersonal social forces affecting the individual, and of the concept of universal human perfection to be achieved through society. This latter notion, Knorr Cetina points out, runs through Enlightenment thought from Rousseau to Condorcet, and takes on one of its most meaningful forms precisely in 'Marx's vision of a socialist age.

> The question then is what replaces the social imagination. In the sciences that focus on the human world, the answer is plain: it is now the individual rather than society.
>
> (Ibidem, p. 77)

This focus on the individual emerges in numerous forms: in the ever-increasing emphasis on the self and on self-improvement[28] as the main path to the advancement of man; in the related explosion of *subjectivity thinking* in human sciences; and in the predominance of a group of cultures and of scientific theories that 'empower the individual as the unit that seeks information, calculates behavioural outcomes, and, through these mechanisms, engineers his or her fate' (Ibidem, p. 77).[29]

> The remarkable rise of subjectivity thinking thus harbours tendencies that bridge the gap between the human and the natural sciences.
>
> One tendency is the orientation towards concepts such as the notion of life. The second tendency is the orientation towards research and explanations that assimilate humans with other forms of life. Both play into a more general culture of life.
>
> (Ibidem, p. 77)

In general terms, we are thus faced with an interpretation of post-human development that considers the latter as the product of bidirectional relationships between cultural transformations and advances in scientific calculation.

In the vein of the argument already developed in the previous chapter, I believe that, while the transition from human to life alludes to something extremely important, that something should not, to my mind, be considered in the light of a cultural transformation; nor should it be immediately interpreted on the basis of the scientific processes which that transformation is apparently in a bi-univocal relationship with.

What I intend to do instead, is consider post-human enhancement in light of the question that I previously broached as an issue of the dominion of lived-experience; of the dominion of life, as life *lived through live-experience*.

In order to understand the 'distinctive nature' of post-human enhancement, we must, in my opinion, come back to the question of the dominion of lived-experience by trying to investigate the *completion* of that dominion (which means, at the same time the completion of the dominion of machination and the completion of the correspondence between machination and lived-experience) in the age of the 'end' of philosophy. As we shall see, that completion has a deal with the decisive moment of the posthuman: the 'transformation' of the relationship between man and things.

Here, however, a doubt arises.

Previously, we considered a certain idea of human development (of development of man in the total richness of his manifestations and possibilities) in relation to one of the foremost moments in the history of metaphysics: Marx's ontological thesis and its implications in terms of the conception of the human being and her relationship with nature.

But what did we see in Marx, according to Heidegger's interpretation?

In his ontological thesis, did we not recognize the determination of the being of beings as man's vital productive activity – the vital activity which jointly produces nature and man himself?

And did we not then accept Schild's suggestion to consider Marx as the thinker for whom man obeys to the imperative of Machenschaft to the very heart of his lived-experience – and as the thinker in whom the correspondence between machination and lived-experience comes to the open in a very peculiar way?

Is not Marx the philosopher for whom the making of man corresponds to *living* in a truly human manner, for whom man, by living, constantly produces himself as a more humanized man, and produces a more humanized nature?

But then, if the post-human development of man is a development that at first sight appears to us to be connected to man's making himself in things (created and produced by man) and, at the same time, as something that takes place as an enhancement of life *on the basis of life*, does the root of this development not already exist entirely complete *in Marx*?

Answering this question involves seeking to consider the phenomenon which Heidegger refers to as the completion of the history of metaphysics. In this completion, which metaphysics enters thanks to Marx and then to Nietzsche, it is no longer philosophy – and thus a particular determination of the being of beings – which sets the course and gives direction.

Let us recall once more what Schild (2011) says. According to that *metaphysical thinker*, Marx, being in the world of human beings consists in obeying the demands of *Machenschaft* to the very heart of *man's* experience. In Marx, *Machenschaft* – that which reigns supreme over all the metaphysical determinations of the being of beings – is exposed for the first time in its co-belonging with the dominion of lived-experience, and this coming out into the open, we might say, occurs as the setting-up of the demands of 'self-making' (and therefore of *power* as machination) at the heart of man's lived-experience.

I suggest now – as we will see later, and will try to understand in what way we might say this – that when, in the age of the end of philosophy, the power of lived-experience develops in a certain way, we will no longer be able to talk, as we do in the case of Marx, of the lived-experience *of* man.

Let us begin by examining a passage of section 58:

> now for the first time everything is 'experienced live' *[erlebt]* and every undertaking and performance drips with 'lived experiences' *[Erlebnisse]*. And this 'lived experience' proves that now even *man as a being* has incurred the loss of be-ing and has fallen prey to his hunt for lived-experiences.
>
> (Heidegger, 1999a, p. 86)

This passage at first glance seems difficult to understand, whereas on the other hand it seems easier – although it is not at all certain that this is indeed the case – to understand that by treating beings as calculable resources, man finds that he himself becomes nothing more than a *human resource*.

What does it mean that by dint of dealing with beings as lived-experiences (as providers of lived-experience for man) man himself becomes the quarry of his own pursuit of lived-experiences – that man himself, *human* life, falls itself under the rule of *Erlebnis*?

Does it mean, for example, that man's life is formed as a totality of lived-experiences? That life counts as human life only insofar as it is a totality of domains, of moments, of dimensions, of occasions of lived-experience? That life is all the more human the more it manages to *develop itself*, seizing this expanding totality of possibilities of living?

This is, in fact, what I alluded to in previous sections of this work, when I focused on the total 'lived' quality of life and its relationship with a conception of man's life as a totality of 'lived-experiences' in constant expansion.

This conception of man continues to exercise a strong hold even today, which means that the contemporary West is still under the grip of that particular form of dominion of the lived-experience that occurs in Marx.

Yet, in order to understand the completion of the trajectory of power and calculation (and its relationship with *life*), we should not remain at Marx; and not even nor at Nietzsche, the metaphysical thinker in which life will come on the scene in the most explicit and powerful way, when *will to power*, that will be determined as the being of beings, will be the basic character of *life*[30] (Heidegger, 1991).

We must instead consider the extreme outcome of that dominance of lived-experience: the outcome in which live-experience[31] 'attains the utmost of what is its ownmost' (Heidegger, 1999a, p. 349).

In the age of the cybernetic fulfilment of metaphysics, man – *together with* beings – will be under the rule of lived-experience and of machination in an unprecedented way.

To try to grasp the quality of this 'perfecting', we must tackle the interpretation of an extraordinarily dense passage in section 274.

> And in the moment when planning and calculation have become gigantic, a being in the whole begins to shrink. The 'world' becomes smaller and smaller, not only in the quantitative but also in the metaphysical sense: a being as a being, i.e. as object, is in the end so dissolved into controllability that the being-character of a being disappears, as it were, and the abandonment of beings by being is completed.

> The metaphysical diminishing of the 'world' produces a hollowing-out of man. The relation to a being as such loses, in and with this being, all purpose; the relation as comportment of man extends itself only to itself and to its methodical [*planmäßig*] enactment. The feeling of feeling feels only feeling, feeling itself becomes the object of enjoyment. The 'live-experience' attains the utmost of what is its ownmost, lived-experiences are lived. The lostness into beings is lived as capability of transforming 'life' into the calculable whirlwind of empty circling around itself and of making this capability believable as something 'true to life'.
>
> (Ibidem, p. 348–349)

In the first part of this passage, Heidegger focuses on the phenomenon of the dissolution of *a being as a being*. This being, which throughout the history of modern metaphysics is taken up as an object – and therefore as an object unconditionally available for manipulation, for control and planning – ends up by losing its *being-character.*

This dissolution of the being-character of beings is also referred to by Heidegger in section 67, in which Heidegger considers the misshaping of beingness in terms of its co-belonging with the misshaping of man (which occurs in his relation to beings and to himself).

> How machination and lived-experience (initially concealed as such for a long time, nay even concealed up to now) mutually drive each other into the extreme and thus, according to their utmost abandonment, unfold the *misshapings* of beingness and of man, in his relation to beings and to himself and in these misshapings mutually drive toward each other and form a onefold, which conceals all the more what enowns the onefold: the abandonment of beings by any truth of be-ing and ultimately even *by this* [be-ing] itself.
>
> (Ibidem, p. 93)

In section 274, Heidegger jointly refers to this 'deformation' of beingness and of man and to a sort of radical 'transformation' of the relationship between man and beings.

We must view this relationship between man and beings as a relationship that, throughout the history of metaphysics, has taken place under the banner of the 'experienceability' of beings in the register of lived-experience (and then of their representability as objects).

According to Heidegger, however, this relationship of man with beings ends by losing all purpose. This means that lived-experience develops in an increasingly self-referential and 'procedural' manner, bearing relation to nothing but itself and its own progress, to the methodical enactment of its development.

The dominion of lived-experience proceeds, that is – as strange at it may seem– without having anything further to do with man and beings. It advances, yet no longer proceeds as a relationship between man and beings – between man and the beings he deals with as lived-experiences.

In order to understand what this might mean, let us try to consider lived-experience in a different manner than we have done – and with some reason – until now. In other words, we should no longer understand the phenomenon of *Erlebnis* by looking at the unconditional transition from one lived-experience to another lived-experience, or from *one being* experientially lived by man to *another being* experientially lived by man.

Now lived-experience is not anymore, so to speak, a matter of man and beings; it obeys to nothing else than the demands of its own constant advancement.

There is a change of tune in the dominion of lived-experience and this change of tune should be understood as a completion and perfecting of the correspondence between *Erlebnis* and *Machenschaft*. What we are faced with is the most 'extreme' correspondence between living and self-making: lived-experience is no other than its own self-making, we might say.

In this movement, man and beings become *nothing* other than *resources* for the lived-experience's procedural self-making, where only the latter counts. It is not man who makes himself by living and by relating himself to beings as lived-experiences, for man's life enhancement (for the enhancement of life as a total of lived-experiences). The dominion of *Machenschaft*/*Erlebnis* does not occur, as it did before, by passing through the usual 'roles' of man and beings.

What we must focus on, then, is precisely the co-belonging between the extreme self-referentiality of the making of lived-experience and the fact that man and beings are, in an unprecedented way, hollowed out. When machination and lived-experience draw ever closer to each other until they form *a onefold*, the 'status' of man and beings and the nature of their connection radically change.

This does not mean, of course, that beings and man disappear, but that all beings (including man) become involved in what Heidegger names, in section 67, a *relation of non-relationality.*

In other words, the new dominance of lived-experience implies a new relationship between human and non-human beings.

What we should try to understand is how this 'transformation' of the relationship between man and beings is something *calculative*. And today, it seems, we have somehow the opportunity to look at the extreme outcome of this calculative transformation of man and beings: all we have to do is look at what is taking place before our very eyes under the banner of post-human enhancement.

What have we in fact seen at the disquieting heart of such enhancement? What prospects are foreseen by the developments of the 'post-human' sciences?

Man makes himself in machines, in bits, in networks, in organs, in prostheses, where these are *taken for* human, considered *as* human, which means, however, experienced *as* human.

We must keep precisely this *as something* in mind, in order to understand in what sense the above phenomenon is calculative.

Where man makes himself in any given being considered as and *lived* as a man, machination can proceed *by itself*, or, as noted above, without the need for beings as man's lived-experiences or the need for man as he who 'experiences' beings. Let us read once again the supremely important passage of section 67, paying particular attention to what is said about the link between machination, non-relationality and calculation.

> What does *machination* mean? That which is let loose into its own shackles. Which shackles? The pattern of generally calculable explainability, by which everything draws nearer to everything else equally and becomes completely alien to itself – yes totally other than just alien. The relation of non-relationality.
>
> (Ibidem, p. 92)

Let us ask ourselves: how should we understand what Heidegger is saying here? When confronted with this phrase, we should not turn in haste to something that we believe we already know quite well: the fact that when beings and man become unconditionally manipulable, producible, enhanceable as resources, then everything becomes equal to every other thing.[32]

Instead, we should see this phrase in a more precise manner. The age in which machination attains *the utmost of what is its ownmost* is the age when the zenith is reached by the movement in which every being draw near to any other being but is no longer in a relationship with itself (with the being that it is).

This happens when *Machenschaft* and *Erlebnis* become a onefold; but also when the imperative of self-making and of calculability co-belong ever more completely.

Machenschaft means 'the pattern of generally calculable explainability'. The expression *generally calculable explainability* means precisely what it says in German. In other words, it points directly to *Rechnen* and to what it means, based on the way in which it perceives the legacy of the Latin verb *reor*. *Rechnen* means taking something for something else, considering something as something else.

But we must not stop at understanding *Rechnen* in the sense in which it is used, as long as metaphysics has not reached its fulfilment. We must not stop, in particular, at considering the phenomenon that I previously examined as the correspondence between *Rechnen* and *Vor-Stellen*, between calculation and the representation of beings for man as a subject.

When we consider *Rechnen* in its metaphysical form, we think of the *take for*, the *take as*, on the basis of *man* taking one being for another being, considering one being as another being. And we consider this movement to be that which allows the representability of a being as an object for a subject, and then as an object which is systematically measurable, controllable, manipulable, organizable, decomposable and, ultimately, unconditionally *available*.

Here we should consider this *taking as* in a radically different way. We are no longer confronted with man who represents things through calculation by taking something for something else from the standpoint of man himself (and ending by calculating himself). Here, instead, we have man and beings which, by living, each make themselves by taking the one *as* the other, the one for the other.

In the era of the 'end' of metaphysics, that *as something* that is contained in Rechnen resonates in an even freer, more powerful tone.

It is no longer beings and man, we might say, who make themselves by themselves, by obeying the imperative of self-making in a certain way; that is, by playing the game of subjectivization/objectivization and thus of representation and calculation (which lived-experience, as what confirms the anthropological perspectives, is complicit with).

Here, it is the *as something* that dominates in an unconditional and self-referential way; and this precisely when man and beings are left to take themselves one as the other.[33] The more this dominion reaches completion, the more the relation of non-relationality now involves every human and non-human being.

It is in the light of the above considerations that we must understand that the extreme completion of the dominion of machination and lived-experience (which is the extreme completion of their correspondence) is also, in a certain sense, the extreme completion of co-belonging between machination and calculation. And it is again in that light that we should understand the significance of the fact that modern technology, in bringing itself to perfection, speaks, ever more precisely, the language of calculative thinking.

When we think of modern technology in the present day, we primarily have in view a set of phenomena: systematic measurement, arrangement, ordering, manipulation, control, management, production, organization and planning, *resourcification* or, from another perspective, performance, efficiency, accountability and *resourcefulness*.

When technological calculation and power are viewed in relation to Heidegger, however, our thoughts turn, and with good reason, to what Heidegger refers to as the essence of modern technology, the *Ge-Stell*[34] – the latter, we might say, is the configuration that machination assumes in the age of modern technology and of its perfection, which occurs under the rule of cybernetic control on beings.

When the essence of modern technology – Heidegger (2011c) writes in the well-known pages of the essay on technology – manifests itself as *Ge-stell*, beings will not anymore present themselves as *objects*, but as standing-reserves; and man, who thinks of himself as the supreme orderer of the standing-reserves, will end up to be he himself a standing-reserve.

It precisely by having in mind the joint dissolution of man and beings (the disappearing of the being-character of beings and the hollowing out of man), as it is addressed in the *Contributions*, that we can re-read what Heidegger later says about the perfection of technology under the rule of *Ge-Stell*.

The age in which *Ge-Stell* will dominate (letting man and beings lie *next to each other* as standing-reserves) will coincide with the ever more complete deployment of the relation of non-relationality; and this deployment, in turn, coincides with the ever more extreme dominion of lived-experience as self-making, of lived life as self-making. Power lets itself dissipate through beings; but precisely through beings that, as the joint misshaping of humans and things progresses, ends up being no more than mere resources for the self-making of the lived-experience. The unconditionality of power, we might say, now becomes the unconditionality of the lived-experience.

Let us now return to the extract from Heidegger and comment on the final part, in order to try to better determine the way in which we should consider the transition from human to life.

How do I interpret the last part of the quoted passage?

Life, precisely in becoming nothing other than lived life, closes on itself, closing itself to things: in other words, it screws itself down on beings; the latter lose their *being-character* and dissolve as beings, together with man. This means that life transforms itself into – becomes lived as – nothing but a calculative whirlwind. In this whirlwind, life makes itself in the transition from one possibility of lived life to another.

However, according to Heidegger, this movement is the movement in which this life, which makes itself in this way, constantly ensures itself as *true* life.

Here, we are confronted with the crucial question that we broached earlier, when we mentioned the post-human debate. What, in fact, is the main question that animates that debate? It is this: what remains of the truly – authentically – human in 'post-human' life? To what extent is that life which makes itself and makes itself lived beyond man (beyond his body and his mind, in machines, in man–machine hybrids, in cyborgs and in robots) – still real life? To what point, that is, is it *truly human* life?

In my opinion, what we should consider is that the further the cybernetic age advances, the less the truth of life plays on a human scale.

True life is not truly *human* life. The human is no longer the standpoint for measuring the truth of life.

Throughout the history of metaphysics – and following the succession of determinations of the being of beings in that history – the true plays on the human scale (and the truth of life plays on the same human scale of the truth of beings, which is a truth based on man and on his life).

Let us consider the first and the penultimate modern metaphysical giants.

What is truth for Descartes? It is the certainty of representation. It is the certainty of the representation of beings as objects for a subject; for the self-securing of man as a certain subject.

And what is truth for Marx? What, for him, is the real truth of life, that which makes life truly human? It is nothing other than the humanization of man. The truth of life – that activity that produces at the same time both man and things – plays on the same scale of truth of man and truth of beings. This scale is, in fact, that of the ever more complete humanization of man, which is achieved through the complete socialization of man himself, as he becomes truly total man insofar as he is truly social.

However, what does truth become, ever more decisively and completely, in the cybernetic era? What does truth correspond to? To calculation. Truth is increasingly completely defined by the performance itself of the calculation. It is a *performative truth*, defined by the sole need to produce results and by the ability to pass from one result to another.

What has happened to make life fall under the dominion of this truth – and therefore have to ensure its own truth, with reference to nothing but that truth?

Life makes itself as a lived life. The truth of life is therefore, we might say, the truth of lived-experience. But the truth of lived-experience, in accordance with what I said earlier, is no longer the truth of lived beings from the standpoint of the human subject who lives them. The truth which the lived-experience must obey is no other than the *methodical enactment* of the self-referential progress of the lived-experience itself.

In order to properly address post-human enhancement, we should, in my view, keep the whole argument developed above in view and particularly the co-belonging between the self-making of life, the 'new' relationship between beings and the completion and perfecting of calculability.

The more we will be able to grasp, in the age of the completion of calculability, the essential nature of calculation, the more we will grasp the nature of the possibility which is contained in the perfection of modern technology.

We should not regard the 'final' season of calculation as the extreme point of a process of decay, of decline, whereas the perfecting of technological power would trigger a sort of shock capable of awakening Western man.

We should not primarily regard the emptiness characterizing the present technological age as an emptiness *produced* by technology and technological calculation, the latter being ever more manipulative, de-humanizing, de-historicizing and draining. Nor should we consider that emptiness to be the effect of a techno-scientific reduction, of a capitalist reduction, of a reduction of everything to a resource – it is neither in terms of reduction, nor in terms of annexation of man to the rule of power that we should primarily think.

We should not remain at those manifestations that we are more or less accustomed to recognizing in terms of, for example, the power and pervasiveness of the techno-capitalistic or bio-capitalist assimilation of life, of the extreme commodification of the human or of the extreme stage of biopolitical manipulation of life.

This does not mean at all underrating the ways in which calculation and power manifest themselves, nor does it mean to deny the value of the interpretations of the development of bio-capitalism and bio-power. This means, instead, preventing the interpretation of calculation and power to which we are accustomed from blocking the possibility of grasping the proper nature of the completion of calculative thinking and thus the opportunity it contains.

When life and self-making speak the same language more and more decisively and indeed speak the same language of calculation, they in fact speak only the language of non-relationality. This remains to be considered, and it remains difficult to consider.

Relation of non-relationality means that beings say nothing more to man (not even something in the order of the provision of lived-experiences to the human subject). It means that, in an extreme way, beings lose the possibility of stimulating, of enchanting man. The relationship with beings, with a certain, individual being, is no longer the opportunity – and this is the case in an extreme manner – to open man to his finitude, which is the access to that which is not in the league of the calculating subject.

Let us further consider the issue of (non) relationality, by focusing on some moments of contemporary social theory.

3.3.2 Translations between man and beings: Notes on Latour

The argument that I have developed above allows to look in a certain way to some contemporary lines of thought and may contribute to a sort of clarification of the 'relationships' with Heideggerian reflection. By this, I mean that this clarification might give a different and more precise tone to the criticism, rejection – or even acceptance – of what Heidegger says. If that were to happen, it might then be of some interest to those for whom Heidegger's work constitutes neither a point of reference nor an opportunity for reflection.

I will focus again on the question of the *relation of non-relationality* and I will try to review this issue with an eye turned to the work of Bruno Latour.

Latour has established himself in recent decades as one of the world's most celebrated and influential intellectual figure – as a social theorist, theorist of science and philosopher.

The significant crop of critical contributions that has sprouted around his work has often targeted precisely the relationship between Latour and Heidegger.[35]

Here, I am not directly interested in a critique of the way in which Latour interprets and rejects Heidegger's thought, nor even in the possibility of detecting points in common or potential convergence between Latour and Heidegger.

I intend, in fact, simply to see how the question of relationality can be seen at work in Latour's thought.

One of the issues central to Latour's work is a profound and radical rethinking of the way in which the relationship between human and non-human has been conceptualized in the Western world.

For Latour, the world does not consist of human subjects that relate to natural objects, nor of a cultural sphere that can be detected and then perhaps crossbred with the sphere of nature. The world is not made of humans who represent, interpret, construct, objectify, calculate and produce non-human beings, silent, inert and soulless.

The world is made up of actors, or more precisely of actants, human and non-human. It is possible, within certain limits, to distinguish between human and non-human actants, but certainly not on the basis of an acknowledged privilege that the former rather than the latter might possess.

What is an actant? Or rather, what does it do?

All things, even the inanimate objects, as Harman (2009) reminds, are 'actors endowed with the capacity to translate what they transport, to redefine it, to redeploy it, and also to betray it' (Latour, 1993, p. 81, quoted in Harman 2009).

Things are mediators, translators, convectors; they are the mediators of relationships with other things. They are 'defined' precisely by the relationships they build with other actants, and more specifically by the continuous 'trials of strength' that they carry out with other things.

It is not possible to consider a thing separately from its relationships and associations. Each element 'is to be defined by its associations and is an event created at *the occasion* of each of those associations' (Latour, 1999, p. 165, quoted in Harman, 2009, emphasis added by Harman).

As Harman (2009, p. 83) sums up in his useful interpretative investigation of Latour's thought, for Latour actors 'are both human and non-human, lasting only as their alliance endures, more real the more alliances they have, and linked only through another actor capable of translating one into terms of the other'.

Considering that the relationship is what makes all beings, makes the metaphysical category of *essence* resonate in a decidedly low or even cacophonous tone. This way of thinking denies the right to citizenship, in Latour's world, to those leftovers from the metaphysical category of essence which take the form of an *inner core* of things that can be opposed to their continuous redefinition, or in other words, to the continuous rearrangement of their relationships – of their alliances – with other things. According to Harman (Ibidem, p. 65):

> If we are speaking of instantaneous events, then there is no essential inner core that lies beneath the shifting accidents of the moment. And if we are speaking of trajectories or transformations,

> then there is still no cryptic domestic essence on the interior of a thing that could endure across time – here a thing is still found on the surface of the world, but it is now a surface unfolding through a succession of various shapes rather than a cinematic frame of absolute specificity. A merely apparent essence will gradually condense from this grand drama of instantaneous points and flying trajectories; even once it crystallizes, the essence will have only a pragmatic value in helping us identify certain things as the same.

Latour's main target is precisely modernity, and therefore modern metaphysics. Latour's argument is based on the denial of the fact that modernity has really been able to bring to fruition its insane plan: that of purifying the world by separating it into opposite spheres of human and non-human, of culture and nature. *We have never been modern* means above all this: that this impossible task was not accomplished and therefore there is no need to be the victims of any modern illusion that prevents us from recognizing the world in its relationality.

The fact that this world, for Latour, is not made of subjects and objects, but of quasi-subjects and quasi-objects, should not lead us astray. That *quasi*, in fact, does not speak the language of approximation, but that of radical distancing.

Let us read a passage from another famous work:

> For the thing we are looking for is not a human thing, nor is it an inhuman thing. It offers, rather, a continuous passage, a commerce, an *interchange* between what humans inscribe in it and what it prescribes to humans. It translates the one into the other. The thing is the nonhuman version of the people, it is the human version of things, twice displaced. What should it be called? Neither object nor subject. An instituted object, quasi-object, quasisubject, a thing that possesses body and soul indissolubly.
>
> (Latour, 1996, p. 213)

In this sentence we find the impossibility of considering human and non-human things – and even the distinction between the human and the non-human – except in terms of their relationships. And this, as Latour points out provocatively in a passage from *Pandora's hope*, applies precisely to *all things*:

> this is true for the lactic acid ferment, as well as for the city of Rouen, the Emperor, the laboratory on the rue d'Ulm, God, and Pasteur and Pouchet's own standing, psychology, and presuppositions.
>
> (Latour, 1999, p. 165, quoted in Harman, 2009)

In this context, then, what becomes of the age-old question on man and the human? Let us read some further passages of *We have never been modern*:

> Must we solemnly announce the death of man and dissolve him in the play of language, an evanescent reflection of inhuman structures that would escape all understanding? No, since we are no more in Discourse than we are in Nature. In any event, nothing is sufficiently inhuman to dissolve human beings in it and announce their death. Their will, their actions, their words are too abundant.
>
> (Latour, 1993, p. 137)

And then what can we say about the human, according to Latour?

> If the human does not possess a stable form, it is not formless for all that. If, instead of attaching it to one constitutional pole or the other, we move it closer to the middle, it becomes the mediator and even the intersection of the two. The human is not a constitutional pole to be opposed to that of the nonhuman. The two expressions 'humans' and 'nonhumans' are belated results that no longer suffice to designate the other dimension. The scale of value consists not in shifting the definition of the human along the horizontal line that connects the Object pole to the Subject pole, but in sliding it along the vertical dimension that defines the nonmodern world. Reveal its work of mediation, and it will take on human form. Conceal it again, and we shall have to talk about inhumanity, even if it is draping itself in the Bill of Rights. The expression 'anthropomorphic' considerably underestimates our humanity. We should be talking about morphism. Morphism is the place

> where technomorphisms, zoomorphisms, phusimorphisms, ideomorphisms, theomorphisms, sociomorphisms, psychomorphisms, all come together.
>
> Their alliances and their exchanges, taken together, are what define the *anthropos*. A weaver of morphisms – isn't that enough of a definition? The closer the *anthropos* comes to this distribution, the more human it is.
>
> (Ibidem, p. 137)

This entire passage, including the last sentence, deserves special attention. Here, we might say, the totality in expansion is no longer – as it is, for example, in Sen, based on Marx – a totality of possibilities of life of man and for man. Here, the totality is the totality of relationships in its constitutive expandability: not of the relationships between man and beings, but the relationships that make the actants, both human and non-human.

Thus, here is man. Or in other words, here are the relationships – the translations, exchanges, alliances – that make man (and beings).

> Ecce homo: delegated, mediated, distributed, mandated, uttered.
>
> [...]
>
> The human is in the delegation itself, in the pass, in the sending, in the continuous exchange of forms. Of course it is not a thing, but things are not things either. Of course it is not a merchandise, but merchandise is not merchandise either. Of course it is not a machine, but anyone who has seen machines knows that they are scarcely mechanical. Of course it is not of this world, but this world is not of this world either. Of course it is not in God, but what relation is there between the God above and the God below? Humanism can maintain itself only by sharing itself with all these mandates. Human nature is the set of its delegates and its representatives, its figures and its messengers.
>
> (Ibidem, p. 138)

In this long passage, we find the most decisive theorization of a complete and total relationality: non-human things, human things – and even divine things – make themselves in the translations that they continually set in motion. Human life exists only in the translation –

in the continuous mediation and interchanges that man effects with things and with himself (with the human forms which, in their interchanges, make the human).

The *as something*, we might say, becomes, in Latour, what should be held primarily in view, by holding in view the continuous passage from one *as something* to another. Man makes himself in the passage from one morphism to another, in the continuous exchange of forms.

The few notes that we have dedicated to Latour have already enabled us to understand how, in the framework of his thought, the post-human and trans-human question plays in a scale of obviousness. The making of man in things (molecules, bits, networks) only *adds* new possibilities to a phenomenon that, according to Latour, has always existed, provided the distorting lens of modernity does not prevent us from recognizing it. Even if someone wished to say that Latour's thought is consistent with what goes by the name of post-human (and in this case, much more precisely, trans-human), this would, in my opinion, mean that his thought places the trans-human issue on the level of the self-evident.

It is not my intention here, however, in the face of Latour's arguments, to conduct an in-depth critical analysis, in search perhaps of aporias. Here, instead, I want to ask myself just one question: in what sense may we see a *consonance* between Latour's thought and what Heidegger sees as the direction that thinking takes in the in the era of the 'end' of metaphysics?

What is, from my point of view, the meaning of that *relation of non-relationality* that Heidegger speaks of? That things and man make themselves in the most unbridled self-making of their 'relationships', the more these relationships take place in the refusal of that which is not of the order of calculable beings; of that which man has a privileged relationship with, and regarding which he has a duty to do.

On further thought, however, this might be, so to speak, well acknowledged by Latour. For the latter, recognizing that the human and non-human world is a matter of relationships – of translations, mediations, alliances, trajectories of transformation – becomes possible precisely when one abandons the illusion that there is something to which man must answer – something that is beyond the league of the 'relational' self-making of things and man. It is only by freeing himself from the illusion that man ought to deal with something that is beyond the sphere of 'calculative' exchanges that man can be himself – in other words, he can be made as the relationships and mediations which, through their continuous transformation, make him.

Except that, for Heidegger, the unbridled development of calculative relationships is what characterizes the age of the completion of modern metaphysics. As such, it is a danger which contains an opportunity. This opportunity, for which it is not easy to be prepared, is the possibility for man of experiencing the fact that he is claimed, and challenged and *needed* by what is not of the order of the calculable.

For Latour, on the contrary in my view, the same phenomenon is neither a danger nor an opportunity. It is something that goes by itself. I do not mean by this that it is something natural, something in the nature of things and of man. It is something that simply goes by itself and that simply asks to be acknowledged, provided one frees itself from the fantasies of modernity, of postmodernity and even of the phenomenology of Heidegger who, according to Latour, sees *Dasein* as opposing the world.

Something lets itself to be seen in the completion of metaphysics although this does not in any way mean that it automatically leads to the possibility of truly grasping it or that we are ready to do so.[36] However, this something may seem to some to be the most precious of opportunities, and at the same time it may appear to others not as an opportunity at all, but rather as something that, in order to be duly comprehended, must be understood in its very manifestness.

The possibility which, for Heidegger arises precisely when man and beings are hollowed out, is the possibility for man of preparing himself for the task which belongs to him.

As far as our experience shows, Heidegger (2011a, p. 155) says in his *Letter on humanism*, man, *as a mortal*, has a duty that does not pertain to other living beings: that of thinking 'the essence of his Being'.

According to Heidegger, as long as we are mortal, we have a job to do. And just when it seems this work no longer needs to be done – just when it seems that we have rid ourselves of it – it is precisely then that the opportunity to do it arises.

This is the duty that Latour may reject, in a singularly resolute and complete manner. He may reject it, moreover, as the duty of man and of other *living beings* – and we may ask ourselves, on the basis of what we have read, whether for Latour not just horses and sheep, but even bricks and streets, fall into this category.

3.3.3 'Lived' quality and post-human enhancement

There is a passage in a recent paper on the post-human that is worthy of the greatest attention as far as the argument that I am developing is concerned. That passage interprets, we might say, the transition from 'human development' to 'post-human development' precisely from the perspective of quality of life.

> The ethical debates on the standards of quality of 'human life' are now already extended to more metaphysical questions on what qualifies as 'human life'.
>
> (Hellsten, 2012, p. 4)[37]

Today, the relationship between quality, life, man and his development seems to take on a new tone.

At first, the issue of quality of life seemed to be a question of measurement and improvement of human life. When human development takes on the forms of trans-human and post-human enhancement, quality becomes an issue of what *qualifies* life as human life, in a situation where the problem lies in the human quality of the self-enhancing life.

This somehow echoes the transformation that the reference to quality undergoes in Rose's thought, in the transition from the Rose (1992) of the early 1990s (when he wrote of the transfiguration of existential questions in the most effective ways of improving 'quality of life') to the Rose of the new millennium, who speaks of the evaluation of the relative and comparative 'quality of life' of differently composed human beings and different ways of being human.

What does it mean, from my point of view, that, while calculation and development resonate in a post-human timbre, quality of life continues to resonate and even takes on new tones?

To understand the link between quality of life and post-human enhancement we must focus on an issue that we have previously tackled: that of the relationship between 'lived' quality, human life and things. The 'transformation' of the man-beings relationship is, indeed, what we previously saw as the key to understanding the leap in the domination of lived-experience, and thus the phenomenon of the 'self-referential' advance of lived-experience itself.

The relationship between man and beings under the heading of quality is something I have already addressed in the previous chapter, when I considered the catalogue of qualities – that catalogue in which quality of life seems to sit next to quality of things (of landscape, environment, emotions, affections, relationships, cultural experience, etc.).

And already, in the way things remain next to each other, we have seen the mark of a particular lack of distinction between things (and between things and life). When quality becomes a matter of calculable, lived *quality of everything*, what is then called into question, in a specific way, is the individuality of a being. In other words, the capacity that a being has – as the being that it is – of saying anything to man, of stimulating him, of 'provoking' him, is challenged.

However, until a certain moment, so to speak, the quality of human life could be considered as the total of the qualities of the things that make life, and, therefore, human development could be seen as the constant expansion of the total of qualities.

What we ask now is: in what chord does quality resonate when the enhancement of life no longer resonates in the 'traditional' chord of human development and when the relationship between man and things develops on the post-human scene? We must prepare ourselves to understand the fact that quality remains on the scene, precisely when its presence seems to resonate, ever more completely, in a void.

Let us read a quote from one of the protagonists of the so-called *democratic trans-humanism*.[38] It is a passage from the introduction of a book on the cyborgization of man, which proposes an interpretation of the phenomenon centred on the possibilities of democratically regulating it Hughes argues that transhuman technologies.

> can radically improve our quality of life, and that we have a fundamental right to use them to control our bodies and minds. But to ensure these benefits we need to democratically regulate these technologies and make them equally available in free societies. Becoming more than human can improve all our lives, but only

> new forms of transhuman citizenship and democracy will make us freer, more equal and more united.
>
> (Hughes, 2004, p. xii)[39]

This passage seems to indicate a criterion for the management of trans-human technologies: the latter can and should be freely put to the test, provided that there is a democratic debate about their actual ability to increase the quality of life.

'Whose quality of life?', we might ask.

As long as the issue of trans-human transformation of man is a matter of application of 'improving' prostheses that leave man himself basically intact, the words of Hughes might appear in a certain, well-known light.

But the question that post-human development poses – and it poses it both for apologists and for critics of such development – is precisely the 'extreme outcome' of such technologies; in that outcome (as the distinction between cyborg-like entities and humans and between intelligent, conscious machines and human minds seem to be dissolved), the subjectivity which evaluates life as it is transformed by science is no longer, we might say, necessarily human.

The problem of the post/trans-human *is* its extreme outcome, irrespective of the opinions that each of us might have on the actual likelihood of achieving those possibilities that science allows us to glimpse – independently, that is, of the fact that the extreme possibilities of post-human transformation are considered to be either just around the corner, or still in the science-fiction imaginations of the few.

The point – in its banal simplicity – is in fact this: who can set limits to calculation? And from what standpoint? The post-human is already advancing towards its extreme possibility, precisely when the possibility of imposing limits[40] on man's self-enhancement arises in an increasingly marked absence of reference.

Thus, if we must consider the issue of trans-human in its extreme character, Hughes' phrase would sound something like this: we can advance towards the trans-human, provided we democratically measure the quality of the life of that trans-human (be it cyborgized man, intelligent machine, robot with pieces of human brain, human body with an electronic mind, or human mind transferred to a computer network).

While we ask ourselves what on earth this means, let us consider another author. This time, it is the case of one of the 'extreme' prophets of the post-human. As noted above, Kurzweil speaks of conscious machines, *spiritual* machines, machines that 'will claim to have spiritual experiences' (2000, p. 6) and of machine-based intelligences that will 'claim to be human' (Ibidem, p. 280).[41]

> There will be no distinction, post-Singularity, between human and machine or between physical and virtual reality. If you wonder what will remain unequivocally human in such a world, it's simply this quality: ours is the species that inherently seeks to extend its physical and mental reach beyond current limitations.
>
> (Kurzweil, 2006, p. 9)

How should we view these words? It is not so much, to my mind, a question of distancing ourselves from it and denouncing it as a typical phrase for effect, the result of futuristic exaggerations.

Rather, this statement is, in my view, simply imprecise, if subjected to a careful phenomenological inspection.

What would remain *unequivocally human* in the age of post-human development would be man's constant self-making beyond himself – that is, beyond those limits, corporeal and psychical, that determine man at a given time. If, for Kurzweil, this means that the demands for enhancement is a distinctive trait of the human compared to the non-human, then the analyses I have previously carried out make it impossible for me to agree.

This extending beyond limitations that Kurzweil speaks of, in my perspective, is nothing but the demands for power, which is the demand for overpowering of power itself; but then unconditional obedience to this demand is in no way something that distinctively distinguishes the human with respect to the non-human. In the season of calculative perfection, the demand of power is something which man and beings obey *together*. This means that this demand takes place as the calculative switching of man and beings – or, as I said previously, in the enhancement of man and of beings which occurs when man makes himself in the movement that takes the being *as* a man and vice versa.

Writing something along the lines of Kurzweil's statement thus risks, in my view, precluding to properly address the phenomenon of post-human development; and this can be seen precisely when quality is brought into play.

Quality, we might say, is in fact no longer the quality of man (or even the lived quality of man's life as a total of lived-experiences), nor is quality still the quality of beings (or even of beings experienced by man as components of his lived life).

What is it then? Let us give in to the temptation of writing this: it is the quality of living, that is, the quality of self-making. Yet at precisely this point, we become troubled. What can possibly be meant by bringing quality into the equation when man and beings seem to be hollowed out? What is the meaning of talking of quality, when we can no longer say quality *of man* and quality of *beings*? What is this quality without man and without beings, without the gift that man and beings bestow on each other?

We feel the extreme point of the metaphysical consumption of quality as the basic character of the *quale*, of the what, of the ownmost. Specifically, we feel the extreme loss of man's relationship with that quality; the loss of that relationship which – despite the ever more decisive metaphysical 'transformation' from quality into a category, from the what into the metaphysical *what*, from the *ownmost* into 'essence' in a metaphysical sense – continues in a certain manner to speak to man throughout the long season of metaphysics itself. Throughout the parabola of metaphysical thought man continued to feel, *in a certain sense*, that he is a matter of quality.

The withdrawal of being in the cybernetic age therefore takes man out of the equation when that withdrawal deprives man of his relationship with the 'basic character' of the quale, of the what, of the *ownmost*. Man has a very unique relationship with what metaphysics reduces to the range of 'essence'. This is because he is existentially destined, as a man, 'to think the essence of his Being.'

> What man is – or as it called in the traditional language of metaphysics, the 'essence' of man – lies in his ek-sistence.
>
> [...]
>
> Ek-sistence can be said only of the essence of man, that is, only of the human way 'to be'. For as far as our experience shows, only man is admitted to the destiny of ek-sistence. Therefore ek-sistence can also never be thought of as a specific kind of living creature

> among others – granted that man is destined to think the essence of his Being and not merely to give accounts of the nature and history of his constitution and activities.
>
> (Heidegger, 2011a, p. 155)

If the task of giving accounts of one's nature and history is something that the intelligent, spiritual machine will maybe able to do (even better than humans do, if I understand correctly the Kurzweil's argument), the ek-sistential task of thinking Being remains a task that is exclusively reserved to man.

The withdrawal of being leaves, then, man without quality, because quality is left resonating in the void of the relation of non-relationality. In that void quality seems to say only this: the self-making as living and living as self-making. This means also that quality can only mean *making quality* or, in other words, it can only speak the language of the self-overpowering of power.

Quality remains on centre stage, and in the limelight. It remains on the scene, silently pointing towards something. This something, if we give credence to Heidegger's work, is precisely the withdrawal of being in the cybernetic era – it is being that withdraws in the cybernetic age.

It is perhaps precisely when we are faced with the question of quality that we can try to see something of the way in which being withdraws when metaphysics reaches its completion.

Quality therefore remains on the scene, and yet it resonates increasingly *emptily*. And this is, in my view, the root of the enigmatic *dogmaticity* of quality which is felt with disquiet in scholarly reflection – a disquiet that I believe is destined to grow.

The fact that quality remains as a sign resonating in the void echoes the fact that the perfection of calculation leaves man in the dimension of extreme emptiness, and more precisely, in an *evident*, manifest emptiness. It is precisely this manifest emptiness that we must learn to deal with, if the task we face is what Heidegger talks of, during his interview with *Der Spiegel*:

> I do not see humans' situation in the world of global technology as a fate that cannot be unraveled or escaped. Instead, I see the task of thought precisely in thinking along at its limits, so that humans

> can even first achieve an adequate relationship to the essence of technology.
>
> (Heidegger, 2009b, p. 330)
>
> [...]
>
> The *Ge-Stell* holding-sway means: Humans are beset *[gestellt]*, claimed, and challenged by a power that manifests itself in the essence of technology.
>
> It is precisely in humans' experience of being forcibly beset [*Gestelltseins]* by something that is not they and that they do not control, that the possibility exists of realizing that Being needs humans. Precisely the possibility of experience, of being needed, and of being prepared for these new possibilities is concealed in the ownmost core of modern technology. To assist with this realization is all that one can expect from thought, and philosophy is over.
>
> (Ibidem, p. 326–327)

In my view, we will be ready for the possibility which Heidegger evokes if, faced with the most evident, tangible emptiness – and with the emptiness of quality – we resist the temptation of looking back or of passing ahead. We will be ready, that is, if we resist the temptation of taking refuge in the romantic remembrance of what was (perhaps calling into question an old humanism, a new humanism or even a new post-humanism) and also resist the temptation of just contemplating the enactment of calculation and enhancement.

4
Towards a Conclusion: Towards a New Look

On the subject of calculation, much of today's human and social science literature presents us with a reference to the *extreme:* to the extreme proliferation of calculative 'practices'; to the extreme power of such practices and logic; to their extreme pervasiveness in the social sphere, right to the very heart of human life.

The picture that appears is that of an increasingly cogent coalescence between various pathways of calculation and enhancement. The increasingly intensive 'managerialization' of social life in response to the demands of efficiency and performance; the accountability and 'resourcification' of the human that goes far beyond the limits of work; the 'calculative' degeneration of the relationship between debtor and creditor that is at the heart of the might of modern finance; the manipulation of man as a set of genes, cells and bytes of information: all these phenomena hold each other and mutually give each other tone, maintaining complex bi-univocal relationships with a set of social and cultural transformations.

When calculation and power are interpreted as being phenomena internal to the morphogenesis of capitalism – as Magatti (2009) did, in his rich sociological analysis on *techno-nihilistic capitalism* – the analysis must recognize a particularly disquieting closeness between capitalism and its critique. As Magatti himself emphasized with reference to the analyses of Thrift (2005), the catchwords of contemporary capitalism (network and 'vitalism') are the same as those used by a significant number of the critics of capitalism itself.

The picture takes on even more extreme hues when the focus is on the post-human; and when calculation touches on the humanity itself of humankind, the question of critique seems to be radically reshaped. On the one hand, the analysis takes on tones of the most extreme concern and vehement condemnation; on the other hand, positions emerge that acknowledge the pre-eminence of the transformation on the traditional forms of critique.

The analysis that I have carried out in this work is intended to help prepare the ground for a fresh look at this 'extreme' perfection of the trajectory of calculation.

Within my perspective, the extreme stage of calculation is not seen merely and primarily starting from the impact of calculative ordering on man and his life; and even less is it seen as the extreme perfecting of the capitalist process or of the evolution of biopower. The possibility that arises within a new look is, therefore, the possibility of not seeing in the current era that which lets itself be seen first of all and which, in a certain sense, strikes the eye: that is, the involvement of man in the ever-enlarging realm of calculation and power.

In particular, we must resist the temptation of thinking in terms of *calculative reduction* and of that particular reduction which is the reduction of man to things: *reification*.

This expression seems particularly appropriate to describe one of the fundamental traits of the age in which we live, and it may seem, but it is not the case in my view, that Heidegger provides arguments in support of this expression when he speaks of *lostness into beings*.

Yet in my opinion, it is a case of understanding that thinking in terms of reification means still considering in a metaphysical manner that which happens at the end of metaphysics itself. By so doing, we still consider the extreme moment of the history of calculation as merely the outcome of a history in which man calculates beings and himself (and calculates himself in relation to beings, and beings in relation to himself). This means that we consider calculation as something that happens in man's relationship with things and with himself, without seeing in the completion of calculation anything other than the degeneration of that relationship – a degeneration in which man becomes the victim of his own interpretation of beings as calculable objects.

What we can experience in the age of calculative perfection is, instead, precisely calculation as something that calls into question man and beings and the relationship between man and beings in the most radical and extreme way; in an even more extreme way, we might say, than that indicated by the annexation of man to the realm of manipulable things, to be eventually countered by appealing to human dignity.

The opportunity contained in the final season of metaphysics arises precisely when, faced with the very nature of the calculative, man cannot look at calculation as a relationship between man and beings and thus as a matter of beings and man (for example, at the predominance of calculation as a 'perversion' of the relationship between the quantitative and the qualitative, which deprives man of the incomparable singularity of things).

In the *Der Spiegel* interview, Heidegger says that man can become aware of the fact that he is claimed by something that he is not the master of. That 'something' is *being*: in other words, it is the dominion of *Machenschaft* as the way in which being holds sway, by withdrawing.

The fact that man can realize that he is not the master of technology is something that may sound familiar even beyond the 'Heideggerian' perspective.

But what does truly mean that man can realize that he cannot control technology? And that he can experience this precisely in the age of the end of philosophy? It does not merely mean that man can recognize the paradoxical situation in which he becomes a slave to himself – or in other words, to the metaphysical understanding of man himself. It does not mean that he can experience his own process of becoming objectifiable, manipulable, available, plannable. It belongs indeed to metaphysical thought the possibility of considering the 'technological' destiny of man as the submission of man to an empire of power and calculation which he has created himself. The possibility of *reacting* to all this – for example through the denunciation of technology and of its dangers – also belongs to this thought. In so doing, however, metaphysical thinking reacts against itself on the basis of itself. All this, in other words, is not the precondition for a new look; rather, it is the precondition for metaphysics, in its own final season, to stay in its own cage.

What man, instead, has the chance of experiencing, if he manages to direct a certain look at the perfectioning of calculation, is the fact that everything that happens in modern technology is nothing other than the way in which man is challenged by that which is not of the order of the calculative securing of man and things.

What Heidegger tells us about 'calculation', already in his working notes of the 1930s, is thus perhaps of some importance. In fact, he not only tells us with some precision, that what matters in what we call 'calculation' should not merely be seen as corresponding to unconditional and unlimited quantification, or numerical measurement of everything (although, as noted above, such measurement has its own very special importance[1]). He tells us that one day we might see calculative perfection as something that, if seen for what it truly is, contains the chance of experiencing the fact that man is claimed and *needed* by that with respect to which he has an unavoidable task which no-one else can do in his place. The possibility that is stake, in the age of the completion of metaphysics, is precisely the possibility of entering in a new relationship with finitude, as an access to what is not of the order of man as a self-securing calculating subject.

It is worth emphasizing that this possibility is, of course, not *at all* the possibility for man of *representing himself* as mortal, of calculating himself as mortal, of taking account of himself as mortal; in other words, this possibility does not have to do with those strategies of 'managing' and 'calculating' mortality and immortality, which have been deeply analyzed by Bauman (1992). Yet we should not take this 'ambiguity' lightly because we must see calculating someone/something as a mortal as the extreme way in which modern technology proceeds, with its head in the sand, in denial of mortality. This way of behaving, however, advances not on the grounds of the human in the 'traditional' sense, but on the grounds of that calculative switching between man and beings which I reflected on previously.

By this, I mean that it is significant that, in an age in which man has come to be represented as potentially immortal, intelligent machines come to be somehow represented as potentially endowed with something like mortality. The techno-scientific projects aiming to build intelligent machines also aim, as we know, not merely at the production of increasingly powerful machines in terms of computation, but of machines that are ever more capable of experiencing human emotions, ever more spiritual, ever more capable of communicating with humans, feeling the emotions of joy, of sadness, of anxiety. But does not man perhaps experience all this as a *mortal*?

We might therefore say that the post-human techno-scientific project aims to produce machines as living machines, as machines that live as the human living being, that feel 'emotions' as the human being and, for doing so, may need to experience something such as death. But all of these *as* resonate in a calculative tone; or rather are in fact properly calculative, since calculation is precisely the dominion of the 'as something'.

When mortality becomes a matter of calculation (and as such can be 'produced'), it no longer resonates on the scale of man, or even on the scale of *things*, such as machines. Instead, it resonates on the scale of man who makes himself as a machine and of machines that make themselves as human beings.

For Heidegger, the finitude that man can experience is instead something radically different from that; it is something that eludes all representability, all calculation, and all assurances.

The possibility of experiencing this finitude arises, however, at the moment of extreme closure. In the 'final' season of calculation, there is a distinctive 'closeness' between the opportunity for a new look and the blocking of this kind of look.

This is in fact the very question of modern technology. The 'problem' of technology lies in the fact that technology has no relation to its own truth,[2] because it refuses the relationship with that truth.

The more we consider technology in its extreme perfecting, the more the dominion of technology definitely seems to us to be a dominion which keeps man in a certain condition, but above all is that which keeps the focus on something. This something is the way in which technology lets itself be seen.

This something which catches the eye is no other than the *going by itself* of technology. This going by itself is the 'simpleness' of the gigantic which the philosopher talks of in the *Contributions* – that 'simple', obvious going by itself. This is the simplicity that covers the emptiness of technology, which is the fact of having no relationship with its own truth, or in other words, with the fact of being *a matter of being*. And even when this going by itself reveals itself in its own emptiness, it nonetheless keeps its gaze on nothing other than itself.

It is worth pointing out once more that the stance which coincides with this unmoving focus of the gaze is not merely the stance of those who willingly accept and favourably welcome calculation and 'technological' enhancement as something obvious and natural.

This unswerving gaze – which we might all be victims of, myself first and foremost – also takes the form of simple contemplation of technological power (which seems all the more intriguing the more it seems to us to occur without foundation, without meaning, without reference). The gaze can take the form of contemplation of the coalescence of forms and manifestations of technology (from the derivatives market, to the atomic bomb, to bio-technological manipulation); it can also take the form of rejection, of criticism, of condemnation, or of an anti-technology stance.

And yet, it is worth emphasizing again, this extreme closure, for Heidegger, is not such that an opportunity can no longer be seen in the perfecting of calculation.

Today we can somehow experience everything I have mentioned: we can touch it with our hands, in anticipation of being ready to grasp it properly – and this is so, precisely because of the issue of quality.

Let us once more consider the enigmatic power of quality and how it manifests itself in *managerialism*, which is clearly not a phenomenon that merely pertains to the field of organizations, as we commonly understand them.

Today, the *mot d'ordre* is quality. Simply quality. We do not need to specify making quality, or achieving an ever greater level of quality. We do not even need to specify that it is a matter of taking quality into account, and therefore also of measuring it to know whether we are increasing it. Nor do we need to specify that this quality we want to measure, in order to be true quality, must be lived quality, or in other words, quality *calculated* as lived quality, and measured as it is experienced, felt, lived. And finally, we do not need to specify that this quality is the quality of everything, of life and of all things, of all the things that make life – including death, naturally.

Quality goes by itself, as the banner of the present day. When we say quality, everything that should go by itself, resonates by itself, without even coming along with man.

We can maybe direct a certain look at what Heidegger is saying in the *Contributions* when he says that the 'quantitative' (which ultimately is modern technology) becomes quality. This also means that, in the final stage of modern technology, quality becomes no other than the *by itself* of the advance of self-making, of that empire of self-making that in fact proceeds by itself, goes by itself.

Quality, that precious word which, if understood in its original sense, points towards the dimension of the *in itself* – of the dwelling in itself – connotes, in its empty obviousness, the emptiness of modern technology's obvious going by itself.

Perhaps, then, the *Contributions* can offer a rather important contribution to the debate on quality, even though the word quality appears very few times in that work. But here, precisely, it is not a question of quantity: it is quality that counts.

It is a case, then, of actually learning to deal with the emptiness with which quality dominates in the times in which we live. Questioning the enigma of calculable quality means indeed questioning the way in which calculative perfection calls into question the finitude of human beings.

Quality is no more than a question of finitude; at the very core of the question of quality – that quality which Heidegger speaks of in the *Contributions* – we find the truly incalculable relationship of the human being with finitude. Man – as metaphysical thought knows, in its own way – has a very special relationship with quality. But man is a question of quality precisely because of his own finitude.

What is the meaning of that 'individuality' which is the decisive trait of human life?

Human life is singular because it has a completely unique relationship with finitude. Finitude is what gives the fundamental tone and direction to life and to the relationship with the things that occur in man's life. Human life thus has a very special relationship with death compared to the relationship that life itself may have with things.

The relationship that human life has with death is a truly incalculable relationship – and therefore is an unrepresentable and unavailable relationship – because it is a relationship that, in the most profound way, eludes the possibility of being taken for something else, considered as something else.[3]

That relationship is also incalculable in an 'other' sense: in the sense, that is, that the relationship that each person has with death cannot be taken for another person's relationship. Life's unique relationship with death is unique to each person, and that relationship, which each person experiences *in the first person* – is what all humankind has in common.

It is for this reason that death is never a thing, and it is for this reason that man's life itself is never a thing in the order of other things. It is for this reason, too, that human life can never be a total of lived-experiences, a total of events, of moments, of 'spheres' of life, including death.

We experience this resistance to treating life as one thing amongst others when we cannot 'measure life', when by life we truly mean life, life as life (and not, for example, the length of life itself). On the other hand, strangely enough, we can say with the utmost nonchalance 'measure the quality of life'.

However, while life, by virtue of its incalculable link with death, is not a thing, human life, precisely by virtue of that relationship with finitude, is capable of having a relationship with the individuality of things. In other words, human life is capable of encountering a thing *as a thing*, of encountering a thing as the thing that it is. Thanks to its unavoidable relationship with finitude, the human being is able – as we all know, at heart – to experience life in its wholeness (and not in its totality) by encountering an 'individual' thing at a given time. As a mortal, man can be 'stimulated' and provoked by beings; and it is due to finitude that beings can provoke and 'enchant' man.

Thus, if the question of 'calculative' quality has to do with the calculation through which the individuality of things and of life becomes a mere matter of liveability (until this liveability is no longer a matter of man and of beings), this question in fact has a great deal to do with the extreme denial of finitude. And this happens precisely in the age in which the question of mortality – a question which tends to be glossed over by sociology, according to Bauman (see Jacobsen and Tester, 2007) – resonates in an unprecedented tone.

It is not by chance that the 'relationship' between finitude and quality appears before us, in a very specific way, in that manifestation of the extreme perfecting of calculation which we categorize under the title of post-human enhancement. Whenever this enhancement radically calls the finitude of human beings into question, it implicates quality in human life and in things.

In a recent article, O'Brien (2011) addresses from a Heideggerian perspective the question of the *future of humanity* in the face of what the post-human might promise or threaten.

O'Brien's primary critical target is the post-human school of thought – of which, as previously mentioned, Nick Bostrom is one of the main proponents – that envisages a potentially indefinite extension of human life.

In view of Bostrom's theses, which according to O'Brien can only be based on an interpretation of human life as a matter of things (and, for example, of molecules, of molecular change), O'Brien (2011, p. 42) himself responds as follows:

> Part of the difficulty here relates to what Heidegger, I believe, would see as the loss of an ability to identify differences, to make distinctions, to avoid a monochromatic view of ourselves and the world we inhabit. Depending on one's interpretive filtering lens, the differences between certain events, objects or actions can *seem* relatively inconsequential. For example, if we were to describe the activity of plunging a knife into a mattress with, say, the carcass of a pig, and if we are to describe things on a purely molecular level, the differences might appear to be simply matters of degree and not kind. However, if the pig is alive, we might find ourselves baulking at the idea that the only language which is relevant here is the one that describes things on a molecular level. The difference involved when one brings suffering into the equation, and perhaps loss of life, seems inadequately treated under the rubric of molecular change. We don't necessarily have to make the further leap to human beings for the difference to appear to be one of kind and not degree which demands that we speak with a language which *does not* restrict us to mere changes of degree in this example.

Later, clarifying the link with modern technology, of which for Heidegger *Ge-Stell* (Enframing) is the essence, O'Brien (2011, p. 44) adds:

> Enframing dupes people into the belief that the technical language of the exact sciences must be adopted at the *expense* of all other languages. Yet nowhere is it demonstrated that there is *one* language appropriate to human experience or life at the expense of every other mode of discourse *and* that it is the language of science or mathematics.

In the first passage quoted, O'Brien is talking about quality, in the form of the quality-quantity relationship which is so important in the history of metaphysics. In the techno-scientific post-human project, the finitude of the human being tends to be ever more decisively denied or 'de-recognized' in its incalculability (in the incalculability of the 'temporality' of *Dasein* in its relationship with mortality), and is represented instead as a problem which can be addressed by constantly increasing the life duration of post-human beings (such as 'cyborgized' man, brains uploaded into machines or thinking machines).

Precisely in this project, the differences between things seem to evaporate. It is not, in my view, just a matter of the difference, which O'Brien draws attention to, between the living and the non-living (and between human living beings and non-human living beings): precisely in the completion of metaphysics, we might say, all things are living beings in the sense that they all obey the demands of living as self-making. This is the difference between all things: in other words, it is the ability to confront something as the thing which it is. The increasingly extreme denial of this possibility coincides with the most extreme forgetfulness of finitude.

It is necessary, however, to understand precisely *in what way* this denial of quality and finitude comes about; to understand, that is, in what way it involves man and things.

While, as I have already said, the phenomenon should not be merely considered as a reduction of man to beings, neither should it be seen as a reduction of beings to man as the *rational living being*. It is not the fact (and it seems to me that O'Brien's reasoning carries the risk of directing thought down this route) that each being is reduced to its scientific-rational representation. Nor is it the fact that beings are, so to speak, endowed with the vitalistic power of man, of life as power. In other words, we must not – in the case of living/intelligent post-human machines, for example – merely conceive of something as a *super-being*, vitalistically over-powerful. As I have said perhaps too many times, when lived-experience attains its own extreme fulfilment, it is no longer, for Heidegger, a matter either of beings, or of man.

In my opinion, therefore, it is not a case – and here I am again distancing myself from O'Brien's interpretation – of postulating a reduction of language to a mere techno-scientific language which would be incapable of expressing the human or the difference between human and things. By so doing, we would, moreover, run the risk of seeing calculation of quality as a reduction of the qualitative to what can be expressed in the 'quantitative' language of systematic measurement – and I have refused to do this throughout this whole work.

Instead, it is a case of looking at the issue of quality – and therefore of finitude – focusing on what happens in the completion of metaphysical history: namely, the extreme 'closeness'[4] between the *by itself* and the *in itself*. It is a case, in other words, of confronting the fact that the most unconditional power of machination conceals in the most resolute way the dimension of the dwelling *in itself* in which quality and finitude reside. When quality designates nothing other than the 'characteristic' of machination – that is the *going by itself* of machination, it denies in the most extreme way the possibility for man of being in relationship with himself, through encountering things in their individuality.

It is by facing quality and its current emptiness that man can, in a certain way, experience his own finitude, in the age of its extreme denial. This means, once again, experiencing not only being claimed, but also being needed by something that is not in the order of the calculable. And this something – this famous *being* – is not, however, something that could ever be seen in any way as infinite or absolute.

Man's finitude must be maybe understood in the light of what Heidegger, creating a veritable philosophical scandal, calls *the finitude of being itself*. And perhaps when Heidegger considers quality in such a strange and obscure manner – as *the basic character of be-ing itself* – he is in fact pointing in the direction of the question of the finitude of being. Man has a relationship with quality – and therefore with the possibility of *dwelling in himself* – not because of his relationship with an absolute transcendence, but by virtue of his relationship with that which has the nature of finitude.

However, here we are touching questions that go far beyond the scope of this work. If the possibility that emerges in the completion of metaphysics is the possibility of experiencing something which is basically 'simple', this, at the same time summons up the very awkward task of addressing the abyssal question that, for Heidegger, is that of the knowing awareness of the first beginning of the *history of be-ing*.

This should not prevent us, however, from trying to look as clearly as possible – from the perspective of quality and calculation, in our case – at what happens in the age of the completion of metaphysics. By doing so, we might perhaps open our eyes to the new 'view' at which Heidegger hints.

On which pathways can we meet the opportunity which quality offers us – that of turning our attention to the possibility of a life that does not deny finitude?

This opportunity is, in fact, something that we can grasp if we deal with the issues that we recognize as being crucial to social and economic life.[5] That is to say, it is something we can grasp, even if we do not look directly at the issue of post-human 'transformation' of man, in which the denial of finitude, especially in the techno-scientific production of immortality, stands out with a very specific force and evidence.

The question which quality points towards is precisely the one that stands out from the background when, in a radical way, we confront the most important issues for the work of contemporary social sciences. I am thinking, for example, of the issue of the nature of management and of money as the fulcrum of economic life.

Money and management are quality issues. This does not mean that we must investigate the quality of management or the quality of money (for example, in terms of efficiency of *money-making* and of monetary calculation). It means, rather, that economic and managerial life – precisely in an era in which they are subject to the ubiquitous power of calculation – have the opportunity of asking, in an unprecedented way, about themselves. In other words, they have the possibility of asking what exchange is, what the relationship between debtor and creditor is, what managerial decision and the responsibility of the manager are, from a perspective in which the question of finitude is not a fluke to be eschewed with annoyance and a shadow to be rejected with increasing resolution.

Let us consider the very lively debate which arises today around the issues of management and *managerialism*. One of the major issues that stir this debate is the question of the demand for unconditional measurement and unconditional enhancement.

This is the issue of some approaches to management that, addressing the managerial *derecognition of finitude* (Costea, Crump and Amiridis, 2007), focus on the 'paradoxical' unmeasurability of the performance of that human resource, which is left to enhance itself indefinitely *without measure*.

The fact that the derecognition of finitude, as Costea, Crump and Amiridis understand it,[6] results in an *epistemological* problem deserves attention.[7]

In my personal interpretation, the phenomenon which Power (1999) points to, referring to that *programmatic affirmation* of auditing which goes *beyond empirical knowledge*, is one concerning the risk for management of being deprived of its own way to take measure and of its own way to know how to take measure. What is at stake is, in other words, the possibility of *knowing* about management; a possibility that is at risk when the practice and the science of management are to obey to the demand of unconditional techno-scientific calculative assurance. However, precisely against this risk, a chance emerges (and preparing oneself to grasp it has nothing to do with any anti-technological or anti-scientific attitude): the chance for a form of acting and knowing, in managerial, social and economic life, which speaks another language with respect to that of *assurance*.

Again, something important can be seen here precisely from the perspective of quality.

It seems there is no other route for rigorous management but calculating everything indefinitely. Management is faced with this demand for indefinite calculation[8] precisely when it comes to quality (as it constantly does); and management's relationship with quality proceeds under the banner of increasingly decisive assurance.

Responsible management is committed to systematic measurement of the quality of everything with a view to increasing quality itself. This entails measuring these qualities ever more precisely according to how they are actually *experienced*, in the scope of an organization, a city or a nation.

It is a case, therefore, of calculating each component of total quality and each specific decision which might have anything to do with them. Every act of decision-making thus depends on a calculation that seeks to calculate ever more accurately and more profoundly how all the 'components' of life are experienced, perceived, evaluated and 'lived' by an ever wider range of stakeholders. What matters, we might say, is the contribution that the act of decision-making and planning makes to increasing the total quality of life.

This form of managerial responsibility as a responsibility based on calculation belongs to *business management* (the more so the more the company views itself as a 'producer' of social value) and, by definition, to *public management*. And although the question of public sphere marketization is a very serious one, I do not think that the calculative drift of responsibility can be merely interpreted from the standpoint of *marketization*. Nor should that calculative drift be understood as the effect of a quantitative obsession to which management falls victim – just as the issue of quality should not be interpreted in terms of a 'technocratic' quantification of quality itself, to be eventually contrasted by calculating quality in an increasingly socialized and politicized manner, attentive to the diversity of interpretations and conceptions of quality itself. What we must first and foremost focus our attention on is not merely the effects of an involution, or a degeneration of managerial practice.

We should begin to look at the self-referential dominion of calculation as something that, in the deepest and most precise sense, is *beyond* the control of management; the more this is able to be experienced, the more the extreme completion of calculation can be an opportunity for management.

When we are faced with the calculation's extreme capacity for assurance, this demand for assurance can begin to be truly experienced as a removal of responsibility and therefore as a radical deprivation. It is not just the fact that decision and choice are deprived of something, namely of completing the demanding and thankless task that every choice involves: it is also the fact that those same *values* that are now transformed into parameters of calculation are, in a particularly decisive way, deprived of that which, as De Gennaro (2006) noted, we sense in them, that is to say, of their being valid *in themselves*.

Where every managerial ethic responds only to calculation – management can experience the deprivation of that which is its own task: that of managing *when one cannot calculate*.[9] In the face of the extreme power of calculation, the manager can experience choice and decision-making as the access to a dimension of radical incalculability – to that dimension which human beings have a relationship with by virtue of their own finitude.

What may be experienced is therefore the shadow that quality projects, precisely in the age of its extreme calculative withdrawal: the shadow of that incalculable, which is what sustains the possibility of making choices and forming judgments as well as the possibility of measuring *in a measured manner.*

It is precisely against this scenario, that in, in my opinion, we must pay close attention to what is said, in the context of a phenomenological approach to the philosophy of management, about the possibility of considering ethics in management, not by surrendering to the advance of calculation, but by learning to keep a steady gaze with regard to the dimension of the incalculable.

I am thinking, in particular, of a recent work by De Gennaro (2006), in which the question of managerial ethics is posed in terms of the preparation for *leadership,* starting from the question of what leadership and managerial responsibility mean when they point to something different from the obedience to the demands of calculation and to *empowerment to performance.*

The reference to a new 'sense' of leadership should be read as pointing towards a possibility of managerial action and leadership grounded in *thinking* and as such able of preparing itself to measure up with the incalculable. This means posing the issue of freedom in management in a new way.

> This is to say that the possibility for management to be free, and therefore responsible, consists in a form of action which, though encountering things in the domain of empowerment to performance, is not *entirely* delivered to this trait; this action in the first place sustains the difference, i.e., *thinks,* and can therefore *calculate responsibly.* A management that thinks does not change the dominant trait – which is beyond the scope of human action –, nor can it eliminate the pressures that its self-empowerment entails; however, it *interrupts the absoluteness* of this trait, thereby opening the way for measured, moderate action as attuned by the sustained ontological difference. Thinking itself becomes the fundamental action of management and the grounding for its responsibility.
>
> (De Gennaro, 2006, p. 86)

Precisely in the age of extreme calculability– of the dominion of the demands of calculation and enhancement which is the *empowerment to performance* which De Gennaro speaks of – the social and political responsibility of management finds itself, so to speak, at a crossroads.

On the one hand, there is the drift of management's responsibility in response to the unconditional demands of calculability. On the other hand, however, there is the possibility that management might learn to enter into a relationship with itself, or in other words, that it might learn to enter into a relationship with the dimension of radical incalculability in which every decision, every choice and every human responsibility is grounded.

What is at stake is not anything as the recovery of a 'subjectivist' or solipsistic dimension of choice and judgement (against a systematic and de-personalizing calculation), which refuses to recognize and to dignify *the other*. Rather, it is a case of beginning to consider choice as a shared responsibility, although not on the basis of common obedience to the demands of assurance, but based on a common exposure to the incalculable and to the incalculable relationship with finitude that all humankind shares.

Thus, perhaps, management can reclaim its relationship with the dimension of *measure*. This dimension still calls us in the age of the calculative, systematic measurement of everything. Indeed, that dimension points, in Heidegger's thought, towards the fundamental structure of human comportment towards things. It points towards the decisive phenomenon of man's *measuring up* to a thing, to what a thing is, as the thing that it is; it speaks thus a radically different language in respect to the calculation of a thing and to the calculation of its *quality*. Let us read this passage from the Zollikon Seminars (Heidegger, 2001, p. 100), that provides a hint towards the abyssal question of measure.

> All measuring is not necessarily quantitative. Whenever I take notice of something as something, then I myself have 'measured up to' [*anmessen*] what a thing is. This 'measuring up' [*Sich-anmessen*] to what is, is the fundamental structure of human comportment towards things.
>
> In all comprehending of something as something, for instance, of the table as a table, I myself measure up to what I have comprehended [...] The relationship of the human being to measure is not entirely comprehended by quantitative measurability. Indeed, it is not even raised as a question. The relationship of the human being to what gives a measure is a fundamental relationship to what is. It belongs to the understanding of being itself.

Measure (if understood in its difference from quantitative-scientific measurability) and quality (if understood not as a category) point to the dimension of the incalculable; and they do so as they point to the basic phenomenon of the relationship of man with a thing as the thing that it is.[10]

The problem of measure (which, as we are beginning to see, has something to do with quality) is key in considering the issue of money. I am thinking here primarily of Amato's (2010) and Amato and Fantacci's (2011) important meditation on money, credit and finance.

Amato's meditation is carried out in discourse not only with Heidegger's thought, but also with some of the highlights in the tradition of economic thought and particularly with the work of Keynes, that giant of economic thinking who has still much to tell us about measure, calculability and incalculability.[11]

How does calculation and enhancement need to be addressed from the perspective of money and finance? What is the meaning of calculating the relationship between debtor and creditor and making it available for endless enhancement, in which debts are always paid tomorrow, which is to say, never? What does it mean that money – whose own function is that of being the measure of exchange – becomes ever more decisively a calculable commodity?

The extreme calculability of money is, according to Amato (2010), the extreme outcome of an initial hesitation in the history of metaphysics. This is the hesitation to consider money as an institution, and specifically as the institution that makes exchange *true and meaningful* for those taking part in it.

But money is an institution by virtue of its relationship with that which is not of the order of the calculable – with that radically incalculable dimension to which man has access precisely by virtue of his own finitude.

It is precisely by virtue of its relationship with the incalculable that money proper can and must *disappear*; it is precisely because of its relationship with the incalculable that money *that is truly money* must be capable of disappearing once it has completed its task, in favour of exchange.

Considering forms of money and finance that measure up to what money and finance properly are thus entails considering the possibility of economic life in which exchange and the debtor-creditor relationship are alive to that in which they are grounded – a ground that, insofar as it concerns finitude, is radically incalculable and non-assurable.

Thinking about money and finance in this way thus means not thinking in terms of assurance. It means, for example, not thinking at all in terms of a better quality of financial markets – by which I also mean a better social and democratic quality. It means, instead, considering the possibility of an economic and social life that is based on sharing. To be precise, this does not mean that it is based on sharing the imperative of assurance (which is indeed something that we cannot share, but that we can at least obey together), but is instead based on sharing the dimension of lack, of loss, of sacrifice, that is at the heart of any economy that is truly such.

It is in light of the above that we can say that money and management are questions of quality. It is also through the question of management and money that we can grasp the chance which is contained in the age of perfected calculability. And the more we renew questioning on the calculation of quality – a task which I attempted to contribute to in this work – the more we can grasp this chance.

What is at stake is not the possibility of setting limits to calculation: the *unlimited* deployment of calculation (of quality) is not merely the effect of a degeneration of calculation itself, but something which belongs to the calculative, if properly understood. This is something than we have the chance of considering, precisely when we are faced with the disquieting post-human dimension. What happens on the frontier of the post-human can represent indeed an opportunity to re-direct our look; provided we do not read it as a perversion of techno-scientific calculation, but as a phenomenon pointing towards what calculation *essentially is*: something which man cannot fully master and something which, in its perfection, challenges man in an unprecedented way.

What we can experience – as difficult as it may be – is the possibility of a *measured measure*. The latter is not merely a matter of methodological prudence or of the construction of an open debate (which remains, by the way, useful) on the forms, criteria and rationalities of measurement; it is, instead, a matter of a measure than do not deny the incalculable, but can instead measure up with the incalculable in managerial, economic, social and political life. Such a possibility is not lost; this is not anything we have lost and that we had once, and it is not something that is inevitably destined to be lost, as far as calculation reaches perfection.

However, the point is: with which attitude should we look at the contemporary practices of calculation of quality in order to grasp that possibility?

A new look towards quality does not require moving away from the way in which quality currently allows itself to be calculated, if by this we mean that we wish *to know no more of* such calculation. Nor this new look implies the denunciation of calculation, calculable quality, or the socio-political intents of quality measurement.

First and foremost, it is worth emphasizing, it is a case of renouncing every attitude of condescension towards what is, at heart, the political significance of that calculation.

The calculation of quality of life – at least, as long as this still refers to *human* life – takes place with the intention of doing *justice to man* (to the richness of the human being) and of aiming at better *justice among humankind*. And it may well be the case, however, that this work is capable of producing results.

Let us consider, for example, the work of Amartya Sen and his argument on the calculation of the total quality of life in light of the concept of *capability*. Who would deny that such a calculation may make it possible to expose the state of serious and extreme deprivation in which some – indeed, many – human beings live?

And yet today, we have the possibility of seeing that, if we indefinitely pursue the calculability of quality (and even if we do so with the best of intentions), we will have nothing behind us but totality and vitalism – that vitalism whose ultimate root is no other than the dominion of lived-experience. Moreover, this 'totality' and this vitalism no longer play to the tune of the human but instead play to the tune of the post-human, of post-human quality of life, of the quality of the post-human city.

The opportunity we have is that of experiencing that the *lived total in expansion* (whether human or post-human) is something that does not measure up to the possibility of being human that human beings have; and this has nothing to do with a 'traditionalist' return to a humanity that we *no longer* have, to a *measure* that we no longer have, and to a *quality* that we no longer have.

This opportunity, however, is to some extent denied to us if we think purely in terms of a critique of capitalism or of (bio)-power and therefore if we exclusively interpret quality – 'managerial' quality but also quality of life – as an element of governmental rationalities, aimed at masking interests and positions of power.

These interests and positions of power do truly *exist*, and the analysis of the instrumental use of quality discourses and techniques is something to which we must show not only the greatest respect but also the utmost care – or I do so, at any rate, in my own case.

However, in my view, the more we address in a certain way the extreme deployment of calculation, the more should we recognize that calculation and enhancement cannot be merely considered from the standpoint of the transformations of bio-capitalism and bio-power, which nonetheless remain matters of the greatest importance.

If we manage to acknowledge this, we can be freer to experience something, precisely on the very frontier of calculation and quality. This may happen in the most diverse places, starting from the ones we are most familiar with.

There is, in my opinion, in the recent social science literature, a particularly emblematic passage, as regards the argument I am advancing here. This passage is contained in the aforementioned dialogue between two scholars, John Law and Michel Callon, who cannot be presumed as being on the same wavelength as the one I propose in this work.

The passage is as follows:

> JL [...] I wilt when I have to account for myself. And I don't think this is because I'm a bad teacher. It is because teaching, when I do it well as I think I sometimes do, is outside *any* possibility of accountability. It is a labour of love. And the passion that it is carried in is dried up when I have to account for it.
>
> MC You are a philosophical romantic, my dear colleague!
>
> (Callon and Law, 2005, p. 724–725)

Here, in my view, Law speaks of quality, without even having to mention it explicitly.

He speaks of the quality of that thing, which for him is very serious, which is the job of teaching – of that thing which is at risk of the most extreme deformation when it is the subject of systematic calculation of the quality of teaching. This calculation justifies itself as the most responsible and transparent way of taking account of the right of the other (the student, in this case) to ever more and ever better *secure* this right.

Regarding this calculation, however, Law speaks the language of another quality.

He speaks the language of doing one's work well. In other words, he speaks the language of the possibility of excelling, with respect to oneself above all, by dwelling in oneself. This opportunity to do one's work well is sometimes successful and sometimes not, and when it is not successful we are disappointed because there may, perhaps, be another opportunity – but there will not continue to be other opportunities eternally since, until proven otherwise, we are mortal.

He speaks the language of passion and of love; of that love which is perhaps something that is not concerned with the immeasurable proliferation of life that negates death, but which perhaps appears as a possibility precisely on the basis of the condition of finitude of human beings.

In short in my opinion, he speaks the language, even if not explicitly, of responsibility: the responsibility with regard to oneself and to others; the responsibility that teacher and students share. They share this responsibility, however, in the openness to something that belongs to no-one and cannot be guaranteed to anyone; something that is *common* precisely because it is incalculable.

Precisely against the advance of calculability, a possibility of sensing in a new way the issue of incalculability arises. And this possibility arises when we are confronted by the present banal, obvious emptiness of quality – by its simple *going by itself.* This possibility, in my view, has an essentially political nature; and the very question of quality and calculation deserves indeed not only to keep on being a cutting-edge topic for social, political and managerial studies, but also to be put at the core of a public debate, which should be as *free* as possible.

Provided, however, that the political dimension, as a democratic dimension, is not conceptualised from the standpoint of a certain idea of democracy as a process – a process which portrays itself, more and more decisively, as being *democratically calculative* and *calculatively democratic.*

Within the horizon of this conception of the democratic process, which establishes itself as increasingly obvious, it seems that, in the face of the question of quality and of the shadow which quality casts, there is nothing to be done but this: produce new concepts and new constructions of quality, and take ever more precise account of the ways in which quality is perceived, conceived, lived.

It seems, in other words, that in the democratic process the possibility of a *halt* with regard to a phenomenon is prevented at its very roots. This halt is the hallmark of that work – undoubtedly arduous, but not exclusively reserved to only a few – which is thought.

What quality points to, as a political issue, is precisely the possibility of inquiring in common, and therefore the possibility of feeling in common the possibility of an economic and social life that measures up to what we all, still, share: and that is the incalculability of life as grounded in finitude.

The possibility of an economic and social life – and of justice – which has a relationship with finitude still resonates today in a faint tone which is vaguely esoteric or mystical, excessive and disturbing. Perhaps instead if, in this very day and age, we see calculation for what it really is, we can begin perceiving the distinctive quality of this possibility: that of *sobriety*.

Notes

1 Calculation, Quality and Life: A First Look at the Debate

1. The reference here is to the role – so important in Foucault's thoughts on biopolitics – of the techno-scientific apparatuses of economic, statistic and demographic sciences (for some classical studies on statistics and statistical thinking, see Desrosières, 1988; Hacking, 1990; Porter, 1986). The development of economic and statistical theory has dense biunivocal relationships with the issue of life insurance (see Porter, 2000), as it is highlighted, for example, by the crucial question of the standardization of human life. See Lampland and Leigh Star (2008) and Lengwiler (2008).
2. See Rabinow and Rose (2006) for an analysis of the meanings (in terms of truth discourses and authorities considered competent to speak that truth, strategies of intervention and modes of subjectification) that the notion of biopower, which in Foucault is surrounded by a certain ambiguity, has assumed in the interdisciplinary debate.
3. See Miller (1992), who emphasizes that the calculative practices of managerial accounting cannot be in any way reduced to double-entry bookkeeping, but are, instead, composed of a variety of technologies and forms of rationality.
4. In which, as Vollmer (2003) reminds us, it contributed to a profound renewal of the scenario of the sociological analyses on the role of accounting practice.
5. See, on the ability of accounting of creating and shaping organizational realities, Hopwood (1978; 1987) and Vollmer (2003). The debate on the performativity of calculative practices has considerably developed in recent years, within and beyond Foucauldian perspectives. See, for example, on how various technological instruments shape and reshape markets, Callon, Millo and Muniesa (2007), on the 'performativity' of financial models, MacKenzie (2006) and on the way in which the use of calculative tools shapes the practices of risk management, Kalthoff (2005). See also Knorr, Cetina and Preda (2005).
6. See, for example, Fineman (2004).
7. See Foucault (2007; 2008).
8. See Rose and Miller (1992), Hopwood (1987; 1992), Vollmer (2003).
9. Lemke mentions, beyond the works of Rabinow and Rose, various lines of research, among which those of Dillon and Reid (2001), Flower and Heath (1993), Haraway (1991) and Rheinberger (2000). On 'posthuman medicine', see Waldby (2000).
10. For an analysis of the conceptualizations and definitions of quality in the field of management, see Reeves and Bednar (1994).

11. For a critical interpretation of the transformation of organizations, under the banner of Total Quality, with regard also to organizational models based on customer and supplier links, see Tuckman (1994).
12. See Kurunmäki and Miller (2006) on the diffusion of practices of performance measurement: in the rhetoric of the British *Modernising Government* agenda, performance measurement is promoted with the aim of increasing the capacity of the centre to monitor and control local service provision, in a frame in which one of the most important issues concerns the need for encouraging local autonomy while improving central control.
13. See, for example, Travers (2007).
14. See, for example, Borraz (2007) on standards. On policy instrumentation, see Lascoumes and Le Gales (2007).
15. The reference is, for example, to European ecological labelling, to the certification of environmental management systems and to indicators for local environmental quality and sustainability.
16. On some aspects of the role of quality in EU territorial policy, see Doria (2006).
17. On *quality assurance* in the field of education, see European Parliament and Council (2006).
18. On the EU efforts in the growing and controversial field of the measuring of the quality of regulatory 'products,' see http://ec.europa.eu/governance/better_regulation/index_en.htm, accessed on 30 October 2012. See, concerning the Organisation for Economic Co-operation and Development (OECD) countries, Jacobzone et al. (2007).
19. Under the umbrella of quality, the relationships between various 'dimensions' of development and between various policy domains, more than being measured in their controversial and prospective aspects, seem rather to be 'anticipated' by a meta-code of connection that pre-assures their integration. See Doria (2009).
20. It is in partially because of the very vagueness of quality of life – Armstrong and Caldwell (2004) argue, mentioned by Benzer (2011) – that quality of life itself could be invoked as a common goal across different political programmes.
21. Concerning the origins of quality of life as a major political issue, see Rapley (2003) and Benzer (2011). With regard to the United States, Rapley (2003) noted the publication of the 1969 *Toward a Social Report*, which identified the dimensions of health and illness; income and poverty; the physical environment; public order and safety; social mobility; learning, science and art; participation and alienation. On the subject of the origins of the process of producing social indicators in the European countries, Rapley drew attention to the *Dutch Biennal Social and Cultural Report* (first published in 1974), the UK's *Social Trends* (first published in 1970) and France's *Données Sociales* (first published in 1973).
22. See, for example, the OECD project on national well-being measurement and comparison http://www.oecdbetterlifeindex.org/#/01151110511, accessed on 30 October 2012.

23. This also concerns the 'disadvantaged' categories of citizens, taken on as *enterprising selves* engaged in choosing among various care programmes. Cf. Rapley (2003).
24. See Rapley (2003), who emphasizes the coexistence of subjective and objective measurements both at the individual level and at the level of the population at large.
25. The report was produced by the *Commission on the Measurement of Economic Performance and Social Progress*, and coordinated by Stiglitz, Sen and Fitoussi.
26. The report identifies three macro-sides: *Classical GDP issues, Quality of life* and *Sustainable Development and Environment.*
27. This is the case, for example, of the Mercer *Quality of Living Survey*, the ranking of the most liveable cities produced by *The Economist*, the Monocle *Liveable Cities Index.*
28. See, for example, the *Urban Audit* project carried out by Eurostat with the aim of measuring various aspects of the quality of urban life in European cities.
29. See Doria (2006; 2009). For a taxonomic approach to the evaluation of local identity, see Mignolli and Nijkamp (2001).
30. On the measurement of cultural quality, see Belfiore (2004) and Gray (2006).
31. See Rogerson (1999) and Tremblay, Rogerson and Chicoine (2008).
32. 'For the audit explosion has been driven less by an empirically grounded understanding of the productive benefits of audit and more by a pervasive belief, almost ideological in form, in the need for the discipline which it provides. It is ironic that in many instances audit practices are themselves insulated from the market forces and ideals of deregulation which they serve' (Power, 1994, p. 36).
33. 'We seem to have lost an ability to be publicly skeptical about the fashion for audit and quality assurance; they appear as "natural" solutions to the problems we face. And yet, just as other fashions have come and gone as the basis for management thinking, the audit explosion is also likely to be a passing phase' (Power, 1994, p. 32).
34. 'In the end, we probably measure more things in more detail than is functionally necessary and we do so for reasons that are often cultural and psychological, rather than technical. The job of social science is to find out these reasons, although social scientists always need to be reminded of their own constitutive role in social demands for the measurement of everything' (Power, 2004, p. 780).
35. See Strathern (2000).
36. On the possibility of resisting the politics of quality in the context of higher education see Worthington and Hodgson (2005).
37. 'It is as if society had fallen prey to a mysterious and enervating sickness whose principal symptom is a neurotic demand for checks and double checks without end. Institutional self-strangulation is a predictable result' (Lock and Lorenz, 2007, p. 416–417).

38. For a critical reading of the role that those technologies play in reshaping the international and supranational regulatory environments, see Higgins (2006).
39. For an analysis, from the perspective of juridical studies, of the issue of environmental responsibility which addresses also the issue of quality, see Fabre-Magnan (2012).
40. This points to Legendre's reflection on management, in the framework of his *dogmatic anthropology*. See Legendre (1998; 2001).
41. As Callon, Méadel and Rabeharisoa (2002) remind, the consideration of the role of the processes of 'qualification' is also at the core of the French school of conventions. See Eymard-Duvernay (1994), Salais and Storper (1993), Thévenot (1993). See also Musselin and Paradeise (2002) and the other contributions to the monographic issue of *Sociologie du travail, Dossier/debate La Qualitè* (vol. 44, n. 2, 2002).
42. Qualification takes place through *objectification* processes (which define and stabilize the properties of a given good and allow property laws to apply to it), as well as through *singularization* practices, which render a good comparable, but not identical, to other goods. A product may be constructed as a marketable good once it has been located in a field in which it can be linked (also through the establishment of new relationships) and compared to other similar goods. By means of these processes, a physical or non-physical entity can be transformed into a good *attached* to the consumer. Through qualification, a good can be made calculable, and the purchaser can give it an economic value, expressed in the form of a price or of a range of prices that the purchaser himself is willing to pay (see Callon and Muniesa, 2005).
43. A given operation of framing, which defines the relevant elements for the construction of a certain market, is followed by the emergence of relationships and processes which exceed the frame and proliferate in the social body. Within the qualification dynamics, a possibility arises of the transformation of not only the network of the actors, but also of the *identities* of the subjects involved. Hence there is a 'politicization' of markets and a re-conceptualisation of the market itself. The latter, as a *calculative collective device* (Callon and Muniesa, 2005), would then no longer be characterized by the tendency to impose impersonal laws, but would instead form a sort of a diversified device, constantly reshaped by the actors and by social sciences (Callon, 1998). See Barry and Slater (2002) and Callon, Méadel and Rabeharisoa (2002).
44. See, on this point, Slater (2002).
45. One of the fields in which the cooperation between different actors developed is that related to the development of innovative medicines and therapies. In that context, patients cooperate with scientists and other actors in the definition of both technical-scientific and ethical issues. See, for example, on this topic, Rabinow (1999).
46. On the proliferation of numerical ordinal ranking (or ratings) in the current socio-economic scenarios, see Guyer (2010).

47. Making incalculabilities, according to Callon and Law (2005), takes a lot of effort and develops through different strategies, amongst which *rarefaction*, the withdrawing of the necessary resources to qualculate (i.e. to frame, to figure, to display things, to build relationships among them).
48. On the relationship between quality of life and the concept of risk, see Benzer (2011).

2 Quality and Calculation: A Phenomenological Journey

1. This work, unanimously acknowledged as extremely important has been, despite the linguistic difficulties, object of a growing number of analyses, even beyond the border of philosophical studies. See, for example, Elden (2003; 2005).
2. '*Be-ing*', as the translators of the *Contributions* note, translates *Seyn*, which is the eighteenth century orthography that Heidegger uses to designate *Sein* – being – when being is not grasped metaphysically. See Heidegger (1999a, p. xxii).
3. The history of philosophy is, for Heidegger, the history of metaphysical thinking, as that thinking devoted to think the being *of beings*. As Heidegger writes in the *Letter on humanism*:

    > Metaphysics does indeed represent beings in their Being, and so it thinks the Being of beings. But it does not think the difference of both. Metaphysics does not ask about the truth of Being itself. Nor does it therefore ask in what way the essence of man belongs to the truth of Being.
    >
    > (Heidegger, 2011a, p. 154)

    Let us read also the following passage from 'The end of philosophy and the task of thinking':

    > Philosophy is metaphysics. Metaphysics thinks beings as a whole-the world, man, God-with respect to Being, with respect to the belonging together of beings in Being. Metaphysics thinks beings as beings in the manner of a representational thinking that gives grounds. For since the beginning of philosophy, and with that beginning, the Being of beings has shown itself as the ground (*archē, aition*, principle). The ground is that from which beings as such are what they are in their becoming, perishing, and persisting as something that can be known, handled, and worked upon.
    >
    > (Heidegger, 2011b, p. 312)

4. 'This means: the matter itself stands in the way it stands to us, before us. To "put oneself in the picture" about something means: to place the being itself before one just as things are with it, and, as so placed, to keep it permanently before one. But a decisive condition in the essence of the picture

is still missing. That we are "in the picture" about something means not just that the being is placed before, represented by, us. It means, rather, that it stands before us together with what belongs to and stands together with it as a system. To be "in the picture" resonates with: being well informed, being equipped and prepared. Where the world becomes picture, beings as a whole are set in place as that for which man is prepared; that which, therefore, he correspondingly intends to bring before him, have before him, and, thereby, in a decisive sense, place before him'.

(Heidegger, 2002, p. 67)

5. 'In reckoning, something is imputed, not arbitrarily and not in the sense of a suspicion; what is imputed is that due to which a matter is the way it is. What is thus imputed, computed is that upon which something rests, namely what lies present before us, supportive, what is reckoned in a reckoning; *ratio* is therefore the basis, the footing, that is, the ground. In imputing, reckoning represents something as something. This representing of something as something is a bringing-before-oneself that deals with some particular thing that lies present, and in such a dealing-with perceives the condition it is in vis-à-vis that in terms of which and by which it is reckoned. Reckoning, *ratio*, as such a perceiving, is Reason'.

(Heidegger, 1996, p. 104)

6. If the ever more complete annexation of all beings to the realm of objectification and calculation, is the form of calculation's perfecting that we feel most familiar with, we must however, understand perfecting in at least two other senses. We have to understand it as the constantantly perfected assurance of man's self-installation, as subject, in the world as a picture. Perfecting should be understood, at the same time, as movement aimed at making the essence of the calculation ever less recognizable as something that belongs to the way in which being holds sway, by withdrawing.
7. 'The gigantic shows the magnitude of the self-certain *subjectum* which builds everything on its own representing and producing' (Heidegger, 1999a, p. 311).
8. For some notes on the theme of quality in the *Contributions*, see Livingston (2003).
9. This is a consequence of the fact that 'be-ing' abandons being, leaving it to beings. See, for a discussion on these crucial points, Schild 2013.
10. While it is not possible in this work to comment on this decisive issue in Heidegger's thinking (see, just as an example, Heidegger, 2009a), let us read what Heidegger writes about the Greek experience of beings in above mentioned essay on *Weltbild*. For the Greeks, Heidegger says commenting on Parmenides:

    The being is that which rises up and opens itself; that which, as what is present, comes upon man, i.e., upon him who opens himself to what is present in that he apprehends it. The being does not acquire being in that man first looks upon it in the sense of representation that has the character of subjective perception. Rather, man is the one who

> is looked upon by beings, the one who is gathered by self-opening beings into presencing with them. To be looked at by beings, to be included and maintained and so supported by their openness, to be driven about by their conflict and marked by their dividedness, that is the essence of humanity in the great age of Greece. In order to fulfill his essence, therefore, man has to gather (λέγείν) and save (σώζείν), catch up and preserve, the self-opening in its openness; and he must remain exposed to all of its divisive confusion. Greek humanity *is* the receiver *[Vernehmer]* of beings, which is the reason that, in the age of the Greeks, the world can never become picture.
>
> (Heidegger, 2002, p. 68–69)

11. Livingston (2003) himself, in his essay on machination and lived-experience, addresses some moments of the Heidegger's thinking on *physis* and *techne*.
12. *Machenschaft*, that which belongs to the sway of being, as 'what is precisely *not* ownmost to the beingness of beings', seems to emerge in the modern era 'into the openness of interpretation of beings' (Heidegger, 1999a, p. 89). That is because, in some forms, in the modern era, the dominion of *Machenschaft* seems to be able to be recognized; in the form, in particular, of the recognition that the modern era is dominated by calculation. Yet, in modernity, *Machenschaft* does not *at all* allow itself to be grasped in its ownmost. This is because it is concealed behind that which appears to be its opposite, that being *Erlebnis*.
13. The difficulty in thinking *Erlebnis* and its co-belogingness with *Machenschaft* lies also in the issue of non-simultaneity. Although the very root of the dominion of lived-experience can be traced in the basic metaphysical interpretation of man as the rational living being, *Erlebnis*, so to speak, comes into the open in modernity, showing itself as the opposite of machination.
14. Livingston (2003), referring also to the Heidegger's argument in *Being and Time*, mentions Dilthey, Husserl, Bergson and Scheler as adherents to the philosophical orientation which is based on *life* and *lived-experience* of individual persons.
15. Vernon describes the relationship between *Machenschaft* and *Erlebnis* (better, what in my view, should be considered *one* dimension of that relationship) thus:

> While technology makes lived-experiences available to individuals, it also takes the wonder out of them precisely through the calculation that make the new experience open to all. Our boredom is not relieved by any particular lived-experience, for each can only be lived insofar as it is *not* wondrous and estranging, but is *necessarily* calculable and predictable. As a result, we yearn again for new lived-experiences that break the newly-produced tedium. [...] the desire for individual *Erlebnisse* is not opposed to the expansion of machination; rather, machination both satisfies (by providing new lived-experiences) and

> re-invigorates (by making them immediately boring) our yearning for them.
>
> (Vernon, 2008, pp. 114–115)

16. See also Heidegger (2011b).
17. It is worthwhile noting that Heidegger, in the midst of his discussion of the gigantic and the quantitative, says that: 'here it is not a matter of reversing the "quantitative" into something qualitative' (Heidegger, 1999a, p. 95). This means, in my interpretation, that a proper understanding of the 'quantitative' and the 'qualitative' does not involve any form or reversing the relationship, any overturning of the relationship between quantity and quality as categories and any 'requalification' of quality.
18. These and the following quoted phrases of Fédier (2003) are translated here from the Italian text.
19. Here we encounter a configuration of the *accessibility* and *publicness* which characterize the dominion of lived-experience. It seems, indeed, that the calculation of the subject's lived-experiences through the measurement of how they are continuously *perceived* by the subject and by others has something to do with the movement in which 'the present "lived-experience" will continually be interpreted historically [*historisch*] and in which its *publicness* will be conveyed to everyone by this interpretation as quickly and accessibly as possible' (Heidegger, 1999a, p. 107).
20. For a description of recent lines of research on this theme see Economist Intelligence Unit (2010).
21. Values will become in Nietzsche, as Heidegger notes in his interpretation, the conditions for the domination of *will to power*. When in the Nietzsche's metaphysics, the being of beings, will be determined as will to power, values will become the conditions under which the will to power, according to its essence, stands. Value thinking, in the last metaphysical thinker, will come to belong essentially to the very being of will to power. See Heidegger (1991).
22. It is a case to remind that these phenomena, according to Heidegger, cannot be measured (and not even to 'objectified') without violating them in their quality of phenomena.

> How do we measure sadness? Evidently, one cannot measure it at all! Why not? If one approached sadness with a method of measuring, the very approach would already be contrary to the meaning of sadness. Thus, one would preclude sadness as sadness beforehand. Here, even the claim to measure is already a violation of the phenomenon as a phenomenon. But do we not also use quantitative concepts in our speech about sadness? One does not speak of an 'intense' sadness, but of a 'great' or a 'profound' sadness. One can also say 'He is a "bit sad"' but that does not mean a small quantity of sadness. The 'a bit' refers to a quality of mood. This very depth, however, is by no means measurable. [...] Regarding the depth of a feeling of sadness, there is no

> reason or occasion whatsoever to estimate it quantitatively, let alone to measure it.
>
> (Heidegger, 2001, p. 82)

23. Although the quotation refers to subjective aspects, in my view, similar considerations can be made for the objective aspects.
24. Undoubtedly the indicators that the social sciences constantly put forward are not only explicitly indicators of quality. These days we continously deal with indicators for development, sustainability, efficiency, performance, justice and so on. When it is a question of measuring phenomena that concern human life and which therefore are irredeemably *complex* and multi-dimensional, ever-increasing sets of indicators are required.

    However, we must consider that nothing is more worthy of being indicated than quality; by this I do not mean only that quality is the most important thing to be indicated, but that, in the dimension of calculative thinking, the movement of indicating (as a movement which fixes and assures by projecting something and keeping it projected) is needed precisely when quality is at stake.
25. Precisely in the age of the extreme calculability (of the incalculable), the incalculable is projected as a shadow, whose knowledge is refused. As Heidegger (2002, p. 72) says, at the end of *The Age of the World Picture*:

    > This incalculability becomes the invisible shadow cast over all things when man has become the *subiectum* and world has become picture [...]. Through this shadow the modern world withdraws into a space beyond representation and so lends to the incalculable its own determinateness and historical uniqueness. This shadow, however, points to something else, knowledge of which, to us moderns, is refused.
    >
    > [...]
    >
    > Man will know the incalculable – that is, safeguard it in its truth – only in creative questioning and forming from out of the power of genuine reflection.

26. For Aristotle, a quantity is a plurality if it can be numbered; it is a greatness if it is measurable. A plurality is the name for that which can be divided into non-continuous parts; greatness is that which is divisible into continuous parts.
27. Concerning this reductionist character of biopolitical power, Brusa and Tarizzo remind us of the warnings of Edmund Husserl on the methods used to objectify the human psyche and the technical turn taken by such procedures that have a tendency to transform psychology into an exact science, into a science of measurement. What comes to my mind is, instead, what Heidegger says about Husserl (Heidegger, 1999b, p. 56–57):

    > For Husserl, a definite ideal of science was prescribed in *mathematics* and the mathematical natural sciences. Mathematics was the model

> for all scientific disciplines. This scientific ideal came into play in that one attempted to elevate description to the level of mathematical rigour [...]. Is it justified to hold up mathematics as a model for all scientific disciplines? Or are the basic relations between mathematics and other disciplines not thereby stood on their heads?
>
> Mathematics is the least rigorous of disciplines, because it is the one easiest to gain access to. The human sciences presuppose much more scientific existence than could ever be achieved by a mathematician. One should approach a scientific discipline not a system of propositions and grounds for justifying them, but rather as something in which factical Dasein critically confronts itself and explicates itself. To bring mathematics into play as the model for all scientific disciplines is unphenomenological – the meaning of scientific rigor needs rather to be drawn from the kind of object being investigated and the mode of access appropriate to it.

28. We can find, in the *Contributions*, some illuminating notes on the relationship between the way of thinking of sciences (which is particularly manifested in mathematical physics) and the scientific explainability of life.

    After referring to thinking in 'causalities', that is, in terms of 'if-then' relationships, Heidegger writes:

    > To assume that one is able, with this apparently 'free' causality, to grasp more easily what is 'alive' merely betrays the secretly kept conviction that one will one day bring what is alive *also* under the jurisdiction of explanation.
    >
    > (Heidegger, 1999a, p. 102)

    This outcome, according to Heidegger, was very close at hand because human sciences, through the 'historiographic' treatment of the human, were working, in their own way, towards calculating human existence in terms of causal relationships, consigning the unexpected, the accidental and the chance to the bin of non-calculable exceptions.
29. In order to properly consider the scientific treatment of the human (a task that is traditionally in charge of the human sciences and that, for Heidegger, requires much effort), we must take very seriously the words of Heidegger (1999a, p. 104) in the section dedicated to 'Propositions about Science' in the *Contributions*.

    > Moreover, execution of rigour in the human sciences in terms of performance always remains much more difficult than carrying out the exactness of 'exact' sciences.

30. It is from that perspective that we can prepare ourselves to address the convergence between the human sciences and the natural sciences to which Heidegger refers in paragraph 76 of the *Beiträge*: 'the objective and methodical difference between the natural and the human sciences will recede more and more' (Heidegger, 1999a, p. 107).

3 Calculation, Quality and Enhancement

1. It is worth noting here that *power* develops, in the entire metaphysical history, together with the imperative of self-making. The demand of power (as the demand of the constant self-overpowering of power), which marks all the metaphysical trajectory and manifests itself in the forms of technological power which we are accustomed to, should be understood precisely in its very intimate relationship with the *empire of self-making*. Power (as *Macht*) dwells at the very core of *Machenschaft*. As Schild 2013 discusses, following the interpretation of physis which occur at the beginning of metaphysical history, the being of beings comes to be determined in such a way that beings cannot recognize anything other than something that is *out of themselves*. It is by considering this very phenomenon, that we should address the demand for overpowering power which accompanies the trajectory of machination along the whole metaphysical history. However, a possibility and the task remains of thinking, so to speak, the origin of power in a more original way. This means addressing Heidegger's thought on the 'relationship' between power and physis, before that, at the beginning of metaphysical thought, *Machenschaft* comes to force. For some notes on this crucial pathway of thinking, see Schild 2013.
2. As we read in the Seminar in Zähringen: 'My Marx interpretation, Heidegger explains, is not political. It is concerned with being and the manner in which it destines itself. It is in this perspective and from this vision that I can say that with Marx the position of the most extreme nihilism is reached!' (Heidegger, 2003, p. 77).
3. 'With the reversal of metaphysics that was already accomplished by Karl Marx, the uttermost possibility of philosophy is attained. It has entered into its end' (Heidegger, 2011b, p. 313).
4. For Marx, communism is fulfilled naturalism; it is humanism, and insofar as it is fulfilled humanism, it is naturalism. This means that human work, as the humanization of nature, is at the same time that which naturalizes man, brings him back to his human essence, humanizes him. The humanization of man is therefore the achievement of the *naturalness* of man by means of the complete *humanization* of nature (Bee, 2010).
5. As Bee (2010) duly notes, for Marx man's completeness, his essence, consists precisely in being as far as actually possible – that is, at the maximum of his potential for becoming – *working material*.
6. As Bee (2010) suggests, we must grasp the 'epistemological' implications of this issue in the light of the ontological significance of the issue of human development in Marx. All science – the science of man and the science of nature – is nothing more than a science of human development; it is nothing other than the total science of the development of the total social man who produces himself, objectifying nature. For Marx the science of man, as well as natural science, can be no other than a science which deals equally with social production and the transformation

of nature, and with the fulfilment of human needs. It is a science, therefore, of the humanization of nature and of the naturalization of man; thus at the same time it is also a science of the humanization of man.

7. It is only as social man, or in other words as the social product of man himself, that man can manage to achieve self-sufficiency or 'independence'; that is to say, he can succeed in being a being who owes his very existence to himself. See also on this point Bee (2010).
8. See the *Grundrisse* (Marx, 1993).
9. For Sen, seizing this opportunity to live fully can be achieved by conceptualizing human development in a non-reductive manner. Such a conception of development must relinquish, in particular, thinking in terms of an exhaustive causal relationship between the production of material well-being and the enrichment of man.

   > There are, therefore, really two distinct issues here. First, economic prosperity is no more than one of the means to enriching lives of people. [...] Secondly, even as a means, merely enhancing average economic opulence can be quite inefficient in the pursuit of the really valuable ends.
   >
   > (Sen, 1989, p. 42–43)

   A conception of development worthy of the constitutive richness of man must, therefore, also distance itself from the intention of calculating what might indeed be a broad concept of 'quality of life', but which would in fact merely be based on the contribution that material abundance (such as income) provides to quality of life itself. In such a case, this would be 'commodity-based accounting of the quality of life (involving a confusion of means and ends)'.
10. As Sen writes:

    > In the view that is being pursued here, the constituent elements of life are seen as a combination of various different functionings (a 'functioning n-tuple') [...] The claim is that the functionings are constitutive of a person's being, and an evaluation of a person's well-being has to take the form of an assessment of these constituent elements.
    >
    > (Sen, 1989, p. 44)

11. The quoted passage is taken from the translation of McLellan (1977).
12. See Nussbaum and Sen (1993).
13. For Sen (1989) the difference between an instrumental and an intrinsic conception of choice is significant. Although both conceptions may be useful, in the intrinsic conception not only the choice between available alternatives is taken into account, but also the possibility of choosing among other alternatives.
14. In the work in question, Sen (1989, p. 45) recognizes this issue in the following terms:

    > There are many ambiguities in the conceptual framework of the capability approach. Indeed, the nature of human life and the content

> of human freedom are themselves far from unproblematic concepts. In so far as there are genuine ambiguities in the underlying objects of value, these will be reflected in corresponding ambiguities in the characterization of capability.

15. Sen (1989, p. 45–46) writes:

> It should be noted also that there is always an element of real choice in the description of functionings, since the format of 'doings' and 'beings' permits additional 'achievements' to be defined and included. Frequently, the same doings and beings can be seen from different perspectives, with varying emphases. [...] There is no escape from the problem of evaluation in selecting a class of functionings as important and others not so.

16. On the Hardt and Negri's interpretation of Foucault's thought on this point – an interpretation that considers Foucault's analyses also as the potential for the production of alternative subjectivities – see Hardt and Negri (2009).
17. 'Focusing on the making of the multitude, then, allows us to recognize how its productive activity is also a political act of self-making' (Hardt and Negri, 2009, p. 175).
18. The notion of flesh is discussed here with reference to the Merleau-Ponty's thought.
19. Biopower's attempt to recover forms of control over biopolitical value should therefore be understood, according to Hardt and Negri, as an intervention on the flesh of life, aimed at reducing the latter to controllable sequences.
20. To Hardt and Negri, the regressive nature of Heidegger's thought appears evident, precisely because that thought seemingly brings phenomenology, 'back to classical ontology not in order to develop a means to reconstruct being through human productive capacities but rather as a meditation on our telluric condition, our powerlessness, and death' (Hardt and Negri, 2009, p. 29).
21. As Hardt and Negri write:

> The production of subjectivity is always a process of hybridization, border crossing, and in contemporary history this subjective hybrid is produced increasingly at the interface between the human and the machine. Today subjectivity, stripped of all its seemingly organic qualities, arises out of the factory as a brilliant technological assemblage. [...] The cyborg is now the only model available for theorizing subjectivity. Bodies without organs, humans without qualities, cyborgs: these are the subjective figures today capable of communism.
>
> (Hardt and Negri, 1994, p. 12–13)

22. 'This revolutionary process of the abolition of identity, we should keep in mind, is monstrous, violent, and traumatic' (Hardt and Negri, 2009).

23. For Negri, this making of life, in its singularity, as the process of its own expansion, can be seen in terms of the body as *living labour*:

    > When we look at bodies, we realize that we are not only in the presence of a multitude of bodies, but we also understand that *every body is a multitude*. Crossing each other in the multitude, crossing the multitude with the multitude, bodies intermingle, become subject to *métissage*, become hybridized, transform themselves; they are like the waves of the sea, in perennial movement and in perennial reciprocal transformation. The metaphysics of individuality (and/or of the person) are a fearsome mystification of the multitude of bodies. *There is no possibility for a body of being alone*. One cannot even imagine it. When one defines the human being as an individual, when one considers this being as an autonomous source of rights and of properties, one renders this being solo. But one's self does not exist except in relation to the other.
    >
    > (Negri, 2008a, p. 120)

24. On the interpretation of the multitude of singularities as a recomposed swarm, see Negri (2011).
25. NBIC stands for nanotechnology, bioengineering, information science and cognitive research.
26. On some aspects of the post-human scenario, see Lafontaine (2004).
27. See, for example, Fukuyama (2002) and, for a reflection on the ethical implications of genetic engineering, see Habermas (2003).
28. 'The self-help literature consistently asserts an individual's right and obligation to make a strong commitment to him/herself. But it also affirms that it is a person's "life" that should be improved; the goal of the commitment to oneself is life enhancement – an idea that not only means increased enjoyment but also reflects on biological life as improvable and extendable' (Knorr Cetina, 2005, p. 77).
29. The spread of *rational choice theories* based on the pillar of maximization of utility is, according to Knorr-Cetina (2005), a notable form of this cultural macro-trend. The recent developments in economics – and, in particular, the growth of *behavioural economics* – represent one of the frontiers in the evolution of a scientific representation of man which adheres to *subjectivity thinking* and propels the latter towards its most extreme possibilities.
30. With Nietzsche, Heidegger says in the *Contributions*, the final and crucial approach of the history of metaphysics is reached; in that approach, reason as the property of man as *animal rationale* ('and everything that, under other headings, revolves within the sphere of this "property" of living being' Heidegger, 1999a, p. 310) will be 'reduced' to life. This means that the *appeal to life* that marks Nietzsche's metaphysics must be understood in its constitutive co-belongingness with the dominion of calculative reason.

    When will to power will become the basic character of beings, reason will become *living reason*, as bodying reason. Man's rationality will be transposed into animality in the sense of bodying will to power; where the 'name *body* identifies the distinctive unity in the constructs of domination in all drives, urges, and passions that will life itself' (Heidegger, 1991, p. 218 of vol. III).

31. Live-experience – *Erleben* – denotes in the *Contributions* the basic demand that decrees that everything turns into lived-experiences.
32. And, we might say, this occurs precisely when all things are produced and represented in their *irreducible specificity*.
33. This means that beings and man make themselves together, passing from one *as something* to another, but they make themselves in this way precisely when the humanity of man and the beingness of beings mutually advance towards dissolution.
34. On *Ge-Stell* see Schild (2004). *Ge-Stell* designates the coalescence of the forms of *Stellen* that, the more modern technology advances towards its own fulfilment, the more it perfects itself as coalescence and perfects its hold on man and beings.
35. See Riis (2008), Kochan (2010) and Khong (2003).
36. What is the risk we run in relation to the correspondence between *Machenschaft* and *Erlebnis*? It is the risk that, by presuming of understanding the extreme point of the perfection of the calculation as an unveiling of its original movement, we can grasp the essential co-belonging of machination and lived-experience. That co-belongingness that has remained hidden for so long, hiding behind the veil of the *utmost oppositionality* between *the machinational* and *lived-experience*; that co-belongingness that now the dominion of the calculable quality of life seems to place in front of us in a manner so clear that we cannot avoid grasping it.

    As Heidegger writes:

    > When thinking-mindfulness (as questioning the truth of be-ing and only as this) attains the knowing awareness of this mutual belongingness, then the basic thrust of the history of the first beginning (history of Western metaphysics) is grasped along with that, in terms of the knowing awareness of the other beginning.
    >
    > (Heidegger, 1999a, p. 89–90)

    However, the fact that, according to Heidegger, the possibility of knowing the co-belongingness of *Machenschaft* and *Erlebnis* and thus the first beginning of Western philosophy is still denied us, must not be a presupposition for abandoning any questioning on the subject. It is maybe by ever better grasping the opportunity which is contained in the completion of metaphysics that we can prepare ourselves for a task which remains yet to be done.
37. The fundamental question which contemporary man seems to be left within his post-human expansion is, according to Hellsten (2012, p. 2) for example, one that considers the 'accurate quality for human life: what kind of life is worth of living – what kind of life is *human enough* for human beings'?

38. Hughes (2004, p. xv) present the trans-humanist point of view (which embodies different positions) as follows:

    > After 400 years of democratic citizenship gradually being extended to include working men, women and all races, trans-humanists argue that rights should now be extended to all self-aware minds. In bioethics, this view is known as 'personhood theory': Only self-aware persons can have rights. 'Persons' don't have to be human, and not all humans are persons. The bioLuddites, on the other hand, advocate 'human racism,' the idea that only human beings can be citizens. Just as European racists once denied citizenship to Africans and believed that allowing Africans to have rights would destroy democracy, the human-racists want to deny citizenship and the right to exist to post-humans, intelligent animals and robots.

39. Hughes (2004) also refers in his book to some methodologies of quality measurement, such as the *Quality-adjusted Life Year.*
40. The embarrassment in which the post-human scenario leaves contemporary man manifests itself when he acknowledge the necessity – and, at the same time, the difficulty – of making distinctions within the processes of the manipulation and enhancement of human life. This emerges, in my view, in some critical contributions on the post-human future, such as that of Fukuyama. The issue which philosophical tradition has addressed as the essence of man qualifying all human beings – what Fukuyama defines as a Factor X – becomes ever more translated into a calculative scene in which the critical point becomes the finite or infinite – conditional or unconditional – malleability of the human essence.

    > We may be about to enter into a post-human future, in which technologies will give us the capacity gradually to alter that essence over time. Many embrace this power, under the banner of human freedom
    >
    > [...]
    >
    > But this kind of freedom will be different from all other freedoms that people have previously enjoyed. Political freedom has heretofore meant the freedom to pursue those ends that our natures had established for us. Those ends are not rigidly determined; human nature is very plastic and we have an enormous range of choices conformable with that nature. But it is not infinitely malleable, and the elements that remain constant – particularly our species-typical gamut of emotional responses – constitute a safe harbor that allows us to connect, potentially, with all other human beings.
    >
    > (Fukuyama, 2002, p. 217–218)

    The issue of the difficulty of making distinctions on the scene of post-human enhancement is also addressed by O' Brien (2011).
41. These are some developments which, according to Kurzweil (2000, p. 280) can be foreseen to take place before the end of this century.

> There is a strong trend towards a merger of human thinking with the world of machine intelligence that the human species initially created.
>
> There is no longer any clear distinction between humans and computers.
>
> Most conscious entities do not have a permanent physical presence. Machine-based intelligences derived from extended models of human intelligence claim to be human, although their brains are not based on carbon-based cellular processes, but rather electronic and photonic equivalents. Most of these intelligences are not tied to a specific computational processing unit. The number of software-based humans vastly exceeds those still using native neuron-cell-based computation.
>
> Even among those human intelligences still using carbon-based neurons, there is ubiquitous use of neural-implant technology, which provides enormous augmentation of human perceptual and cognitive abilities. Humans who do not utilize such implants are unable to meaningfully participate in dialogues with those who do.

See also the following passage concerning the 'presuppositions' of the enhancement processes:

> Regardless of the nature and derivation of a mental experience, spiritual or otherwise, once we have access to the computational processes that give rise to it, we have the opportunity to understand its neurological correlates. With the understanding of our mental processes will come the opportunity to capture our intellectual, emotional, and spiritual experiences, to call them up at will, and to enhance them.
>
> (Ibidem, p. 151)

4 Towards a Conclusion: Towards a New Look

1. Without forgetting, however, that numbers are not, in themselves, a matter of measurement. See how this crucial issue is evocated by Bill Maurer (2010), in his reflection on the theological unconscious of the mathematical techniques of financial derivatives.
2. See on this point David (2001). What is at issue here is the question that Heidegger addresses in the well-known passages of the essay on modern technology (Heidegger, 2011c). The danger that is contained in modern technology does not have to do with the effects of technological machines and apparatuses. The danger lies in the fact that *Enframing* – which translates *Ge-Stell*, the essence of modern technology – is a destining of revealing, that conceals itself as a way of revealing.

   The kind of revealing that is proper to Enframing – and that is characterized by the unconditional regulating and securing of the standing-reserves – 'drives out every other possibility of revealing' (Ibidem, p. 232). Furthermore, Enframing 'not only conceals a former way of revealing (bringing-forth) but also conceals revealing itself and with it that wherein uncolealment, i.e. thruth, propiates' [...] 'The rule of enframing threatens man with the possibility that it could be denied to him to enter into a more original revealing and hence to experience the call of a more primal thruth' (Ibidem, p. 232).

3. 'There is only *one* thing against which all violence-doing directly shatters. That is death. It is an end beyond all completion, a limit beyond all limits. Here there is no breaking forth and breaking up, no capturing and subjugating. But this un-canny thing, which sets us simply and suddenly out from everything homely once and for all, is not a special event that must also be mentioned among others, because it, too, ultimately does occur. The human being has no way out in the face of death, not only when it is time to die, but constantly and essentially. Insofar as humans *are*, they stand in the no-exit of death'.

   (Heidegger, 2000, p. 168–169, quoted in O'Brien, 2011)

4. Where, precisely in the face of this closeness between the *by itself* and the *in itself,* the possibility arises of comprehending the abyssal difference between the two.
5. We might say: in all the 'dimensions' of social and economic life, especially when we do not see these as being merely parts of a total, or components of the total quality of social life.
6. 'We introduce the notion of *derecognition of finitude* to capture this basic trend of contemporary managerialism, which exhorts every individual to see her/himself as a unique "finite infinity" who ought to seek in labour the path to find, inhabit, perform and activate his/her own particular endless resourcefulness' (Costea, Crump and Amiridis, 2007, p. 247).
7. 'Liberated from dogmatic shackles, the foundational question of this novel world-view is how the "self" is to carry the burden of absolute freedom. Certain transformations occur in the function, meaning and applications of particular metaphors, such as self-actualization, self-realization, performance, excellence, total quality, knowledge or talent. The problem of absolute freedom and the problem of finitude become problems of *measure* in both ethical and epistemological terms. The projection of endless potentialities of the self in the exercise of this newly found freedom is perpetually in search of a measure: if the self always possesses something in "excess" of what it already is, what is the normative framework, or conceptual specification, that makes this "surplus" accessible? Excess of potentiality is a paradoxical notion: it is not a "beyond" but always something immanent and somehow accessible whilst remaining always an aspiration. Without a measure (a "hypermetron") of the journey to actualize potentialities, the invocation of excellence, total quality or continuous improvement is always running the risk of being fraught with the sense of "being out of reach"'.

   (Costea, Crump and Amiridis, 2007, p. 258)

8. This demand not only entails unconditional use of quantitative tools: it implies, rather, letting oneself follow the flow in which all things

(environment, equity, affections, emotions and justice) are calculated as the parameters for performance growth. On this point, see De Gennaro (2006).

9. See how De Gennaro (2006) comments on this point, referring to the management's expert Malik.
10. It is worthwhile noting that, in the Zollikon Seminars themselves, Heidegger also further clarifies how the nature of measurability – as what characterizes the scientific approach to things and particularly the approach of natural sciences – must not be understood by merely focusing on the production of numerical results. The meaning of quantitative measurability, instead, should be grasped precisely by looking at the phenomenon of *calculability* – and thus at the movement of calculating in advance – which lies at the very core of the scientific method.

    > If scientific research and its theme – nature – is characterized by measurability, then we have an insufficient concept of this measurability if we believe that it is merely a matter of acquiring some definite numerical statement. In fact measurability means calculability, that is, a view of nature guaranteeing knowledge of how we can, and how we must, count on its proceses. Measurability means calculability in this characterization. But measurability means *precalculability*. And this is decisive because the point is *control* and *domination* of the processes of nature.
    >
    > (Heidegger, 2001, p. 104–105)

    On the question on measure in Heidegger, and its decisive relationship with the poetic dimension, see Kleinberg-Levin (2005).
11. See for a Keynesian interpretation of money, interest and calculation Fantacci (2010). On the theme of calculation and money see also the other contributions in Amato, Doria and Fantacci (2010).

References

Amato, M. (2010), *L'enigma della moneta e l'inizio dell'economia* (Milano: et al. edizioni).

Amato, M., L. Doria and L. Fantacci (eds.) (2010), *Money and Calculation. Economic and Sociological Perspectives* (Basingstoke: Palgrave Macmillan and Bocconi University Press).

Amato, M. and L. Fantacci (2011), *The End of Finance* (Cambridge: Polity Press).

Armstrong, D. and D. Caldwell (2004), 'Origins of the concept of quality of life in health care: a rhetorical solution to a political problem', *Social Theory & Health* 2, pp. 361–371.

Ball, S. J. (2003), 'The teacher's soul and the terrors of performativity', *Journal of Educational Policy* 18(2), pp. 215–228.

Barratt, E. (2003), 'Foucault, HRM and the ethos of the critical management scholar', *Journal of Management Studies* 40(5), pp. 1069–1087.

Barry, A. and D. Slater (2002), 'Introduction: The technological economy', *Economy and Society* 31(2), pp. 175–193.

Bauman, Z. (1992) *Mortality, Immortality & Other Life Strategies* (Cambridge: Polity Press).

Bee, M. (2010), *Senza alcun bisogno. Dall'autosufficienza alla sostenibilità* (Lecce: Pensa Multimedia).

Belfiore, E. (2004), 'Auditing culture: The subsidised cultural sector in the new public management', *International Journal of Cultural Policy* 10(2), pp. 183–202.

Benzer, M. (2011), *Quality of Life and Risk Conceptions in UK Healthcare Regulation: Towards a Critical Analysis*, Discussion Paper, no. 68, Centre for Analysis of Risk and Regulation, LSE.

Boltanski, L. and E. Chiapello (2005), *The New Spirit of Capitalism*, trans. G. Elliott (London: Verso).

Borraz, O. (2007), 'Governing standards: The rise of standardization processes in France and in the EU', *Governance* 20(1), pp. 57–84.

Bostrom, N. (2005), 'In defence of posthuman dignity', *Bioethics* 19(3), pp. 202–214.

Bostrom, Nick (2007), 'The future of humanity', http://www.nickbostrom.com/papers/future.pdf, accessed on 30 October 2012.

Brusa L. and D. Tarizzo (2009), 'Vite di qualità. Sulla razionalità biopolitica', *Filosofia politica*, XXIII(3), December, pp. 397–412.

Callon, M. (1998), 'Introduction: the embeddedness of economic markets in economics' in M. Callon (ed.) *The Laws of the Market* (Oxford: Blackwell), pp. 1–57.

Callon, M., P. Lascoumes and Y. Barthe (2001), *Agir dans un monde incertain. Essai sur la démocratie technique* (Paris: Seuil).

Callon, M. and J. Law (2005), 'On qualculation, agency, and otherness', *Environment and Planning D* 23(5), pp. 717–733.

Callon M., C. Méadel and V. Rabeharisoa (2002), 'The economy of qualities', *Economy and Society* 31(2), pp. 194–217.

Callon, M., Y. Millo and F. Muniesa (eds.) (2007), *Market Devices* (London: Wiley).

Callon, M. and F. Muniesa (2005), 'Economic markets as calculative collective devices', *Organization Studies* 26(8), pp. 1229–1250.

Charlton, B. G. (2002), 'Audit, accountability, quality and all that: The growth of managerial technologies in UK Universities', in S. Prickett and P. Erskine-Hill (eds.) *Education! Education! Education! – Managerial Ethics and the law of Unintended Consequences* (Thorverton: Imprint Academic), pp. 13–28.

Cochoy, F. (2002), *Une Sociologie du Packaging ou l'Âne de Buridan Face au Marché* (Paris: Presses Universitaires de France).

Cochoy, F. (2008), 'Calculation, qualculation, calqulation: shopping cart arithmetic, equipped cognition and the clustered consumer', *Marketing Theory* 8(1), pp. 15–44.

Cooper, M. (2008), *Life as Surplus: Biotechnology and Capitalism in the Neoliberal Era* (Seattle and London: University of Washington Press).

Costea, B., N. Crump and K. Amiridis (2007), 'Managerialism and "infinite human resourcefulness": A commentary upon the "therapeutic habitus", "derecognition of finitude" and the modern sense of self', *Journal for Cultural Research* 11(3), pp. 245–264.

Cummins, R., E. Gullone and A. Lau (2002), 'A model of subjective well-being homeostasis: the role of personality', in E. Gullone and R. Cummins (eds.) *Universality of Subjective Wellbeing Indicators* (Dordrecht: Kluwer Academic Publishers), pp. 7–46.

Dahlberg, G., P. Moss and A. Pence (1999), *Beyond Quality in Early Childhood Education and Care: Languages of Evaluation* (London and New York: Routledge).

Daston, L. (1988), *Classical Probability in the Enlightenment* (Princeton: Princeton University Press).

David, P. (2001), ' "Comment ça marche?" ou la chance de la technique' in *La fête de la pensée. Hommage à François Fédier*, Textes rassemblés par H. France-Lanord and F. Midal (Paris: Lettrage distribution), pp. 169–184.

De Gennaro, I. (2006), 'Building leadership on the invaluable: Towards the groundworks for a phenomenological approach to the philosophy of management', *Ancilla Iuris* 78, pp. 78–87, http://www.anci.ch/_media/beitrag/ancilla2006_78_de_genarro_leadership.pdf, accessed on 30 October 2012.

Desrosières, A. (1998) *The Politics of Large Numbers: A History of Statistical Reasoning*, trans. C. Naish (Cambridge, Mass.: Harvard University Press).

Diener, E. (1984), 'Subjective well-being', *Psychological Bulletin* 93, pp. 542–575.

Dillon, Michael and J. Reid. (2001), 'Global liberal governance: biopolitics, security, and war', *Millennium: Journal of International Studies* 30(1), pp. 41–66.

Doria, L. (2006), 'Managing the unmanageable resource: Multiple utility and quality in the EU policy discourses on local identity', in L. Doria, V. Fedeli and C. Tedesco (eds.) *Rethinking European Spatial Policy as a Hologram: Actions, Institutions, Discourses* (Aldershot: Ashgate), pp. 235–256.

Doria L. (2009), 'Il potere e il problema della qualità. Considerazioni della prospettiva della sociologia economica', *Studi Organizzativi* (1), pp. 143–170.

Economist Intelligence Unit (2010), *The Quality of Death. Ranking end-of-life Care Across the World*, http://graphics.eiu.com/upload/QOD_main_final_edition_Jul12_toprint.pdf, accessed on 30 October 2012.

Edgerton, R. B. (1990), 'Quality of Life from a longitudinal research perspective' in R. L. Schalock (ed.) *Quality of Life: Perspectives and Issues* (Washington: AAMR), pp. 149–160.

Elden, S. (2003), 'Taking the measure of the beiträge: Heidegger, national socialism and the calculation of the political', *European Journal of Political Theory* 2, pp. 35–56.

Elden, S. (2005), 'Contributions to geography? the spaces of Heidegger's Beiträge', *Environment and Planning D: Society and Space* 23(6), pp. 811–827.

Emad, P. (2007), *On the Way to Heidegger's Contributions to Philosophy* (Madison: The University of Wisconsin Press).

European Parliament and Council (2006), *Recommendation of the European Parliament and of the Council of 15 February 2006 on Further European Cooperation in Quality Assurance in Higher Education*.

Eymard-Duvernay, F. (1994) 'Coordination des échanges par l'entreprise et qualité des biens', in A.Orléan (ed.) *Analyse économique des conventions*, (Paris: PUF), pp. 307–334.

Fabre-Magnan, M. (2012), 'Postface. Pour une responsabilité écologique' in L. Neyret and G. J. Martin (eds.) *Nomenclature des préjudices environnementaux* (Paris: L. G. D. J.), pp. 387–415.

Fantacci, L. (2010), 'What kind of calculation is implied in the money rate of interest?', in M. Amato, L. Doria and L. Fantacci (eds.), *Money and calculation. Economic and sociological perspectives* (Basingstoke: Palgrave Macmillan and Bocconi University Press), pp. 79–100.

Fédier, F. (2003), *Totalitarismo e nichilismo, Tre seminari e una conferenza*, a cura di Maurizio Borghi (Como-Pavia: Ibis).

Fineman, S. (2004), 'Getting the measure of emotion – And the cautionary tale of emotional intelligence', *Human Relations* 57(6), pp. 719–740.

Flower, M. and D. Heath (1993), 'Micro-anatomo politics: Mapping the human genome project', *Culture, Medicine and Psychiatry*, 17, pp. 27–41.

Foucault, M (2007), *Security, Territory, Population: Lectures at the Collège de France*, 1977–1978 (NewYork: Palgrave Macmillan).

Foucault, M. (2008), *The Birth of Biopolitics: Lectures at the Collège de France, 1978–79* (New York: Palgrave Macmillan).

Fukuyama, F. (2002), *Our Posthuman Future: Consequences of the Biotechnology Revolution* (New York: Farrar, Strauss and Giroux).

Gray, C. (2006) 'Managing the unmanageable: The politics of cultural planning' *Public Policy and Administration* 21(2), pp. 101–113.

Guyer, J. I. (2010), 'The eruption of tradition? On ordinality and calculation' *Anthropological Theory* 10(1–2), pp. 123–131.
Habermas, J. (2003), *The Future of Human Nature* (Cambridge: Polity).
Hacking, I. (1990), *The Taming of Chance* (Cambridge: Cambridge University Press).
Hardt, M. and A. Negri (1994), *Labor of Dionysus: A Critique of the State-Form* (Minneapolis: University of Minnesota Press).
Hardt, M. and A. Negri (2000), *Empire* (Cambridge, MA: Harvard University Press).
Hardt, M. and A. Negri (2009), *Commonwealth* (Cambridge, MA: Harvard University Press).
Harman, H. (2009), *Prince of Networks. Bruno Latour and Metaphysics* (Melbourne: Repress).
Haraway, D. (1991), *Simians, Cyborgs, and Women: The Reinvention of Nature* (London: Free Association Books).
Heidegger, M. (1962), *Being and Time*, trans. J. Macquarrie and E. Robinson (Oxford: Blackwell).
Heidegger, M. (1991), *Nietzsche*, Volumes Three and Four, edited by D. Farrell Krell (San Francisco: Harper & Row).
Heidegger, M. (1996), *The Principle of Reason*, trans. Reginald Lilly (Bloomington and Indianapolis: Indiana University Press).
Heidegger, M (1999a), *Contributions to Philosophy (From Enowning)*, trans. P. Emad and K. Maly (Bloomington: Indiana University Press).
Heidegger, M. (1999b), *Ontology: The Hermeneutics of Facticity*, trans. J. van Buren (Bloomington: Indiana University Press).
Heidegger, M. (2000), *Introduction to Metaphysics*, trans. Gregory Fried and Richard Polt (New Haven and London: Yale University Press).
Heidegger, M. (2001), *Zollikon Seminars. Protocols, Conversations, Letters*, edited by Medard Boss (Evaston: Northwestern University Press).
Heidegger, M. (2002), 'The Age of the World Picture', in *Off the Beaten Track*, edited and trans. J. Young and K. Haynes (Cambridge: Cambridge University Press).
Heidegger, M. (2003), *Four Seminars*, trans. Andrew Mitchell and François Raffoul (Bloomington and Indianapolis: Indiana University Press).
Heidegger, M. (2009a) 'As when on a holiday' in *The Heidegger Reader*, edited with an introduction by Günter Figal, trans. Jerome Veith (Bloomington: Indiana University Press).
Heidegger, M. (2009b), '*Der Spiegel* interview with Martin Heidegger' in *The Heidegger Reader*, edited with an introduction by Günter Figal, trans. Jerome Veith (Bloomington: Indiana University Press).
Heidegger, M. (2011a), 'Letter on humanism' in *Basic Writings*, edited by D. F. Krell with a foreword by T. Carman (London and New York: Routledge).
Heidegger, M. (2011b), 'The end of philosophy and the task of thinking' in *Basic Writings*, edited by D. F. Krell with a foreword by T. Carman (London and New York: Routledge).

Heidegger, M. (2011c), 'The question concerning technology' in *Basic Writings*, edited by D. F. Krell with a foreword by T. Carman (London and New York: Routledge), pp. 217–238.

Hellsten S. (2012), ' "The meaning of life" during a transition from modernity to Transhumanism and Posthumanity', *Journal of Anthropology* 2012, pp. 311–325.

Higgins V. and W. Larner (2010), 'From standardization to standardizing work', in V. Higgins and W. Larner (eds.) *Calculating the Social: Standards and the Reconfiguration of Governing* (Basingstoke: Palgrave Macmillan), pp. 205–218.

Higgins, W. (2006) 'How we are governed now: Globalisation, neo-liberal governmentality and the nullification of substantive policy', *Journal of Australian Political Economy* (57), pp. 5–29.

Hopwood, A G. (1978), 'Towards an organizational perspective for the study of accounting and information systems', *Accounting, Organizations and Society* 3, pp. 3–13.

Hopwood, A G. (1987) "The Archaeology of accounting systems", *Accounting, Organizations and Society* 12, pp. 207–234.

Hopwood, A. G. (1992) "Accounting calculation and the shifting sphere of the economic", *The European Accounting Review* 1, pp. 125–143.

Hughes, J. (2004), *Citizen Cyborg: Why Democratic Societies Must Respond to the Redesigned Human of the Future* (Cambridge, MA: Westview Press).

Jacobsen, M. H. and K. Tester (2007) 'Sociology, Nostalgia, Utopia and Mortality: A Conversation with Zygmunt Bauman', *European Journal of Social Theory*, 10 (2), pp. 305–325.

Jacobzone, S. et al. (2007), 'Regulatory Management Systems Across OECD Countries: Indicators of Recent Achievements and Challenges', OECD Working Papers on Public Governance, No. 9, OECD Publishing, http://dx.doi.org/10.1787/5kmjr1g0n8bq-en, accessed on 30 October 2012.

Kalthoff, H. (2005), 'Practices of calculation: Economic representations and risk management', *Theory, Culture &Society* 22(2), pp. 69–97.

Khong, L. (2003), 'Actants and enframing: Heidegger and Latour on technology', *Studies in History and Philosophy of Science Part A* 34(4), December, pp. 693–704.

Kleinberg-Levin, D. M. (2005), *Gestures of Ethical Life: Reading Hölderlin's Question of Measure After Heidegger* (Stanford: Stanford University Press).

Knorr Cetina, K. (2005), 'The rise of a culture of life', *EMBO Reports*6 (S76–S80), http://www.nature.com/embor/journal/v6/n1s/full/7400437.html, accessed on 30 October 2012.

Knorr Cetina, K. and A. Preda (eds.) (2005), *The Sociology of Financial Markets* (Oxford: Oxford University Press).

Kochan, J. (2010), 'Latour's Heidegger', *Social Studies of Science August* 40(4), pp. 579–598.

Kurunmäki, L. and P. Miller (2006), 'Modernising government: the calculating self, hybridisation and performance measurement', *Financial Accountability and Management* 22(1), pp. 87–106.

Kurzweil, R. (2000), *The Age of Spiritual Machines* (London: Penguin Books).
Kurzweil, R. (2006), *The Singularity Is Near: When Humans Transcend Biology* (London: Penguin Books).
Lafontaine, C. (2004), *L'Empire cybernétique. Des machines à penser à la pensée machine* (Paris: Seuil).
Lampland, M. and S. Leigh Star (eds.) (2008), *Formalizing Practices: Reckoning with Standards, Numbers and Models in Science and Everyday Life* (Ithaca, NY: Cornell University Press).
Lascoumes, P. and P. Le Galès (2007), 'Introduction: Understanding public policy through its instruments – from the nature of instruments to the sociology of public policy instrumentation', *Governance* 20(1), pp. 1–21.
Latour, B. (1993), *We Have Never Been Modern*, trans. Catherine Porter (Cambridge, MA: Harvard University Press).
Latour, B. (1996), *Aramis, or the Love for Technology*, trans. C. Porter (Cambridge, MA: Harvard University Press).
Latour, B. (1999), *Pandora's Hope, Essay on the Reality of Science Studies* (Cambridge, MA: Harvard University Press).
Legendre, P. (1988), *Le Desir politique de Dieu* (Paris: Fayard).
Legendre, P. (2001), *De la Société comme Texte. Linéaments d'une anthropologie dogmatique* (Paris: Fayard).
Lemke, T. (2011), *Biopolitics: An Advanced Introduction* (New York: New York University Press).
Lengwiler, M. (2008), 'Double standards: The history of standardizing humans in modern life insurance' in M. Lampland, S. Leigh Star (eds.) *Formalizing Practices: Reckoning with Standards, Numbers and Models in Science and Everyday Life* (Ithaca, NY: Cornell University Press), pp. 149–167.
Livingston P. (2003), 'Thinking and being: Heidegger and Wittgenstein on machination and lived-experience', *Inquiry* (46), pp. 324–345.
Lock, G. and C. Lorenz (2007), 'Revisiting the university front', *Studies in Philosophy and Education* 26(5), pp. 405–418.
Loughlin, M. (1996), 'The language of quality', *Journal of Evaluation in Clinical Practice* 2(2), pp. 87–95.
Loughlin, M. (2002), *Ethics, Management and Mithology* (Oxford: Radcliffe Medical Press).
McLellan D. (ed.) (2007), *Karl Marx: Selected Writings* (Oxford: Oxford University Press, 1977).
MacKenzie, D. (2006), *An Engine, Not a Camera: How Financial Models Shape Markets* (Cambridge, MA: MIT Press).
Magatti, M. (2009), *Libertà immaginaria. Le illusioni del capitalismo tecnonichilista* (Milano: Feltrinelli).
Marx, K. and F. Engels (1947) The *German Ideology* (New York: International Publishers).
Marx, K. (1978), 'Economic and philosophical manuscripts of 1844', in *The Marx-Engels Reader*, edited by Robert Tucker (New York: Norton & Company).
Marx, K. (1993), *Grundrisse: Foundations of the Critique of Political Economy*, trans. M. Nicolaus (London: Penguin Classics).

Massumi, B. (2009), 'National enterprise emergency: Steps towards an ecology of powers', *Theory, Culture and Society* 26(26), pp. 153–185.

Maurer, B. (2010), 'Repressed futures: Financial derivatives' theological unconscious', in M. Amato, L. Doria and L. Fantacci (eds.), *Money and Calculation: Economic and Sociological Perspectives* (Basingstoke: Palgrave Macmillan and Bocconi University Press), pp. 148–173.

Mignolli, G. and P. Nijkamp (2001), *Values and Effects of Local Identity Preservation: A Taxonomic Approach* (Vrije Universiteit Amsterdam: Research Memorandum).

Miller, P. (1992), "Accounting and objectivity: The invention of calculating selves and calculable spaces" *Annals of Scholarship* 9, pp. 61–85.

Miller, P. (2001), "Governing by numbers: Why calculative practices matter," *Social Research* 68(2), pp. 379–396.

Miller, P and C. Napier (1993), "Genealogies of calculation", *Accounting, Organizations and Society*18, pp. 631–647.

Miller, P. and T. O'Leary (1994), "Governing the calculable person", in A. G. Hopwood and P. Miller (eds.), *Accounting as Social and Institutional Practice* (Cambridge: Cambridge University Press), pp. 98–115.

Miller, P. and N. Rose (1990), "Governing economic life", *Economy and Society*19, pp. 1–31.

Morley, L. (2003), *Quality and Power in Higher Education* (Maidenhead: Open University Press).

Musselin, C. and C. Paradeise (2002), 'Où en sommes-nous?', *Sociologie du travail, Dossier/debate La Qualitè*, 44, pp. 256–260.

Negri, A. (1999), 'Value and affect', *Boundary 2,* trans. by M. Hardt 26(2), pp. 77–88.

Negri, A. (2008a), *Reflections on Empire*, trans. Ed Emery (Cambridge: Polity).

Negri, A. (2008b), *Empire and Beyond*, trans. Ed Emery (Cambridge: Polity).

Negri, A. (2011), *Art & Multitude*, trans. Ed Emery (Cambridge: Polity).

Nielsen, K. H. (2003), 'Cultural policy and evaluation of quality', *International Journal of Cultural Policy* 9(3), pp. 237–245.

Nussbaum, M. and A. Sen (eds.) (1993), *The Quality of Life* (New York: Oxford University Press).

O'Brien, M. (2011), 'The future of humanity: Heidegger, personhood and technology', *Comparative Philosophy* 2 July, pp. 23–49.

Porter, T. M. (1986), *The Rise of Statistical Thinking* (Princeton: Princeton University Press).

Porter, T. M. (2000), 'Life insurance, medical testing, and the management of mortality' in L. Daston (ed.), *Biographies of Scientific Objects* (Chicago: University of Chicago Press).

Power, M. (1994), *The Audit Explosion* (London: Demos).

Power, M. (1999), *The Audit Society: Rituals of Verification* (Oxford: Oxford University Press).

Power M. (2004), 'Counting, control and calculation: Reflections on measuring and management', *Human Relations* 57(6), pp. 765–783.

Rabinow, P. (1992), 'Artificiality and enlightenment: from sociobiology to biosociality', in J. Crary and S. Kwinter (eds.) *Incorporations* (New York: Zone Books), pp. 234–252.

Rabinow, P. (1999), *French DNA: Trouble in Purgatory* (Chicago: University of Chicago Press).

Rabinow, P. and N. Rose (2006), 'Biopower today', *Biosocieties* 1(2), pp. 195–217.

Rapley, M. (2003), *Quality of Life Research: A Critical Introduction* (London: Sage Publications).

Reeves, C. A. and D. A. Bednar (1994), 'Defining quality: Alternatives and implications', *The Academy of Management Review* 19, pp. 419–445.

Rheinberger, H. (2000), 'Beyond nature and culture: modes of reasoning in the age of molecular biology and medicine', in M. Lock, A. Young and A. Cambrosio (eds.) *Living and Working with the New Medical Technologies* (Cambridge: Cambridge University Press), pp. 19–30.

Ricci, F. (2008), 'Gagner la Heimatlosigkeit', *Heidegger Studien* 24, pp. 61–102.

Riis, S. (2008), 'The symmetry between Bruno Latour and Martin Heidegger: The technique of turning a Police Officer into a speed bump', *Social Studies of Science April* 38(2), pp. 285–301.

Rogerson, R. (1999), 'Quality of life and urban competitiveness' *Urban Studies* 36, pp. 969–985.

Rose, N. (1989), *Governing the Soul: The Shaping of the Private Self* (London: Routledge).

Rose, N. (1991), 'Governing by numbers: Figuring out democracy', *Accounting, Organizations and Society* 16, 1991, pp. 673–692.

Rose, N. (1992), 'Governing the enterprising self', in P. Heelas and P. Morris (eds.) *The Values of the Enterprise Culture: The Moral Debate* (London: Routledge), pp. 141–164.

Rose, N. (1996), 'Governing "advanced" liberal democracies', in A. Barry, T. Osborne and N. Rose (eds.), *Foucault and Political Reason: Liberalism, Neo-Liberalism and Rationalities of Government* (Chicago, IL: University of Chicago Press), pp. 37–64.

Rose, N. (2001), 'The politics of life itself', *Theory, Culture & Society* 18:1, pp. 1–30.

Rose, N. (2007), *The Politics of Life Itself* (Princeton: Princeton University Press).

Rose, N. and P. Miller (1992), 'Political power beyond the state: Problematics of government', *British Journal of Sociology* 43, pp. 173–205.

Salais, R. (2006), 'On the correct (and incorrect) use of indicators in public action', *Comparative Labor Law & Policy Journal*, 27(2), pp. 237–256.

Salais, R. and Storper,M. (1993) *Les mondes de production* (Paris: Editions de l'EHESS).

Schild, A. (2004), *L' Hiver du monde*, http://www.contrepointphilosophique.ch/Bibliotheque/Pages/AlexandreSchild/HiverDuMonde.pdf, accessed on 30 October 2012.

Schild, A. (2011), 'L'être au péril du faire' in M. Foessel, J.-C. Gens and P. Rodrigo (eds), *Faire monde. Essais phénoménologiques* (Paris: Mimesis France).

Schild, A. (2013) 'Machenschaft' in P. Arjakovsky, F. Fédier and H. France-Lanord (eds.) *Dictionnaire Martin Heidegger. Vocabulaire polyphonique de sa pensée* (Paris: Les Éditions du CERF).

Sen, A. (1987), *Freedom of Choice. Concept and Content,* Wider Working Papers, World Institute for Development Economics Research of the United Nations University, Alfred Marshall Lecture at the annual meeting of the European Economic Association, Copenhagen, 22 August, 1987, http://www.wider.unu.edu/publications/working-papers/previous/en_GB/wp-25/_files/82530817594427220/default/WP25.pdf, accessed on 30 October 2012).

Sen, A. (1989), 'Development as capability expansion', *Journal of Development Planning* 19, pp. 41–58.

Shore, C. and S. Wright (1999), 'Audit culture and Anthropology: neo-liberalism in British higher education', *The Journal of the Royal Anthropological Institute* 5(4), pp. 557–575.

Shore, C. and S. Wright (2000), 'Coercive accountability: the rise of audit culture in higher education', in M. Strathern (ed.) *Audit Cultures. Anthropological Studies in Accountability, Ethics and the Academy* (London: Routledge), pp. 57–89.

Simmel, G. (1950), 'The metropolis and mental life', in K. H. Wolff (trans. and ed.) *The Sociology of Georg Simmel* (New York: Free Press), pp. 409–424.

Simmel, G. (2004), *The Philosophy of Money,* Third Enlarged Version, edited by D. Frisby, trans. T. Bottomore and D. Frisby (London: Routledge).

Slater, D. (2002), 'From calculation to alienation: Disentangling economic abstractions', *Economy and Society* 31(2), pp. 234–249.

Stiglitz J. E., A. Sen and J.P. Fitoussi (2009), *Report by the Commission on the Measurement of Economic Performance and Social Progress.* Web site for the Report (English version) http://www.stiglitz-sen-fitoussi.fr/documents/rapport_anglais.pdf, accessed on 30 October 2012.

Strathern, M. (2000), 'The tyranny of transparency', *British Educational Research Journal* 26(3): 309–321.

Sunder Rajan, K. (2006), *Biocapital: The Constitution of Postgenomic Life* (Durham: Duke University Press).

Supiot, A. (2006), 'Law and labour. A world market of norms?', *New Left Review* 39, pp. 109–121.

Thévenot, L. (1993) *Essais sur les objets usuels: Propriétés, fonctions, usages. Les objets dans l'action. De la maison au laboratoire.*Raisons Pratiques 4, (Paris: Editions de l'EHESS) pp. 85–111.

Thrift, N. (2005), *Knowing Capitalism* (London: Sage).

Townley, B., (1993), "Foucault, power/knowledge and its relevance for human resource management", *Academy of Management Review*18, pp. 518–545.

Travers M. (2007), *The New Bureaucracy: Quality Assurance and Its Critics* (Bristol: Policy Press).

Tremblay R., R. Rogerson and H. Chicoine (2008), 'Place ratings, shifting neoliberalism and quality of life in communities', *Revue Interventions économiques* [En ligne], 37 |, http://interventionseconomiques.revues.org/495, accessed on 28 October 2012.

Tuckman, A. (1994), 'The yellow brick road: total quality management and the restructuring of organizational culture', *Organization Studies*15, pp. 727–751.

Vernon J. (2008), 'Erfahren and Erleben: Metaphysical Experience and its Overcoming in Heidegger's *Beiträge' Symposium (Canadian Journal of Continental Philosophy / Revue canadienne de philosophie continentale)* 12(1), Article 8, pp. 108–125.

Vollmer, H. (2003), 'Bookkeeping, accounting, calculative practice: the sociological suspense of calculation', *Critical Perspectives on Accounting* 14, pp. 353–381.

Vormbusch U. (2008), 'Talking numbers – Governing immaterial labour', *Economic Sociology_The European Electronic Newsletter* 10(1), pp. 8–11.

Waldby, C. (2000), *The Visible Human Project: Informatic Bodies and Posthuman Medicine* (London: Routledge).

Wahlberg, A. (2007), 'Measuring progress: calculating the life of nations', *Distinktion: Scandinavian Journal of Social Theory* (14), pp. 65–82.

Wilkinson, A. and H. Willmott (1996), 'Quality management, problems and pitfalls: a critical perspective', *International Journal of Quality and Reliability Management* 13, pp. 55–65.

Worthington, F. and J. Hodgson (2005), 'Academic labour and the politics of quality in higher education: A critical evaluation of the conditions of possibility of resistance', *Critical Quarterly* 47, pp. 96–110.

Index

Printed and bound in the United States of America